FIFTH EDITION

Working With Words

A Handbook for Media Writers and Editors

Brian S. Brooks
University of Missouri Columbia

James L. Pinson
Eastern Michigan University

Jean Gaddy Wilson
Weiner, Edrich, Brown, Inc.

Bedford / St. Martin's
Boston ◆ New York

FOR BEDFORD/ST.MARTIN'S

Communication Editor: Jennifer Bartlett
Developmental Editor: Sara Slawnik
Editorial Assistant, Publishing Services: Maria Teresa Burwell
Senior Production Supervisor: Joe Ford
Production Associate: Christie Gross
Marketing Manager: Richard Cadman
Project Management: Books By Design, Inc.
Text Design: Claire Seng-Niemoeller
Cover Design: Lucy Krikorian
Cover Photos: (Left) Robert Lewine/Corbisstockmarket;
    (Center) Barry Rosenthal/Getty Images/FPG;
    (Right) George Heisler Photography, Inc./Getty Images/The Image Bank
Composition: Books By Design, Inc.
Printing and Binding: Haddon Craftsmen, an RR Donnelley & Sons Company

President: Joan E. Feinberg
Publisher for History and Communication: Patricia A. Rossi
Director of Marketing: Karen R. Melton
Director of Editing, Design, and Production: Marcia Cohen
Manager, Publishing Services: Emily Berleth

Library of Congress Control Number: 2002103649

For information, write: Bedford/St. Martin's, 75 Arlington Street,
Boston, MA 02116   (617-399-4000)

ISBN: 0–312–39790-9

Preface

"Working With Words" is a writing handbook for journalism students and professionals. It is meant partly as a book to be read and studied, and partly as a reference to track down tricky questions of grammar, usage, style, wordiness and insensitive language. It's meant to be used in classes, as well as on journalists' desks to supplement the AP Stylebook and dictionaries.

"Working With Words" had its beginnings in our own work as newspaper copy editors. We found that our stylebook and dictionary did not always answer the questions that came up every day about grammar, usage, punctuation, compound-word spellings and similar issues. We kept a small shelf of books to consult at such times, but there was no single, comprehensive resource to which a member of the working press could turn for such answers.

One of us remembers searching more than 10 books, for example, just to check the spelling of the phrase "do's and don'ts." Copy editors are expected to get such details right—but often they are also expected to edit and write headlines for about four stories an hour, or one every 15 minutes or so.

Later, when teaching editing to students at the University of Missouri and supervising their work on the daily Columbia Missourian, we realized that if professionals could use a book such as this one, students needed it even more. Grammar is simply not stressed in public schools today, and our students typically tell us that the last time their teachers covered it at all was in middle school—in the sixth to eighth grades.

With employers complaining that too many recent college graduates are deficient in language skills, it's falling more and more on journalism educators to fill the gap that secondary education has too often left. The challenge is to lift even some of our brightest students from what employers consider a remedial level of grammar and usage understanding to that demanded of working professionals.

That's what we try to do in this book, and that's part of what we think sets it apart from others. We've tried to explain the issues as simply as possible. But, at the same time, we haven't tried to make it look easier, as many books do, by leaving out the harder, trickier questions that arise when you make your living working with words. We've aimed at making the book not only an introduction for beginners but also a guide for those same people as they become more advanced.

New to This Edition

In the Fifth Edition, we've continued to make the text simpler for beginners, more comprehensive for seasoned pros and more up-to-date for everyone. We've streamlined the writing by reducing a number of longer passages, especially in the grammar section, to simpler rules. We've tried to make the examples, where possible, more typical of sentences from actual news stories. Throughout the grammar and mechanics chapters, we've added more tips for speakers of English as a second language. We've redesigned the book so it's more attractive and easier to use, and we've added a new feature— tip boxes that provide more specific guidance on grammar and mechanics issues facing journalists on the job.

We've updated material throughout, especially in the chapters on stereotyping (Chapter 13) and writing for online media (Chapter 16). The chapter on verbs (Chapter 5) has been significantly revised and restructured, making it more helpful and easier to use. We've also expanded and reorganized the chapter on punctuation (Chapter 9) by adding more discussion of quotations, attributions and paraphrasing, and by moving this material and other commonly tricky content, such as when and when not to use commas, to the beginning of the chapter. We've continued to offer up-to-date lists of Web resources at the end of every chapter.

As in previous editions, we've kept— and updated— the many useful lists of specific advice for writing and editing. We think when readers become familiar with these lists, they'll keep coming back to the book as a reference, just as they would their stylebook and dictionary. Please see the inside front cover for useful page references.

Unlike other media writing handbooks, "Working With Words" is more than just a grammar and usage manual. It offers three chapters on the key elements of writing for print, broadcast and online media (Chapters 14-16). Because of new technologies such as CD-ROMs and the World Wide Web that increasingly marry print and electronic media, we feel it is increasingly important for all of us to learn how to write for different media. In the Fifth Edition, we've updated these three chapters and grouped them together in a new section called "Writing Methods for Different Media" (Part Four). These chapters build on the fundamentals of grammar, usage, mechanics and style laid out in Parts One through Three and show how word choice, word order, style and even story organization change with the medium.

In closing, we again want to thank our families for their love and support. Thanks also to the many faculty, students, professionals and others who have used previous editions of this book. Thanks especially to students, faculty and media professionals who have sent us suggestions for this new edition. We are further grateful to the following reviewers who graciously offered comprehensive suggestions for this new edition: Thomas V. Dickson (Southwest Missouri State), Terri L. Johnson (Indiana University), Stan Ketterer (Oklahoma State University), Kenneth C. Killebrew (University of South Florida), Kelly A. Taylor (Bowling Green State University) and Jan Whitt (University of Colorado).

Thanks, too, to the staff at Bedford/St. Martin's, who have believed in this book and who have worked with us to make it what it is. We especially want to thank our editor, Sara Slawnik, for her many well-considered, detailed suggestions for making this the best edition so far.

If you'd like to send us questions about this edition or suggestions for the next, here are our e-mail addresses:

Brian S. Brooks	BrooksBS@missouri.edu
James L. Pinson	eng_pinson@online.emich.edu
Jean Gaddy Wilson	jeangaddywilson@aol.com

Contents

Chapter 12   *Conciseness*   235

Chapter 13   *Sexism, Racism and Other "isms"*   269

PART FOUR   Writing Methods for Different Media   299

Chapter 14   *Writing News That's Fit for Print*   301

PART ONE

Grammar and Usage

CHAPTER 1

Grammar Basics

"It will be proved to thy face that thou hast men about thee that usually talk of a noun and a verb and such abominable words as no Christian ear can endure to hear." William Shakespeare, "II Henry VI"

Many people share the suspicion of grammar expressed by the rebel in Shakespeare's play. Even writers, for whom a knowledge of grammar should be one of the main skills of the trade, are often wary of studying the subject.

Many writers rely mainly on what sounds right to them rather than on memorizing rules. To a certain extent, that works. But what sounds right is not always right according to the formal rules of grammar. So what? What good is grammar, anyway? Why should we trust it more than our own ears?

Using Standard English

First, let's understand what grammar is. It's the study of the form and structure of words and their arrangement in speech or writing. The fact is, though, that the way we use words in speech often differs from the accepted standards in writing. Furthermore, there are different standards for informal speech between friends and more formal addresses to a live audience or to people tuned in to the radio or television. There are also different standards for writing for a newspaper, magazine, book or Web page, as opposed to writing for radio or television or writing an e-mail message.

In this book, we mainly focus on the grammar and usage required for more formal media writing or speaking. For some situations—such as live broadcast reports or personal columns or reviews in a newspaper or magazine—a more relaxed standard would be appropriate. But it's easier to lower your standards once you've learned higher ones than it is to raise them if you've never learned more formal ones. By learning the highest standards, you'll be preparing yourself for all occasions.

Why Don't We Write How We Talk?

Why is the informal English we often use when speaking not enough for print or broadcast writing? Why don't we just write the way we talk?

Conversation and written language—even written language to be read aloud—differ in many ways. What sounds right in conversation is often ineffective or inappropriate in writing.

In conversation, for example, we can get across a great deal of meaning through tone of voice, pauses, stress and gestures—meaning that is lost if we merely record the words that were said. Sometimes you notice this in broadcast when the anchor reads words he or she didn't write and the meaning gets lost in the oral interpretation—the wrong word gets stressed, or a crucial tone of voice is missing to convey an irony, for example.

But written language has its own advantages over conversational language. Novelist Kurt Vonnegut Jr. points out one of them: "This is what I find most encouraging about the writing trades: They allow mediocre people who are patient and industrious to revise their stupidity, to edit themselves into something like intelligence."

We normally speak much more loosely and informally than we would care to have recorded in writing. Although news sources often gripe about being misquoted by journalists, nobody seems to insist that newspapers print all the *uhs, ers,* stammers and false starts that a tape would reveal.

If your writing relies on how you talk rather than on what is considered correct in writing, you're using the wrong tool for the job. Too many things can go wrong. For example, the words you learned by ear may not be what you thought you heard. Did you really hear that *d* in *supposed to?* Or the people around you may not have used words in precisely the way that is considered correct in writing. They may have lacked the education; they may have spoken a regional dialect that differs from standard English; or they simply may have spoken informally.

In daily conversation, for example, most people use *their* as a singular pronoun in a situation in which the person could be male or female: *A person should mind their own business.* Most people also use *lay* instead of *lie* to mean "rest," as in *Several employees had to go outside and lay down after the toxic fumes swept through the building.* Either of these sentences would probably go unnoticed in daily conversation but would be considered incorrect if written to be read in print or on the air.

ESL Tip

Students for whom English is a second language should note that the better they are at conversational English, the more they, like native speakers, will need to be aware of how informal conversation differs from media writing.

Conventional Wisdom

When you get down to it, the basic reason for knowing grammar is to communicate better. The same can be said for knowing a topic we take up later in this book: *usage,* or the meaning and use of particular words. Knowing the proper relationships between words and how to use them precisely helps us say what we mean more effectively. Knowing grammar and usage makes us better writers and better journalists.

An astute reader may notice, however, that some of the rules seem more like arbitrary conventions than natural, logical guides. Some rules, indeed, describe conventions, but one should not dismiss them for that reason. Conventions represent agreement, and agreement opens doors to communication.

Actually, a bigger problem is the extent to which the advice in any stylebook, dictionary or grammar book does not represent such agreement. The fact is—although few know it—not everyone subscribes to the same rules of style, spelling and grammar.

Among journalists, the most widely accepted standards for style are set by The Associated Press Stylebook and Briefing on Media Law and the most widely accepted spellings by Webster's New World College Dictionary. We have tried to conform as much as possible to those two books.

Competing Grammars and Stylebooks

On matters of grammar and usage in the media, there is no single standard for matters not covered in the AP Stylebook. We have tried to gather advice from many sources and have included here what we think are the most common, the most reasonable and the most useful standards.

Frankly, though, there are a multitude of grammar and usage guides out there, and they take a variety of approaches. Of the three major current approaches to grammar—traditional, structural and transformational—we have mainly followed the oldest, the traditional, while adopting ideas from the others when they were helpful.

The media as a whole still favor the traditional approach, and that is what journalists are expected to know when they take job tests. But we cannot overlook the fact that about a century of scientific and historical research by linguists has disproved a number of the rules that have been passed on by teachers and editors.

To take one simple example: We're often told not to use the word *hopefully* as a sentence adverb—as in *Hopefully, the snow will miss our area*—because it doesn't say who's doing the hoping. But there aren't comparable rules against other sentence adverbs, such as *frankly* or *strictly speaking,* which likewise don't say who's being frank or speaking strictly.

Our advice for *hopefully* is not to use it except in the sense of "in a hopeful manner"—*She says she looks to the future hopefully*—not because it's illogical to use it as a sentence adverb but because it's so universally condemned, even though the condemnation appears superstitious. Such rules are like the use of the biblical word *shibboleth* and communicate mainly as passwords indicating that the user is "one of us"—the educated.

Why does the media world largely subscribe to traditional grammar and its sometimes outdated rules? Partly because it's been around longer, so it's been more widely taught. But mainly because publishers—news, magazine and book companies—and even broadcast outlets, to a lesser extent, like the *prescriptive* approach of traditional grammar rather than the *descriptive* approach of structural grammar.

Traditional grammar says, "This way is the right way." Structural grammar says, "Anything is right if commonly said by native speakers." The media prefer the consistency of traditional grammar's set rules.

Why? Inconsistencies in the style of a newspaper, online news site, magazine or book draw attention to themselves when readers should instead be concentrating on the content. Deviations from standard grammar or usage in the media industry may cause people in the audience to become confused, maybe even to misinterpret what was said. And when the audience discovers inconsistencies or misused words, credibility is undermined as seriously as if a factual error had been made. In fact, if the language is misused, a factual error can be created.

Besides, consistency saves time and money. Without consistency, a writer might add a comma only to see it taken out by an editor and then put back by a proofreader. If we agree on conventions, we can avoid wasting each other's time—and time, as the saying goes, is money.

But the prescriptive rules have to be amended from time to time to reflect not only changes in the language but also research that proves traditional advice may have been inaccurate. The work of linguists is essential for making such calls on the best evidence available. We have at times noted in this book old rules we think need to be updated.

Grammar and Confidence

Even professional writers often lack confidence in their grammar skills. Many people discover that studying practical grammar not only directly improves their ability to express themselves but also gives them greater confidence in their work. Sometimes, just knowing that you have control over the basics lets you free your mind to concentrate on what's more important—the content and vision of your writing.

Knowing grammar will help you write with greater confidence in the accuracy of what you're writing.

Communicating Well

Grammar is most useful, though, when it's not just helping you conform to conventions or feel confident that you know what you're doing—as important as those things are—but rather when it helps you know how to get your message across better. Granted, many rules of grammar, usage and punctuation seem arbitrary. Those are among the ones most likely to change over the years.

But at their best, grammar and usage rules are the received wisdom of previous writers about how to communicate well and to stay out of trouble. We've edited some sentences that were so ungrammatical and downright confusing, it was difficult or even impossible to understand what the writer was trying to say.

Other times, the mistakes have been unintentionally funny or totally misleading: *As one of the worst examples of a convicted sexual harasser in many years, she said she was shocked at his behavior.* Who's the sexual harasser here: the man, or the woman who was shocked at his behavior? Or does the sentence mean that the woman was one of the worst sexual harassers in many years and that even she was shocked at this man's behavior? Here we have not only confusion but also a possible lawsuit.

If the writer had learned the rule to place modifiers next to what they describe, he or she could have avoided that problem: *She said she was shocked at the behavior of the man, whom she called one of the worst examples of a convicted sexual harasser in many years.*

Talking Shop

Grammar terms are part of the "shop talk" of people who work with words. Just as sports have terms for what happens on the playing field, so speaking and writing have terms to describe what goes on in an utterance. A writer or editor who does not know grammar terminology is like a football player who does not know words for positions and plays.

But grammar terminology is confusing to many people. It's usually something studied too long ago to be remembered clearly. Most people, however, at least vaguely recall learning the eight *parts of speech: nouns, pronouns, verbs, adjectives, adverbs, prepositions, conjunctions* and *interjections.*

You probably also learned another set of terms called the *parts of a sentence: subject, predicate, predicate complement (predicate nominative* and *predicate adjective), direct object, indirect object, noun of direct address, appositive, sentence adverb, prepositional phrase, subject of an infinitive* and so on. It's usually said that the parts of speech refer to what words *are*, the parts of a sentence to what words *do* — that is, how they are used in a sentence.

Then there are the *verbals* — *infinitives, gerunds* and *participles* — that don't fit well in either category. And, of course, there are the terms for groups of words — *phrases, clauses* and *sentences.*

Separating grammatical terms into these categories helps, but don't feel bad if the groupings don't always make sense to you. For example, if you look closely at the definitions in this book, which are fairly standard ones, you'll see that some of the parts of speech are defined by what they are but others are defined by what they do—just as we define parts of a sentence.

Also, if you look in a dictionary, you'll find that many words can be more than one part of speech, depending on how they're used. For example, in the sentence *The mayor likes jogging, jogging* is a noun. But in the sentence *The mayor was jogging down the road, jogging* is a verb. And in the sentence *Jogging down the road, he hurried for help, jogging* is an adjective. Confused?

When English grammarians began in the 18th century to write books about the language, they based them on Latin grammar books. "Parts of speech" is really a mistranslation of the Greek for "parts of a sentence." So, the two categories are not really logically separate. But sometimes, it seems more useful to speak of a word in a sentence as a noun and at other times as a subject or direct object, so you need to know both sets of terms.

Rather than define all the parts of speech, parts of a sentence and verbals right now, we'll introduce the terms as they arise in the following chapters. That way, you will have to take in only as much terminology at a time as is necessary. Meanwhile, consult the index at the back of the book if you need to track down a particular definition.

Quick Start: A Checklist of Common Mistakes

Of all the rules that are presented in this book, aside from spelling and wire-service style, the following are among those we've found to be some of the most violated in student and professional copy.

A

a/an The article *a* is used before a word that begins with a consonant sound when pronounced; *an* is used before a word that begins with a vowel sound when pronounced. In case the following word is an abbreviation, the important thing to remember is that the choice is determined by the initial sound of the following word, not its appearance: *an* (not *a*) *FBI inquiry* because the initial sound is "ef." Many people also get confused by an *h* at the beginning of a word: *a* (not *an*) *historical event* because the initial sound is "hih."

a lot Commonly misspelled as *alot;* change to *many* or *much.*

adjective-adverb confusion Many people confuse these two kinds of modifiers. In the sentence *Everything was running smoothly,* the word *smoothly,* an adverb, is correct; many would incorrectly say *smooth,* an adjective. Remember that adjectives modify nouns or pronouns; adverbs modify verbs, adjectives or other adverbs. In the example, the modifier describes the manner in which something was running—in other words, it modifies the verb. If the sentence had said *Everything* *was smooth, smooth* would be right because *smooth* would be a predicate adjective modifying *Everything*. See Page 85.

adopt/pass   You *adopt* a resolution, but you *pass* an ordinance.

affect/effect   *Affect* is a verb meaning "to influence"; *effect* is a noun meaning "result" and a verb meaning "to cause."

alleged, allegedly   Avoid these words as modifiers, for they don't offer the legal protection many people think. Instead of writing *Smith is an alleged rapist* or *Smith allegedly raped the woman,* write *A man raped the woman, and Smith was later charged with the crime.*

among/between   Use *between* for two items, *among* for three or more.

as/like   *As* is a conjunction and should be used to introduce a clause; *like* is a preposition and should be used to introduce a word or phrase.

as, than   When either of these words is followed by a pronoun at the end of a sentence, the pronoun should be in nominative case because it's the subject of a clause in which the verb may be implied: *She's smarter than I (am)*.

B

blond/blonde, brunet/brunette   The forms without the final *e* are used as the adjective applying to either a man or a woman or as a noun applying to a man only. The forms with the *e* are used only as nouns applying to a woman, although many women would object to being reduced to a hair color. Many people consider these distinctions sexist, but wire-service style maintains them.

C

centers around   Change to *centers on* or *revolves around* because the center is in the middle.

colon   Capitalize the first word after a colon if what follows is a complete sentence; otherwise, the word after a colon is lowercase. See Page 178.

comma   Put a comma before a conjunction such as *and* only if what follows could stand alone as a complete sentence or if, in a series, the *and* could be confusingly read as linking the last two items as one rather than leaving them separate, as in *corn, pork, and beans.* A comma is deleted before an independent clause if you're paraphrasing someone's compound sentence, as in *He said that first he'd write the story and then he would make the phone calls.*

comma-splice sentences   Ordinarily, a comma alone is not enough to connect two independent clauses. Add a conjunction such as *and* after the comma, change the comma to a semicolon, or change the comma to a period and capitalize the next word.

compare to/compare with   Use *compare to* when similarities are stressed; use *compare with* when differences are stressed.

compose/comprise/constitute   The whole *is composed of* the parts or *comprises* the parts. But the parts *constitute* the whole.

conditional mood   With something that is not now true but could be true under the right conditions, use *could* not *can, might* not *may, should* not *shall,* or *would* not *will.* This distinction comes up often in stories about government considering ordinances or laws. For example, don't write *The bill will make gun owners register their automatic rifles.* Instead, write *The bill would make gun owners register their automatic rifles* (if passed into law).

contact   Avoid as a verb. Change to *call, write* or *visit.*

convince/persuade   You're *convinced that* or *convinced of* something, but you're *persuaded to* do something.

────── D ──────

dangling participles   A participle is a form of a verb, usually ending in *ing,* used in place of an adjective. A participial phrase should always be placed next to the word it modifies. If it isn't, the resulting error is called a *dangling participle.* For example, in the sentence *Standing on her head, he watched the yoga teacher,* the participial phrase *Standing on her head* appears to modify *he,* the word it's next to—it sounds as if he's standing on her head. The sentence needs to be rewritten as *He watched the yoga teacher standing on her head.* See Page 91.

debut   Use only as a noun, not as a verb. Don't say that a movie *will debut* but that it *will have its debut.*

different than   Change to *different from.*

────── E ──────

exclamation mark   Generally, avoid except in quotations because it can make a statement sound gushy and introduce an emotional bias inappropriate for most journalism.

────── F ──────

farther/further   *Farther* is used for literal distance, such as *farther down a road; further* is used for figurative distance, such as *further into a subject.*

fewer/less   Use *less* to modify singular words, *fewer* to modify plural words. Remember that a word that is plural in form is sometimes singular in concept, as when *dollars* or *pounds* refers to a set amount as opposed to individual units. Use *fewer* with items that would take *many, less* with items that would take *much: He weighs less than 200 pounds* because 200 pounds is how *much* he weighs, not how *many.*

forbid/prohibit   You *forbid to* or *prohibit from.*

fragments   To be a sentence, a group of words has to have a subject and predicate and express a complete thought. Although fragments are acceptable for certain effects, especially in advertising, be wary of them. See Page 23.

G

gerunds   Gerunds, which usually end in *ing,* are forms of a verb and are used in place of a noun. If a pronoun directly precedes a gerund, the pronoun should be possessive: *They appreciated our* (not *us*) *staying to help.* See Page 45.

H

half-mast/half-staff   Flags are *lowered,* not *raised,* to *half-staff* on land, *half-mast* only on a ship or at a naval base.

hanged/hung   A condemned man was *hanged* by a rope. A picture was *hung* on the wall.

hike   Do not use in place of *increase,* according to wire-service stylebooks.

host   Use only as a noun, not as a verb. Don't say that someone will *host* a party but that someone will *hold* a party or *be host at* a party.

I

if/whether   *If* is used for conditions, as in *If a, then b. Whether* is used to introduce a choice, as in *I don't know whether to go.* (Notice the *or not* that some people add is redundant.) Because many people misuse *if* when they mean *whether* but never the other way around, a handy test is to say the sentence with *whether.* If *whether* will work, it's the right word. If not, use *if.*

imply/infer   A speaker or writer *implies;* a listener or reader *infers.*

its/it's   *Its* is the possessive pronoun. *It's* is the contraction for *it is.*

L

lay/lie   *Lay* is a transitive verb meaning "to set something down." Its principal parts are *lay, laid, have laid, laying. Lie* is an intransitive verb meaning "to rest." Its principal parts are *lie, lay, have lain, lying.*

lead/led   *Lead* is the main present-tense form of the verb *to lead* and also the name of an element that used to be put in paint and gasoline. The past tense of the verb *lead* is *led,* not *lead.*

M

modifier placement   To avoid confusion, place modifiers as close as possible to what they modify. See also *dangling participles.*

murder   A *homicide* is not a *murder* until someone is convicted of the charge of murder—after all, it may prove to be a case of *manslaughter* or even a killing in self-defense. It is permissible to call the trial a *murder trial* before a conviction if murder is the charge the defendant faces, but the crime itself is not a murder until the suspect has been convicted of the charge.

myself   Use only in a sentence in which *I* has been used earlier: *I hurt myself* or *I, myself, believe otherwise.* It should be used only when emphasis is essential.

N

none   The wire services make this word singular when it means, as it usually does, "no one" or "not one," but they make it plural when it means "no two," as in *None could agree.*

not only ... but also   *Not only* must always be followed by *but also* later in the sentence.

P

premiere   Use only as a noun, not as a verb. Don't write that a play *will premiere* but that it *will have its premiere.*

preposition at end of sentence   Most editors prefer that you not end a sentence with a preposition, unless it's impossible to rewrite the sentence to avoid it and to do that conversationally. See Page 97.

presently   This words means "soon," not "now"; change to *at present.*

prior to   Change to *before.*

prioritize   Change to *rank* or *order.* Do not use to mean "make a priority."

pronoun-antecedent agreement   A pronoun must agree in number, person and gender with the word to which it refers. For a variety of tricky situations where this may not be obvious, see Pages 36-37.

pronoun case   Pronouns should use the form that agrees with their function as a part of the sentence. Nominative case should be used when the pronoun functions as a subject of a clause or as a predicate nominative. Objective case should be used when a pronoun functions as any kind of object or as the subject of an infinitive. Possessive case should be used when the pronoun modifies a noun or gerund by showing possession. See Page 35.

proper nouns   Proper nouns should be capitalized, but two problems often arise: (1) The names of many trademarked products, such as *Dumpster, Jell-O* and *Styrofoam,* have become so common that writers sometimes mistakenly think they should be lowercased as common nouns. To avoid legal action over trademark infringement, use the generic equivalent or capitalize the brand name. (2) Compounds such as *German shepherd* seem to fall somewhere between a proper name such as *Fido* and a common noun such as *dog.* In these situations, capitalize only the part of the compound that would be a proper noun on its own. See Page 30.

Q

quotation marks   At the end of a quotation, periods and commas always go inside quotation marks; colons and semicolons always go outside;

and question marks and exclamation marks go inside if they're part of the quotation, outside if they're not. In front of a quotation, after a verb such as *said* attributing the quotation, use a colon to introduce a quotation of more than one sentence, a comma for a quotation of less than one sentence and no punctuation for a partial quotation (less than a sentence). See Page 173.

R

raise/rise   *Raise* is a transitive verb meaning "to lift" something. Its principal parts are *raise, raised, have raised, raising. Rise* is an intransitive verb meaning "to get up." Its principal parts are *rise, rose, have risen, rising.*

restrictive elements   Words, phrases or clauses that modify something they follow are set off by commas if they are a parenthetical afterthought. But if they restrict (are essential to) the meaning of the sentence, they are not set off by commas. For example, in the sentence *The director of "Chloe in the Afternoon," Eric Rohmer, also made the film "Claire's Knee," Eric Rohmer* is set off in commas as a parenthetical afterthought (the sentence means the same without this detail), but *"Claire's Knee"* is not set off in commas because the meaning of the sentence depends on which film this director also made. See Page 19.

robbery   For a crime to be a *robbery,* violence or the threat of violence must be involved. Someone who *burglarizes* a house while its occupants are away did not *rob* the house; instead, the crime should be called a *burglary* or a *theft.*

S

semicolon   A semicolon is used in place of a comma and a conjunction to connect clauses that could stand alone as complete sentences. Sentences with independent clauses linked by a conjunctive adverb such as *however* must contain a semicolon. Semicolons are also used to connect items in a series that may not be complete sentences but have commas inside the items; in such a case, the word *and* at the end of the series should be preceded by a semicolon. See Page 175.

set/sit   *Set* is a transitive verb meaning "to put something." Its principal parts are *set, set, have set, setting. Sit* is an intransitive verb meaning "to take a seat." Its principal parts are *sit, sat, have sat, sitting.*

sexism and racism   It's not enough just to avoid sexist or racist intent in your writing; you also need to beware of language that is likely to be taken as sexist or racist in effect, no matter what you intended. In other words, you need to become more aware of how your audience is likely to interpret what you're saying. See Chapter 13.

split infinitive   Most editors prefer that you not split the *to* from the verb in an infinitive. So instead of *to boldy go where no one has gone before,* they'd prefer you write *to go boldly where no one has gone before.* (See Pages 79-80.

subject-predicate agreement   The verb must agree in number with the subject of the sentence, but many common situations mislead our ears as to whether the subject is singular or plural or even what the subject is. For a detailed explanation, see Chapter 4.

suppose to   Change to *supposed to*.

T

that   Omit *that* wherever doing so wouldn't change the meaning of a sentence. To avoid confusion, do not omit *that* when it follows a time element after the word *said: He said Monday that he would visit.* Without the *that,* it's confusing whether he said this on Monday or would visit on Monday.

that/which   Use *that* to introduce restrictive (essential) clauses that do not require commas, *which* to introduce nonrestrictive (nonessential) clauses that do require commas. See Page 42.

that/who   Use *that* for inanimate objects and animals without names. Use *who* for people and animals with names.

their   Remember that this pronoun is plural. Do not use it in place of *his* or *her* when the context means either a single woman's or a single man's. *Their* is a good choice from both a grammatical and nonsexist perspective, however, when there does not need to be an emphasis on individuality and the entire sentence can be recast in the plural: *Teachers should do their best* rather than *A teacher should do their best* (ungrammatical), *A teacher should do his best* (sexist) or *A teacher should do his or her best* (unnecessarily awkward). See Page 35.

tightening   Use shorter, simpler, more common words whenever possible. Cut any words that do not add to the meaning. Remember, however, not to change the meaning of the passage; the goal is not merely to be brief but to be concise—to be complete as briefly as possible. See Chapter 12.

U

under way/underway   The one-word spelling is used only as a modifier ,in front of something nautical, as in *the underway fleet.*

use to   Change to *used to*.

utilize   Change to *use*.

V

very   Always eliminate, except in quotations.

W

while   For clarity, use only to mean "simultaneously." If contrast is meant, change to *although* at the beginning of a clause, *though* in the middle of one.

who/whom, whoever/whomever *Who* and *whoever* are nominative-case pronouns. *Whom* and *whomever* are objective-case pronouns. A handy way to make sure you use each pair correctly is to begin reading a sentence after the choice between *who/whom* or *whoever/whomever,* adding either *he* or *him* to complete the thought. If *he* works better, use *who* or *whoever;* if *him* works better, use *whom* or *whomever.* See Page 43.

who's/whose *Who's* is the contraction for *who is. Whose* is the possessive form of the pronoun *who.*

Web Resources

GRAMMAR HELP

Several World Wide Web sites provide answers to questions about grammar. Here are some of the better ones.

- The Editor's Pen
  www.pathway.net/dwlacey/gram.htm

- Good Grammar, Good Style
  www.protrainco.com/info/grammar.htm

- Grammar for Journalists
  jcomm.uoregon.edu/~kelleew/j101

- Grammar Now
  www.grammarnow.com

- Guide to Grammar and Writing
  webster.commnet.edu/HP/pages/darling/grammar.htm

- Online English Grammar
  www.edunet.com/english/grammar/index.html

CHAPTER 2

Phrases, Clauses and Sentences

A good sentence has a kind of rightness to it—a clear, exact way of saying something. And when a sentence works well, it has a certain lightness to it as well—a conciseness and charm that let it soar. As Eric Hoffer writes, "There are few things so subtle and beautiful as a good sentence."

We'll start our examination of grammar by taking a look in this chapter at the groups of words that make up a sentence—phrases and clauses—and how they determine whether a sentence hops or plops. We start here because we think grammar may be easier to understand if we begin with the big picture before focusing on the finer details.

But about those details to come, don't worry if you haven't studied English grammar since middle school. There's nothing here nearly so hard as eighth-grade algebra. You'll probably survive this sentence far more easily.

Let's begin with a few definitions and examples. Then, we'll look more thoroughly at what's useful to know about each of these terms.

- *Phrases* are groups of related words that lack either a *subject* (a doer) or a *verb* (an action or state of being) or both:

    to the restaurant

    walking along the beach

    as long as his arm

Phrases can serve many roles in a sentence, taking the place of single-word parts of sentences such as subjects, objects, predicates, modifiers and connecting words.

- *Clauses* are groups of related words that have both a subject and a verb:

    He wants it all.
    [*independent clause*—forms a complete thought independently]

    because he wants it all [*dependent clause*—not a complete thought but depends on something else for it to make a statement]

⬤ *Sentences,* like clauses, are groups of related words with a subject and verb, but, in addition, sentences *must* make a complete statement. Sentences have at least one independent clause and may have any number of dependent clauses:

> He loves to watch television to relax. [one independent clause]
>
> She spends most of her time studying, but she sometimes regrets it. [two independent clauses]
>
> David Letterman's show proved popular even though it was scheduled late at night. [one independent and one dependent clause]

Phrases

Single words can be *subjects* (people or things doing or being), *objects* (receivers of action), *verbs* (actions or states of being), *modifiers* (descriptions) or *connecting words* (sentence glue). So can phrases. The use of phrases in different ways can be especially useful in bringing variety to your sentences.

After the following illustrations, some terms are used to describe the examples more fully. If you're unfamiliar with some of the vocabulary, don't worry. You can look up the terms in the index if you like, but feel free to skip them for now if you prefer. By the time you finish this book, they'll be familiar to you, and when you look back on this later as a reference, the descriptions here will prove additionally helpful.

Phrases as Subjects and Objects

> *Playing the mandolin* is like *plucking a violin.*
> [two gerund phrases, the first used as the subject of the sentence, the second as the object of the preposition *like*]
>
> *To try* is *to succeed.* [two infinitive phrases, the first the subject of the sentence, the second the predicate nominative]
>
> *Over there* is where police found the body.
> [prepositional phrase used as the subject of the sentence]

Phrases as Verbs

> Wagner *had been going* to college for three years at the time.
> [main verb *going* with two helping verbs]
>
> You *shouldn't drink* the water.
> [main verb *drink* with helping verb *should* and adverb *not*]

Phrases as Modifiers

> *Looking through the book,* Chou decided to buy it.
> [participial phrase used as an adjective modifying *Chou*]

SENTENCES

Benitez had been visiting *with his sister* when the accident occurred.
[prepositional phrase used as an adverb modifying verb *had been visiting*]

Phrases as Connecting Words

In spite of that, the commission turned down the request.
[phrasal preposition taking the place of a single one such as *despite*]

The programs are *similar to* each other.
[phrasal preposition taking the place of a single one such as *like*]

Clauses

Clauses come in two main kinds, although the second can be further divided into two types. When we look at sentences, we'll see how clauses are another useful way to vary your writing.

Independent Clauses

○ An *independent (or main) clause* is one that can stand alone as a complete sentence.

You may think of it as a sentence within a sentence because other clauses are often attached to it to make a longer sentence. In a sentence with more than one independent clause, one of the clauses may start with a *coordinating conjunction* or a *conjunctive adverb:*

The City Council approved a budget for next year.

The City Council approved a budget for next year, but it stuck to its promise of keeping increases to 4 percent.
[second clause starts with coordinating conjunction]

The City Council approved a budget for next year; however, it stuck to its promise of keeping increases to 4 percent. [second clause starts with conjunctive adverb, a relatively rare occurrence in newspapers]

Dependent Clauses

○ A *dependent clause* is one that cannot stand alone as a complete sentence but must be joined to an independent clause. That's because dependent clauses work as nouns, adjectives or adverbs rather than as complete statements.

Here are some examples of independent and dependent clauses from a sentence in Ernest Hemingway's "A Moveable Feast":

"If you are lucky enough to have lived in Paris as a young man, then wherever you go for the rest of your life, it stays with you, for Paris is a moveable feast." [*It stays with you* and *Paris is a moveable feast* are independent clauses. The others are all dependent.]

There are two kinds of dependent clauses.

○ *Subordinate clauses* begin with a *subordinate conjunction:*

> The County Commission rejected the idea *because no one really pushed for it.* [subordinate clause acting as an adverb modifying *rejected*]

For more on subordinate conjunctions, see Page 100.

○ *Relative clauses* begin with a *relative pronoun:*

> *Whoever made that rule* no longer works there.
> [relative clause acting in place of a noun as the subject]

> He never did figure out *who had been at the door.*
> [relative clause acting in place of a noun as the direct object]

> The person *who had been there* was long gone.
> [relative clause acting as an adjective modifying *person*]

For more about relative pronouns, see Page 41.

Restrictive vs. Nonrestrictive

Phrases and clauses (and even single words) can be classified as either *restrictive* or *nonrestrictive* (also called *essential* or *nonessential*). Knowing the difference helps you know how to punctuate properly. Understanding about restrictiveness vs. nonrestrictiveness can also help you know whether to use the word *that* or *which* in a sentence. See Page 42.

A *restrictive* word, phrase or clause is essential to a sentence's meaning and *is not* set off by commas. A *nonrestrictive* word, phrase or clause is not essential to a sentence's meaning and *is* set off by commas, dashes or parentheses. We think the clearest way to think of items that are nonrestrictive is *parenthetical.*

○ An easy way to distinguish a restrictive from a nonrestrictive element is to ask yourself whether it could be set off by parentheses. If it could, it's nonrestrictive, so set it off with commas.

Here are some examples of words, phrases and clauses that are *nonrestrictive* (*nonessential* or *parenthetical*) and should be set off by commas:

> "Yes, *Juanita,* I'm over here." [*Juanita* is a noun of direct address and is nonessential—the sentence means the same thing without it.]

> Kansas City's Dwight Frizzell, *an eclectic avant-garde composer,* has just released a new album, "Bullfrog Devildog President." [The phrase *an eclectic avant-garde composer* is acting as an appositive and is nonessential.]

"Beautiful Losers," *the second novel by Canadian poet Leonard Cohen,* combined spirituality and sexuality.
[The phrase *the second novel by Canadian poet Leonard Cohen* works as an adjective modifying *"Beautiful Losers"* and is nonessential.]

That actor — *who had never played professionally before* — won the part.
[The relative clause *who had never played professionally before* works as an adjective modifying *actor* and is nonessential.]

Knowing the difference between restrictive and nonrestrictive elements often makes a difference in understanding what a sentence means. Take a look at this sentence, for example: *Their daughter Dawn arrived with her husband, Kirk.* The absence of commas around *Dawn* indicates that they have more than one daughter, so the name is essential to the meaning of the sentence. *Kirk,* however, is set off by a comma, which indicates that Dawn has only one husband, so his name is not essential to the meaning of the sentence.

Compare these nonrestrictive and restrictive versions of similar sentences:

When he was a child, he said, other boys made fun of him.
[The commas around *he said* indicate that those words are not essential and that a statement was made later in life about incidents that happened during childhood.]

When he was a child, he said other boys made fun of him.
[Here, a comma sets off only the introductory clause. The absence of a comma after *he said* indicates that those two words are essential to the independent clause. In other words, he made the statement when he was a child rather than later in life.]

Journalism Tip
Punctuating Nonrestrictive Phrases and Clauses

Journalists usually avoid parentheses and set off nonrestrictive elements with commas. They use dashes instead of commas, though, when the parenthetical element has commas inside it or if they want a longer pause:

WRONG	Henderson *(the forward)* ran up the left side to receive the pass.
RIGHT	Henderson, *the forward,* ran up the left side to receive the pass.
WRONG	The whole package *(two tickets, two soft drinks and two hot dogs)* cost $40.
WRONG	The whole package, *two tickets, two soft drinks and two hot dogs,* cost $40.
RIGHT	The whole package — *two tickets, two soft drinks and two hot dogs* — cost $40.

Sentences

On the simplest level, a sentence consists of a subject and a verb — that is, someone or something doing or being: *"Existence exists,"* says Ayn Rand in a grammatically simple but philosophically complex sentence. In some sentences, the subject is understood, as in a command: *Run!* Sometimes, the sentence contains a direct object and sometimes an indirect object: *The president sent Congress the bill.* Sometimes, the sentence contains a predicate complement: *"This looks like the big one,"* the general said. Sentences also may contain modifiers and additional phrases and clauses.

Mastering the following forms of sentences gives your writing variety.

○ A *simple sentence* has one independent clause:

> The team is in a slump.

Note that a sentence may have more than one subject and verb and still be a simple sentence because it has just one independent clause:

> The team and the coach are hoping and praying.
> [has a compound subject and compound predicate but only one clause]

○ A *compound sentence* has two or more independent clauses, each expressing a complete thought.

Compound sentences are used to show that thoughts are related and equal. They can be constructed in three ways:

- Independent clauses may be connected by a comma and a *coordinating conjunction (and, but, for, nor, or, yet):*

> The team is in a slump, but the coach is unconcerned.

- Independent clauses may be connected by a semicolon:

> The team is in a slump; the coach is unconcerned.

- Independent clauses may be connected by a *conjunctive adverb (accordingly, also, anyhow, besides, consequently, however, moreover, nevertheless, otherwise, so, still, then, therefore, thus)* along with a semicolon:

> The team is in a slump; however, the coach is unconcerned.

○ A *complex sentence* contains one independent clause and one or more dependent clauses:

> The team was in a slump already when its best pitcher broke his arm.

Dependent clauses are subordinated to the independent clause by *subordinating conjunctions (although, as, as if, as though, because, before, if, since, that, till, unless, until, when, where, whether)* or *relative pronouns (that,*

SENTENCES

that which, what, which, who, whom, whose). If you see subordinating conjunctions or relative pronouns, what follows is probably a dependent clause.

○ A *compound-complex sentence* contains two or more independent clauses and one or more dependent clauses:

> The cat was on the mat, and the dog was eyeing him when Mandeville came home.

Journalism Tip
Using Different Types of Sentences

Media writers should remember the following points about sentences:

○ *Simple sentences* are the easiest to understand and make a great way to stress a point clearly. But too many of them in a row sound choppy and distracting.

○ *Compound sentences, complex sentences* and *compound-complex sentences* should be used only when the writer wants to stress that two ideas or more are closely related. Otherwise, the writing can become illogical or confusing:

WEAK	The Ann Arbor Art Fairs attract about 700,000 visitors, and Ypsilanti holds an annual Frog Island Jazz Festival. [What is the connection between these events? The compound sentence implies there is one but doesn't say it.]
BETTER	The Ann Arbor Art Fairs attract about 700,000 visitors annually. Next door, the town of Ypsilanti also attracts visitors with its annual Frog Island Jazz Festival.
WEAK	Palmer, who also has a master's degree in philosophy, is socially adept when it comes to interacting with her patients. [What is the logical connection between her master's degree and her social skills? The sentence implies one, intentionally or not.]
BETTER	Palmer is socially adept when it comes to interacting with patients. But there's a more solitary, intellectual side of her, as well, as evidenced by her master's degree in philosophy.

○ With *complex sentences,* it's usually clearer not to separate the subject and verb of an independent clause with a dependent clause:

WEAK	The president, although the Cabinet advised against it, vetoed the measure.
BETTER	The president vetoed the measure, although the Cabinet advised against it.

○ Finally, *compound-complex sentences* usually are too long to make good leads for articles, so if you've led with one, consider breaking it down.

Sentence Errors

Unfortunately, sentences sometimes go astray. Here are some common ways.

Fragments

○ A *fragment* is a word or group of words that isn't a complete sentence. Either it lacks a subject or verb or it's a dependent clause:

> A team for all seasons.

> Takes the guesswork out of the game.

> Because he was sick.

Fragments are becoming acceptable to more editors these days, but you shouldn't use fragments unless you have a specific reason. For example, fiction writers use them to capture the way people speak. Ad writers use them to stress a product name: *Joe's Shoes. For people who love their feet.*

Also, some grammarians consider an answer to a question a complete sentence even though it may be incomplete on the surface. They consider the other elements implied: *Why didn't he come? Because he was sick.* Some are also willing to accept a brief transition or a short question as a sentence:

> And now the news.

> Why?

> What more could I do? Sing? Dance?

Fused Sentences

○ A *fused sentence* unacceptably combines two or more sentences without punctuation between them:

WRONG	The mayor left town the auditor did, too.
RIGHT	The mayor left town, and the auditor did, too.
RIGHT	The mayor left town. The auditor did, too.
RIGHT	The mayor left town; the auditor did, too.
	[Journalists usually avoid this approach and either use the comma and conjunction to make a compound sentence or break it into two simple sentences.]

Fused sentences are acceptable only in nonfiction as a quotation from the writings of a semiliterate person.

Comma-Splice Sentences

○ A *comma-splice sentence* unacceptably connects two or more independent clauses with only a comma:

WRONG   The officers were fired, the police chief was, too.

RIGHT   The officers were fired, and the police chief was, too.

RIGHT   The officers were fired. The police chief was, too.

RIGHT   The officers were fired— the police chief was, too.

RIGHT   The officers were fired; the police chief was, too.
[Again, journalists would usually choose one of the previous correct versions rather than use the semicolon.]

Although journalists should normally avoid comma-splice sentences, some writers use comma splices occasionally to imitate conversation. Also, many grammarians now say that a series of short sentences may be connected with commas, if you like, as in Caesar's famous *"I came, I saw, I conquered."* (It could also be translated with semicolons or periods.)

Run-on Sentences

○ A *run-on sentence* may or may not be grammatical, but it usually makes little sense because unrelated items, unimportant details or extra clauses were added as though the writer didn't know when to stop.

Hemingway, however, sometimes used this device to cover ground quickly and let the gaps imply details he didn't want to spell out. The following run-on sentence, although not from Hemingway, is either acceptable or not depending on how effective you judge it:

The blind man's Seeing Eye dog died, and it was a sad occasion, and all the man's friends went to the funeral then went to the bar and drank to his health and said how unfair it was.

Such a sentence might work in fiction, but few magazine or newspaper editors would likely approve it. William Faulkner to the contrary, the best sentences rarely are longer than 2½ typed lines. Sentences containing much technical information shouldn't average more than about 20 words.

Lack of Parallelism

When parallel ideas are not expressed in a parallel manner, the rhythm of the sentence is thrown off and the logical relationships are made less clear. To make ideas parallel, similar items should be written in similar ways. For example, the items in a series should be alike, whether all nouns, all gerunds, all infinitives, all phrases or all clauses. A series of verbs should all be in the same tense, voice and mood.

WRONG He admires Kathy for her intelligence, energy and because she is a good leader. [nouns and clause not balanced]

RIGHT He admires Kathy for her intelligence, energy and leadership.

WRONG First, he walked in, then he smiled, then he says, "Hello." [past and present tenses of the verbs mixed]

RIGHT First, he walked in, then he smiled, then he said, "Hello."

WRONG He enjoyed gathering information and then to write about it. [gerund and infinitive not balanced]

RIGHT He enjoyed gathering information and then writing about it.

WRONG She was presented the award then left. [passive and active voice in same sentence]

RIGHT She accepted the award then left.

WRONG The teacher was both informed, and she cared about her students. [participle and clause not balanced; active and passive voice mixed]

RIGHT The teacher was both informed about the subject and caring toward her students.

WRONG One should be prepared because you never know who might call. [person of subjects not balanced]

RIGHT You should be prepared because you never know who might call.

WRONG The fishing equipment cost as much or more than a bicycle. [conjunctions not balanced because part of one missing]

RIGHT The fishing equipment cost as much as or more than a bicycle.

ESL Tip

If native speakers of English often have trouble keeping sentences parallel, nonnative speakers face a bigger challenge. Students should find, though, that studying the examples here helps them solve some common problems in keeping longer sentences grammatical.

Web Resources

SEARCH ENGINES

The Internet is sometimes called the "world's biggest library." There's a measure of truth in that; all sorts of information can be found there, if you know how to navigate well enough to find what you want. Here are the World Wide Web addresses of the most popular Internet search engines. Using them will lead you to the right place.

- **Alta Vista**
  www.altavista.digital.com

- **Go.com**
  www.infoseek.com

- **Google**
  www.google.com

- **Lycos**
  www.lycos.com

CHAPTER 3

Subjects and Objects

There are many kinds of subjects and objects. Let's start with what words can be subjects or objects before we try tackling all the varieties.

- A *noun* names a person, place or thing, or an idea or quality:

  Susan, Michigan, book, freedom, beauty

Sometimes other words, such as pronouns, gerunds and infinitives, act as nouns.

- A *pronoun* is the most common type of word that takes the place of a noun:

  I, you, him, our, it, theirs, one, someone, everybody

- A *gerund* or an *infinitive* can also take the place of a noun. We'll discuss infinitives in Chapter 5. A *gerund* is a form of the verb, usually ending in *ing, ed, t* or *en,* that is used as a noun:

  His cousin was a state champion in *swimming.* [object of a preposition]

  The whole family enjoys *traveling the country.*
  [gerund phrase acting as a direct object]

- Often, an entire phrase or clause acts as a single noun:

  Johnston said *police have obtained a search warrant to search the suspect's home.*

  Striking city workers walked the picket line outside City Hall for the fifth day today.

To tell whether such a phrase is acting as a noun, try substituting a pronoun for it. If it makes sense, the phrase is acting as a noun. For example:

  Johnston said *it.*

  They walked the picket line.

Kinds of Subjects

In a sentence, nouns, pronouns and other noun substitutes act as subjects or objects. Subjects and objects can be further divided into a variety of kinds.

○ A subject is the noun or pronoun that is doing the acting or being in a sentence. To find the subject, ask "Who?" or "What?" before the verb:

> The *Cornhuskers* won the game.
> [Who won the game? The *Cornhuskers*.]
>
> The *fee* for graduate students is more this year.
> [What is more this year? The *fee*.]

Sometimes, the subject is also called the *simple subject* to distinguish it from the *complete subject,* which is the subject and its modifiers. In the preceding examples, *The Cornhuskers* is the complete subject of the first sentence and *The fee for graduate students* is the complete subject of the second.

○ A *predicate nominative* is a noun or its substitute that follows a linking verb (see Page 58) and restates the subject. Technically, it's a modifier, but think of it as the subject because if the predicate nominative is a pronoun, it should take the same form it would as a subject:

> The change in party control of the Senate became *a problem for the president's agenda.* [linking verb: *became*]
>
> That is *she.* [linking verb: *is*]

○ A *subject of an infinitive* is a noun (or its substitute) that comes between the verb and the infinitive. Oddly, if the subject of an infinitive is a pronoun, it takes the same form it would if it were an object of some kind:

> The police took *her* to be a modern Dillinger.
> [verb: *took;* infinitive: *to be*]
>
> He encouraged *his children* to play sports.
> [verb: *encouraged;* infinitive: *to play*]

Kinds of Objects

○ A *direct object* is the direct receiver of the action in a sentence. To find the direct object, ask "Whom?" or "What?" after the verb:

The board thanked *him* for his 20 years of service.
[Thanked whom? *Him*.]

Two spacewalking astronauts installed new science *equipment* on the international space station Thursday. [Installed what? *Equipment*.]

○ A *predicate objective* (or *objective complement*) sometimes follows a direct object and restates it:

The American public elected him *president*. [direct object: *him*]

The proud parents named their new son *Taylor*. [direct object: *son*]

○ An *indirect object* is the person or thing to whom or to which, or for whom or for which, an action is done. To tell the difference between an indirect object and a direct object in front of a predicate objective, remember that you can put *to* or *for* in front of an indirect object:

He gave the *Detroit Free Press* an exclusive.
[He gave an exclusive to whom? The *Detroit Free Press*.]

She gave *them* the report this morning.
[She gave the report to whom? *Them*.]

○ An *object of a preposition* is a noun or its substitute following a preposition:

In the *movie*, apes rule the planet. [preposition: *in*]

The skidmarks began near this *driveway*. [preposition: *near*]

If the object of the preposition is also acting as the indirect object of the sentence, by convention its role as indirect object takes precedence in labeling it. This may be because usually a prepositional phrase acts as an adjective or adverb, not as a noun or pronoun:

Rogelio recalled for his *parents* the events of that day.
[*Parents* is the object of the preposition *for* but should more precisely be called the indirect object of the sentence.]

○ An *object of a participle* is a noun or its substitute following a participle:

The automaker will take a $200 million charge, resulting from the *write-down* of investments. [participle: *resulting*]

A blond-haired man was spotted carrying a *gun*. [participle: *carrying*]

○ An *object of a gerund* is a noun or its substitute following a gerund:

Playing *poker* with them left him poorer. [gerund: *playing*]

The witness said he didn't believe in naming *names*. [gerund: *naming*]

○ An *object of an infinitive* (or *infinitive complement*) answers "What?" "Whom?" or "Where?" after an infinitive:

> The police want him to answer some *questions*.
> [What do they want him to answer? *Questions*.]
>
> They thought Juanita to be *her*.
> [Whom did they think Juanita to be? *Her*.]
>
> The hostages want to come *home*.
> [Where do the hostages want to come? *Home*.]

Common Nouns vs. Proper Nouns

Let's take a look at when to capitalize a noun and when not to do so.

In centuries past, people capitalized many nouns we wouldn't today. Nowadays, we just capitalize proper nouns (such as *Andrew, Colorado,* or *January*) and lowercase common nouns (generic nouns, such as *truck* or *toothpaste*). But two main problems complicate this: trademarks and names of animals, plants and foods.

○ **Don't confuse trademark terms with generic ones. Generic terms should always be used unless the specific name brand is being singled out.**

Here's a list of some trade names that are often used incorrectly when the generic term is meant.

BRAND NAME	GENERIC
Aqua-Lung	underwater breathing apparatus
AstroTurf	artificial surface
Bake-off	baking contest
Band-Aid	adhesive bandage
Books on Tape	audiotape book
Chap Stick	lip balm
Cheez Doodles	cheese-flavored corn puffs
Coke	cola
Crayola	crayons
Crock-Pot	electric earthenware cooker
Day-Glo	fluorescent colors
Deepfreeze	freezer
Discman	portable CD player
Disposall	garbage disposer
Dumpster	trash bin
Fiberglas	fiberglass

Journalism Tip
Using Trademarks

When a trademark has become so well-known that people start using it generically, the company might lose its exclusive use of the brand name. *Adrenalin, aspirin, heroin, pacemaker, thermos* and *yo-yo* were formerly trademarks but have since become acceptable as generic terms in the United States.

To protect their trademarks, companies often try to enforce their legal claims to brand names by threatening publications with legal action when the terms are used generically. This typically means that a company will send a letter to an offending publication to inform the editors of the trademark violation and threaten legal action if it happens again.

BRAND NAME	GENERIC
Formica	plastic laminate
Freon	refrigerant
Frisbee	flying disk
Fudgsicle	fudge ice-cream bar
Hi-Liter	highlighting marker
Jacuzzi	whirlpool bath
Java	scripting software
Jeep	*jeep* for military vehicle; otherwise, four-wheel-drive vehicle
Jell-O	gelatin
Jockey	underwear
Kitty Litter	cat-box filler
Kleenex	tissue
Kool-Aid	soft-drink mix
Krazy Glue	superadhesive
Land Rover	all-terrain vehicle
Laundromat	coin-operated laundry
Levi's	jeans
Little League Baseball	youth baseball
Lucite	acrylic paint
Mace (short for *Chemical Mace*)	tear-gas spray
Magic Marker	felt-tip marking pen
Moon Pie	marshmallow sandwich
Naugahyde	simulated leather
Nerf	foam toy
Nintendo	video-game player
Novocain	procaine hydrochloride

BRAND NAME	GENERIC
Oreo	cookie
Ouija	fortunetelling board game
Photostat	photocopy
Ping-Pong	table tennis
Popsicle	flavored ice on a stick
Post-it	self-stick note
Quaalude	methaqualone
Q-Tips	cotton swabs
Realtor	real-estate agent
Rollerblade	in-line skate
Rolodex	address-card file
Scotch tape	cellophane tape
Seeing Eye dog	guide dog
Sheetrock	gypsum wallboard
Spam	luncheon meat
Styrofoam	foam plastic
Tabasco	hot-pepper sauce
TelePrompTer	TV cuing device
Vaseline	petroleum jelly
Velcro	adhesive fastener
Windbreaker	lightweight jacket
Windex	glass cleaner
Wite-Out	correction fluid
Xerox	photocopy
Ziploc	zippered plastic bag

● **With animals, foods and plants, capitalize only the parts of a compound name that would be capitalized by themselves:**

> German shepherd, basset hound
>
> Boston cream pie, chocolate fudge supreme
>
> Dutch elm, lily of the valley

Wire-service exceptions include *brussels sprouts, french fries, graham crackers* and *manhattan cocktail.*

The Forms Nouns Take

Nouns in English change their spellings for singular vs. plural *(number)* and possessive or not *(case)*.

A few nouns also change their spellings for *gender,* but these are mostly disappearing. For example, a woman who writes poetry used to be called a *poetess,* but that is seen as a demeaning term today, and the preferred word is *poet* for both men and women. Some words have kept the distinction, but even *actress* and *hostess* are being replaced by *actor* and *host.*

Forming Singulars and Plurals of Nouns

- The rule for making an English noun plural is, in most instances, to add *s* to the singular form. If it already ends in *s* in the singular, as is especially true of some people's surnames, add *es.*

- The plural of nouns ending in *ch, s, sh, ss, tch, x, z* or *zz* is formed by adding *es.*

- The plural of nouns ending with a consonant followed by *y* is generally formed by changing the *y* to *i* and adding *es: try, tries.* If the noun ends with a vowel followed by *y,* generally the *y* stays the same and *s* is added: *day, days.* For proper nouns ending in a consonant followed by *y,* the plural is formed by adding *s: Kelly, Kellys.*

- The plural of nouns ending in *fe* or *lf* is often formed by changing the ending to *ve* and adding *s: knife, knives; self, selves; wife, wives; wolf, wolves.* The plural of some nouns ending in *f,* however, requires adding only *s: roof, roofs; proof, proofs.*

- The plural of nouns ending in *o* is often formed simply by adding *s: duos, ghettos, pianos, radios, solos, trios, zeros.* The plural of many such nouns, however, requires *es: heroes, potatoes, tomatoes, tornadoes, volcanoes.*

- The plural of some words is formed using *en: child, children; ox, oxen; woman, women.* This is a leftover from the Old English tongue (A.D. 450 to 1066).

- Some singular words from foreign languages maintain the foreign plural: *alumnus* (male singular) becomes *alumni; alumna* (female singular) becomes *alumnae.* Similarly, *bacterium* (singular) becomes *bacteria; criterium* or *criterion* becomes *criteria; datum* becomes *data; graffito* becomes *graffiti; medium* becomes *media; memorandum* becomes *memoranda; phenomenon* becomes *phenomena;* and *stratum* becomes *strata.* Notice that many people misuse the plural form of some of these for the singular.

- Some words have the same form in the plural as in the singular: *deer, sheep.*

● The plural of some compound words is formed by adding *s* to the end of the first word: *attorneys general, mothers-in-law*. The plural of a single letter is formed by adding *'s*: *A's*. The plural of a multiletter word or abbreviation, or of a single-digit or multidigit number, is formed without the apostrophe: *ABCs, 1s, 1990s*.

Forming Possessives of Nouns

Unlike in some languages, English nouns are spelled the same whether they're used in a sentence as a subject or as an object. (That is not true of pronouns, as we'll see later in this chapter.) But the spelling of a noun does change if the noun owns something *(the girl's doll)* or has an attribute that's being discussed *(the computer's power)*. When we add an apostrophe or *'s* to the end of a noun, we say that noun is written in *possessive case*.

● The rule for forming the possessive case of a noun is to add *'s* to the end of a singular noun, just an apostrophe to the end of a plural noun: *a boy's goal, the boys' goals*. But there are numerous exceptions, as the rest of this list shows.

● Nouns plural in form but singular in meaning add only an apostrophe: *mumps' effects, General Motors' losses*. But in general, when an inanimate object is doing the possessing, it is better to use *of* or *at*: *the effects of mumps, the losses at General Motors*.

● Nouns that are the same in singular and plural are treated like singulars: *sheep's wool*.

● Singular *common nouns* (generic names such as *tree, child, happiness*) that end in *s* or an *s* sound normally add *'s*: *a witness's testimony*. But if the next word starts with *s* or an *s* sound, the possessive common noun takes only an apostrophe: *for goodness' sake, for appearance' sake*.

● Singular *proper nouns* (actual, specific names) ending in *s* add only an apostrophe: *Jesus' birth*.

● *Compound words* add the apostrophe or *'s* to the word nearest the object possessed: *attorney general's* (singular, possessive) *opinion, mothers-in-law's* (plural, possessive) *affection*.

● In case of ownership by two people, either one or two possessives may be used, depending on the sense: *Mary and Bill's cars* (they own them together, so one *'s* for the two), but *Mary's and Bill's cars* (they own them separately, so each takes *'s*).

○ If you can turn the phrase around and insert *for* between the words, it's merely a descriptive phrase rather than truly possessive and does not need the apostrophe or *'s: citizens band radio (radio band for citizens), teachers college* (college for teachers, not one they own), *writers guide* (a guide for writers).

Sometimes, despite this rule, you have to use *'s* with descriptive phrases because the plural form doesn't end in *s: children's play, women's college.* Sometimes, too, a phrase can be turned around and *for* inserted, but *of* would work just as well: *teachers salaries.* Does this mean "salaries for teachers" or "salaries of teachers"? When it could go either way, the plural often substitutes for the possessive. In this particular example, however, you could drop the *s* and avoid the problem: *teacher salaries.*

Some other exceptions include *baker's dozen, baker's yeast, confectioners' sugar, nurse's aide* and *tinker's damn.*

If the descriptive phrase is used in the name of an organization, use the apostrophe or not according to the organization's preference: *Actors' Equity, Ladies' Home Journal, Borders* (bookstore chain).

○ Some phrases that are merely descriptive rather than possessive are better hyphenated instead:

NOT TRULY POSSESSIVE: three weeks' vacation

BETTER: three-week vacation

○ Some editors insist that inanimate objects that could not really own something should not be made possessive. They would have you write *the power of the computer* rather than *the computer's power,* for example. Such a rule, however, can cause problems with some idioms, such as *a week's pay.* Would anyone really write *the pay of a week?*

○ Double possessives, such as *a brother of Bill's,* occur only when two conditions are met: The word before *of* must involve only some of the possessions—in this case, one brother, not all of them—and the word after *of* cannot be an inanimate object. So, for example, write *a friend of the company,* not *a friend of the company's,* because a company is an inanimate object.

Pronoun Agreement

○ A pronoun must agree with its *antecedent* (the noun or pronoun to which it refers) in *person* (first, second or third), *gender* (male, female or neuter) and *number* (singular or plural).

○ The term *person* is easier to understand by example than by explanation. It refers to who or what is speaking, is spoken to or is spoken about. There are three persons, each of which has particular pronoun forms:

FIRST PERSON   I, we [for when I'm speaking about myself or my group]

SECOND PERSON   you, you [for when one person is speaking to a second person or a group of people]

THIRD PERSON   he, she, it, one, they [when two of us are speaking about a third person or group]

○ A pronoun can be singular or plural. Some common *singular pronouns* include *I, he, she, it* and *one.* Some common *plural pronouns* include *we* and *they. You* can be either singular or plural depending on the meaning. The singular pronouns *thou* and *thee,* found in the King James Bible, have disappeared from modern usage except in religious contexts.

○ Most English pronouns are neuter in *gender,* but the exceptions —some of those in third-person singular, which are masculine or feminine—are common ones:

MASCULINE   he, him, his, himself

FEMININE   she, her, hers, herself

○ When *one* is the antecedent, the pronoun following should be *one* again, not *he* or *you: One does what one has to do.*

○ After *neither ... nor,* the pronoun must agree with the number and gender of the noun that follows *nor: Neither Frank nor Jennifer would do her* (not *his* or *their*) *part.* Better yet, rewrite the sentence.

○ Do not use *they, their* or *theirs* to refer to a singular antecedent that could be either male or female. Sure, *A reporter should check his copy* is sexist, but *A reporter should check their copy* is ungrammatical in formal writing, although common in everyday speech. As for *A reporter should check his or her* (or worse, *his/her*) *copy,* that gets tiresome fast. Best solution: Make the whole thing plural, and write *Reporters should check their copy.* For more on sexist language, see Chapter 13.

Clear Pronoun Reference

○ Make sure it's clear to which noun a pronoun refers. Try repeating the antecedent or otherwise rewriting the sentence:

CONFUSING: The woman spoke loudly because she was hard of hearing—which practically drove her husband crazy.
[What drove the man crazy? His wife's loud speaking or her hearing problem? It's unclear what the antecedent of *which* is.]

CLEAR: The woman spoke loudly because she was hard of hearing—the noise practically drove her husband crazy.

CONFUSING: Juanita's mother died when she was 30.
[Who was 30? Juanita or her mother?]

CLEAR: When Juanita was 30, her mother died.

CLEAR: Juanita's mother died at 30.

POSSIBLY CONFUSING: The Senate passed the bill when it voted on it.
[Readers would probably understand that sentence, but why make them work at it?]

CLEAR: The Senate passed the bill.

In his book "Less Than Words Can Say," Richard Mitchell cites this sentence from a Department of Transportation manual: *"If a guest becomes intoxicated, take his or her keys and send them home in a taxi."* Are we to call a cab for the keys or the guest? Because *guest* is singular and *keys* plural, *them* must refer to *keys*, but many people incorrectly use *them* in a situation referring to a man or a woman.

How about this instead? *If a guest becomes intoxicated, take the car keys and send the person home in a taxi.* By the way, we added the word *car* in front of *keys* because how would the person get in the door if you took the house key, too?

○ It's usually best not to use a pronoun before you introduce the noun to which it refers:

POSSIBLY CONFUSING: If he loses the race, Bennett won't return to his district.

BETTER: If Bennett loses the race, he won't return to his district.

Pronoun Cases

Cases are the forms pronouns take depending on how they are used in a sentence.

○ The *nominative case* is used when the noun or pronoun is the subject, predicate nominative or noun of direct address.

○ The *objective case* is used when the noun or pronoun is the direct object; the indirect object; the object of a preposition, participle, gerund or infinitive; or the subject of an infinitive.

○ The *possessive case* is used to show possession or attribute.

When writing or speaking, use the correct form of the pronouns in the following list according to the preceding rules about their functions in a sentence.

FORMING PRONOUN CASE

Nominative	Objective	Possessive
I	me	my, mine
you	you	you, yours
he	him	his
she	her	her, hers
it	it	its
one	one	one's
we	us	our, ours
they	them	their, theirs
who	whom	whose

Two points about this list are worth adding.

○ *One's* is the only *personal pronoun* (those in the list, except the *relative pronouns who, whom* and *whose*) that uses an apostrophe to show possession.

This is a handy rule to remember to separate *its* from *it's* and to spell *hers, ours, yours* and *theirs*. If we were to look at other kinds of pronouns, as well, we would notice that unlike nouns, the only pronouns that show possession with *'s* end with *one* or *body: anyone's, everyone's, anybody's, everybody's.*

○ When a pronoun has two possessive forms, the first one in the list is used before a noun, the second one after it:

She said that was *her* idea originally.

She said that idea was originally *hers*.

Nominative Case With Pronouns

○ If a pronoun is the subject or predicate nominative (a noun following a linking verb such as *is*), it must be in the nominative case:

She is the *top singer* on the charts in Britain.
[Nouns have only one form for either nominative or objective case, so *singer* is automatically in the correct case as long as it's not possessive.]

It's *she*.

Journalism Tip
Predicate Nominatives in Formal Writing vs. Broadcast

It's she may sound either odd or pretentious to you, but that's because in daily conversation, nominative-case pronouns are reserved mainly for subjects only, not for predicate nominatives. In formal writing, however, *It's she* is preferred over the more conversational *It's her.*

Broadcasters or people writing personal columns may prefer the more conversational use of objective-case pronouns in predicate nominatives.

○ Compound subjects are all in the nominative case:

> *She, he* and *they* were arrested at the demonstration.

○ A pronoun in the complete subject introduced by *as well as* is in the nominative case, even though it does not influence the number of the verb:

> That photographer, as well as *we* two reporters, was in the Soviet Union to cover the summit.

○ A pronoun following *as* or *than* at the end of a sentence is usually in the nominative case, although many people mistake a pronoun in such a position for the object of a preposition. Actually, *as* and *than* are conjunctions, and a pronoun following one is typically the subject of a clause for which the predicate may be implied:

> He finished the test as quickly as *she* (did).

> Aleister Crowley was probably more to blame than *they* (were).

Objective Case With Pronouns

○ If a pronoun is the direct object; indirect object; object of a preposition, participle, gerund or infinitive; or subject of an infinitive, it must be in the objective case:

> Rescuers couldn't reach *them* in time. [*Them* is the direct object.]

> Mia Hamm kicked *her* the ball. [*Her* is the indirect object.]

> His brother borrowed the bike from *him.*
> [*Him* is the object of the preposition *from.*]

> Missing *him,* she wrote a letter.
> [*Him* is the object of the participle *missing.*]

Cleaning *it* up proved difficult. [*It* is the object of the gerund *cleaning*.]

They took *him* to be *me*. [*Him* is the subject of the infinitive *to be*. The object of the infinitive is *me*.]

○ **A pronoun used in a compound object should be in the objective case:**

> WRONG   Between you and *I* ... .
>
> RIGHT   Between you and *me* ... . [The pronouns form a compound object of the preposition *between*. You wouldn't say *between I*.]
>
> WRONG   They invited a friend and *he*.
>
> RIGHT   They invited a friend and *him*. [*Friend* and *him* are compound direct objects. You wouldn't say, *They invited he*.]

○ **If you have a noun or its substitute between a verb and the infinitive *to be*, use the objective case after the infinitive. If not, use the nominative case:**

> Police took Talbot to be *her*.
> [*Talbot* is between the verb *took* and the infinitive *to be*.]
>
> Palmer was thought to be *she*.
> [There is no noun or pronoun between the verb *thought* and the infinitive *to be*.]

The second example at first seems to be an exception to the rule that the object of an infinitive—like any other object—must be in the objective case. But actually, *was thought to be* is functioning here as a linking verb, making the following pronoun a predicate nominative. The easiest way to spot this situation is to note that whenever the infinitive *to be* doesn't have a subject—a noun or pronoun—between it and the previous verb, you should use the nominative case for a pronoun after *to be*.

Possessive Case With Pronouns

○ **Use the possessive case if the pronoun owns something or shows attribution:**

> The president continued *his* address without missing a beat, even when the TelePrompTer failed.

○ **Use the possessive case when the pronoun is followed by a gerund:**

> A producer from Motown Records was there to hear *his* (*not* him) singing that night.

ESL Tip

After verbs, pronouns are perhaps the major grammatical element necessary to understand on the way to mastering a language. First, you have to memorize the various case forms of the personal pronouns (such as *I, me* and *my* or *mine*). Then, you have to learn how to analyze the parts of a sentence to see how the pronoun is used—as a subject, object or possessive adjective—in order to determine which case to use and where to put the pronoun in the sentence. Finally, you have to make sure that each pronoun reference is clear and that the pronoun agrees with its antecedent in number.

Paying close attention to American conversation helps make the proper use of pronouns more automatic, but be aware that conversation often differs from what is considered correct in writing, as some of the examples in this chapter show.

Relative Pronouns

Relative pronouns (who, whom, whoever, whomever, whose, which, that and sometimes *what)* are pronouns that introduce a dependent clause closely connected with the relative pronoun's antecedent. Such dependent clauses are called *relative clauses.* While working as connectives, relative pronouns also serve as the subject or object of the clause in which they occur. The choice of the correct relative pronoun depends on three things: the *antecedent, restrictiveness* and *case.*

If all that sounds complicated, that helps explain why speakers and writers often misuse relative pronouns. But we have a relatively simple solution. We suggest that whenever any of these words appears in a sentence, you run through the following step-by-step procedure:

1. Decide whether the correct pronoun should be from the *that* family (*that, which* or *what*) or from the *who* family (*who, whom, whoever, whomever, whose* or the contraction *who's*).
2. If you decide that the correct relative pronoun should be from the *that* family, choose between *that* and *which* (or possibly *what*).
3. If you decide that the correct relative pronoun should be from the *who* family, choose among *who, whom, whoever, whomever,* and *whose* or the contraction *who's.*

Let's take a look at each of these steps in more detail.

Step 1: How to Decide Between the That and Who Families

⦿ When the word refers back to a *collective noun* (such as the name of an association, business or governing body), a thing (an inanimate object, abstraction and so on) or an animal without a proper name, the relative pronoun should be from the *that* family. When the word refers back to a person or an animal with a proper name, the correct relative pronoun should be from the *who* family.

> Mobil is the oil company *that* (*not* who, *despite the ads*) wants to invite you to support public television. [a business]
>
> The dog *that* bit the child has not been found. [animal without a name]
>
> *Who* is this playwright Horner whom everyone is discussing? [person]
>
> Their cat Fluffy, *who* just had kittens, wasn't straying far from the closet. [animal with a name]

Step 2: How to Decide Between That *and* Which *(or Possibly,* What)

○ Choose *which* to set off something *nonrestrictive* (nonessential to the meaning of the sentence)—or, as we like to say, something *parenthetical.* Choose *that* to set off something *restrictive* (essential)—something you wouldn't put in parentheses.

> RESTRICTIVE: The Nile is the river *that gives Egypt life.*
>
> NONRESTRICTIVE: The Nile, *which flows into the Mediterranean,* gives Egypt life.

○ If you think of a nonessential clause as something parenthetical —an aside—you can remember that *which* introduces a clause set off by parentheses, dashes or commas. *That* introduces a clause not set off by parentheses, dashes or commas:

> RESTRICTIVE: The policy *that critics charged was flawed from the beginning* was amended. [tells which policy of several]
>
> NONRESTRICTIVE: The policy, *which critics charged was flawed from the beginning,* was amended.
> [merely adds a fact parenthetically about the policy under discussion]
>
> RESTRICTIVE: The house *that had a brick front* was theirs.
>
> NONRESTRICTIVE: The corner house, *which had a brick front,* was theirs.

○ Use *what* rather than *that* or *which* mainly in questions and in place of the phrase *that which* or *those which:*

> *What* book has Democrats seeing red these days? [question]
>
> Pundits say he stands a good chance to get *what* he wants.
> [meaning *that which*]

Step 3: How to Decide Between Who and Whom, or Whoever and Whomever

The problem here is that *whom* and *whomever* seem to be on the w in spoken English. Some experts suggest following what many people do in conversation and use *whom* or *whomever* only after a preposition. Others advocate getting rid of *whom* and *whomever* altogether. But **the distinction traditionally drawn, and which most editors still follow, is as follows:**

🔵 Use *who* or *whoever* when the sentence calls for the *nominative case* and *whom* or *whomever* when it calls for the *objective case.* (See Pages 37 to 40).

The hard part, often, is determining which case to use, especially when the sentence has more than one clause. That's because the correct case must reflect the way the pronoun is used in the clause of which it's a part. Look at this sentence:

> Word got out that disgruntled employees were giving free meals to *whoever* asked for one.

Here the preposition *to* would mislead many people into saying or writing *giving free meals to whomever*. Actually, though, the pronoun here is the subject of the clause *whoever asked for one*. This entire dependent clause takes the place of a single noun and acts as the object of the preposition *to*.

Here's another tricky one:

> The police officer asked the witness to point out *whomever* he saw at the scene of the crime.

This time, *whomever* is correct because it's the direct object of the verb *saw*.

If determining the correct case in those last two examples left you scratching your head, help is on the way. It's possible to get *who* vs. *whom* right 100 percent of the time without doing any extensive grammatical analysis. Here's how:

🔵 Begin reading the sentence immediately after the point at which you have a choice between *who* or *whom, whoever* or *whomever.* (If the sentence has more than one clause, this will ensure that you are looking at the correct one.) Then, insert *he* or *him, she* or *her,* or *they* or *them* wherever it makes sense. If *he, she* or *they* works best, use *who* or *whoever.* If *him, her* or *them* works best, use *whom* or *whomever:*

> *Who* did you say wrote "The Red and the Black"? [subject of clause, so nominative case: *Did you say he wrote "The Red and the Black"?*]

> *Whoever* is going had better get ready.
> [subject of clause, so nominative case: *He is going.*]

To *whom* are you speaking?
[object of preposition, so objective case: *Are you speaking to them?*]

Talk with *whomever* you like, and you'll get the same answer.
[object of preposition, so objective case: *You like her.*]

○ To decide when *who* or *whom* needs *ever* at the end, remember that *whoever* is used in place of *anyone* or *anyone who* and *whomever* is used in place of *anyone whom:*

> *Whoever (Anyone who)* was interested could pick up a brochure at the fair.

Whose vs. Who's

○ Don't confuse the relative pronoun *whose* (the possessive form of *who*) with the contraction *who's,* meaning "who is" or "who has." Here, the test is just, "Could I substitute *who is* or *who has?*" If yes, the correct word is *who's.* If no, the correct word is *whose.*

WRONG   *Whose* going to see the new "Star Wars" movie?

RIGHT   *Who's* going to see the new "Star Wars" movie?

WRONG   She said she didn't care *who's* feelings were hurt.

RIGHT   She said she didn't care *whose* feelings were hurt.

Pronouns Ending in *Self* or *Selves*

Reflexive and intensive pronouns (myself, yourself, himself, herself, itself, ourselves, yourselves, themselves) should be used only when the corresponding pronouns or nouns to which they refer have been used earlier in a sentence.

A pronoun is used *reflexively* when something acts on itself: *I hurt myself.* A pronoun is used *intensively* when drawing attention to the noun or pronoun to which it refers: *I, myself, will do it.*

○ The first- and second-person forms of these pronouns come from the possessive case *(my, our, your),* but the third-person forms come from the objective case *(him, her, it, them).* Never say or write *hisself* or *theyselves.*

○ Don't confuse pronouns ending in *self* or *selves* with the properly required pronoun case in a sentence. *Myself* is the biggest offender, especially in a compound subject or object:

WRONG	For JoAnn and *myself*, good night.
RIGHT	For JoAnn and *me,* good night.
	[objective-case pronoun needed for object of preposition]
WRONG	Bill and *myself* are making a list of people who will attend.
RIGHT	Bill and *I* are making a list of people who will attend.
	[nominative-case pronoun needed for subject]

Sportswriter Red Smith said that *myself* is the refuge of idiots taught early that *me* is a dirty word.

Verbal Nouns: Gerunds and Infinitives

○ A *verbal noun* is a noun made from a verb. The two kinds are *gerunds* and *infinitives.* We discuss gerunds here but will discuss infinitives in Chapter 5.

○ A *gerund* is a verb form ending in the present-participle form *(ing)* or sometimes in the past-participle form (*ed, t* and so on) and is used in place of a noun:

Fishing is a relaxing way to spend a morning.

She was one of the *neglected.*

He was a *drunk.*

○ If a *gerund* is directly preceded by a pronoun or noun, the pronoun or noun must be in the possessive case:

He's sorry about his *friends'* bickering.

○ But don't confuse a gerund with a participle. Whereas a pronoun before a gerund should be in the possessive case, one before a participle should be in the objective case:

Can you imagine *(him, his)* singing?

The correct pronoun in that sentence could be either *him* or *his,* depending on what is meant. If the writer is interested in the singing, then *singing* is a gerund and takes *his.* If the writer is more interested in this particular person's abilities, then *singing* is a participle and takes *him.* Say these sentences aloud, stressing the italicized word, and notice the shift in meaning:

Can you imagine his *singing?*

Can you imagine *him* singing?

How can *singing* be an adjective? Substitute another adjective, and it becomes clearer:

Can you imagine him *fat?*

Web Resources

NEWS PROVIDERS

The Internet offers reliable news and other information from many mainstream newspapers, magazines, broadcast networks, and radio and television stations. Editor & Publisher magazine provides a useful index that makes these quick to find by media type or location.

○ **All Links**
   www.all-links.com

○ **Journalist's Guide to the Internet**
   reporter.umd.edu

○ **MediaInfo**
   www.editorandpublisher.com/editorandpublisher/index.jsp

○ **NONCE**
   www.nonce.com

CHAPTER 4

Subject-Verb Agreement

Subject-verb agreement problems are some of the most common ways sentences go wrong. A singular subject needs a singular verb, and a plural subject needs a plural verb. Although that sounds easy enough, some situations can be tricky. It's not always easy to tell whether a subject is singular or plural. Here are some likely sources of trouble.

Conjunctions

A *conjunction* connects words, phrases or clauses. We will discuss conjunctions in greater detail in Chapter 7.

- *And* connecting two or more items in a subject usually makes the verb plural:

    Larson and Shichtman *oppose* the bill.

- The exception is when the words connected by *and* are part of a single thing:

    Pork and beans *is* not exactly the chef's favorite dish.

- *Or* used alone to connect two or more items in a subject makes the verb singular unless one of the items is plural. Then, the verb agrees with the nearest noun or pronoun:

    Mary Teagate or Phil Anderson is answering calls today.

    Mary Teagate or *they are* answering calls today.

- The number of the subject is not affected by phrases beginning with parenthetical words, phrases or clauses that are set off by commas — such as those starting with *along with, as well as, in addition to, including, such as* or *together with:*

47

Blaylock, as well as they, *is* voting in favor of annexation.

⬤ When the correlative conjunctions *not only ... but also* are used, there should not be a comma before the *but also* unless *not only ... but also* connect a dependent and an independent clause. In the first case following, the verb should be plural because the words introduced by *but also* are not parenthetical. In the second case, the verb agrees with the subject of the independent clause:

Not only Mark but also his sister *have* won scholarships.
[There is only one clause here, so there's no comma before *but also* and the verb is plural.]

Not only has Mark won a scholarship, but also so *has* his sister.
[There are two clauses here, a dependent one introduced by *Not only* and an independent one introduced by *but also*. So, there is a comma before *but also*, and the verb following it agrees with the singular subject of the independent clause, *sister*.]

Collective and Uncountable Nouns

Collective nouns are singular in form but plural in meaning. When it comes to verb agreement, form triumphs over function, and collective nouns generally take singular verbs.

Collective nouns include *army, assembly, audience, board, breed, cast, choir, class, club, commission, committee, community, company, corporation, council, couple, covey, crew, crowd, department, faculty, family, firm, flock, furniture, gang, group, herd, jury, mob, orchestra, panel, press, public, remainder, staff, team, union* and *United States*. The names of associations, boards, companies and so on are also considered collective nouns.

⬤ Use a singular verb when the collective noun is being used in the sense of a single group operating together in agreement. Use a plural verb if the noun is used to name a group operating as individuals or in disagreement:

ESL Tip

In British English, collective nouns are typically plural, even when American English treats them as singular:

BRITISH   The government *have* cracked down on terrorists.

AMERICAN   The government *has* cracked down on terrorists.

Assuming you're writing for American media, if you're used to the British approach, you'll need to adjust to the American one.

Journalism Tip
Groups of People in the News

Many news stories focus on meetings of and actions by groups of people—boards, commissions, committees, councils and juries, for example. Remember, although each of these collective nouns names a number of people, the noun itself is considered singular for both verb and pronoun agreement:

WRONG   The City Council *are* holding *their* next meeting at a working retreat.

RIGHT   The City Council *is* holding *its* next meet at a working retreat.

AGREEMENT

The jury *was* seated. [acting as a unit]

The jury *were* split. [Sounds odd, but you can't always trust your ear when it comes to traditional grammar. To avoid the obvious ugliness—to American ears, at least—of this sentence, add the word *members* after *jury*, or, better yet, substitute the word *jurors*.]

○ Unlike other collective nouns, the word *couple* is usually plural rather than singular.

The AP and UPI stylebooks agree to treat *couple* as singular when it refers to a unit and as plural when it refers to two individual people, which sounds like the rule for other collective nouns. But look at these examples:

SINGULAR: A married couple *pays* more under U.S. tax law than two people living together but filing separately. [The *couple* here is two people acting as a unit, filing jointly.]

PLURAL: A couple *were* holding hands in the park. [The *couple* here refers to two people acting as individuals, holding each other's hands.]

In fact, references to *a couple* in American English usually have to be plural. As that great copy editing teacher John Bremner used to point out, if you write that *a couple was married,* then for pronoun consistency, you'd also have to write that *it went on a honeymoon but had a falling out, and it later divorced.*

○ *Uncountable* (also called *noncountable*) *nouns* are nouns that have no plural, although many of them look plural already. They are not so consistent as collective nouns in that some take a singular verb, some a plural.

○ These uncountables take a singular verb: *advice, apparatus, athletics, civics, courage, economics, fun, health, information, jazz, kudos, linguistics, mathematics, measles, mumps, news, remainder, shambles, summons* and *whereabouts.*

AGREEMENT

- These uncountables take a plural verb: *assets, barracks, earnings, goods, odds, pants, pliers, proceeds, remains, riches, scissors, shears, tactics, thanks, tongs* and *wages.*

- These uncountables may take a singular or plural verb depending on the context: *ethics, gross, headquarters, mechanics, politics, savings, series, species* and *statistics:*

    > Politics *is* her favorite subject.

    > Her politics *are* socialistic.

Other Confusing Nouns

- Don't mistake plural nouns ending in *a* with their singular forms ending in *on* or *um. Criteria, data* and *media* are plural, not singular. (For more examples, see Page 33.)

- Units of measurement, such as distances, money, time and weight, sometimes take a singular verb even though they are plural in form. This happens when the amount can be seen as a single amount:

    > Five dollars *is* not too much to ask of a friend.

- In American usage, *majority, number* and *total* are singular if preceded by *the,* plural if preceded by *a:*

    > *The number* of people expected *is* small.

    > *A total* of 50 people *are* expected to attend.

- Fractions and percentages are singular or plural, depending on the noun or pronoun following them:

    > One-third of the *book is* a flashback.

    > One-third of the *customers are* regulars.

    > Fifty percent of the *budget is* for debt retirement.

    > Fifty percent of the *cases are* cured.

Indefinite Pronouns

- *Both, few, many, others* and *several* are plural:

    > Many *were* tragically lost in the terrorist attacks on the World Trade Center.

Another, anybody, anyone, anything, each one, either, everybody, everyone, everything, little, many a, more than one, much, neither, nobody, no one, nothing, other, somebody, someone and *something* are singular, even though some of them seem to refer to more than one:

> More than one *has* deplored the situation.

All, any, each, more, most, none, plenty, some and *such* can be either singular or plural depending on the context:

> All *are* here.
> All *is* lost.

> Some *are* coming.
> Some *is* left.

Some of the indefinite pronouns are worth a special look.

Make *none* singular if it means "no one" or "not one" (which it means most of the time), plural if the sense is "no two" or "no amount":

> None of the people invited *has* arrived. [not one]

> None of the experts *agree*. [no two]

Despite the pleas of most authorities—including Theodore Bernstein, Bergen Evans, William and Mary Morris, and The American Heritage Dictionary—that *none* is more often plural than singular, many people are taught to make it singular all the time, and they will think you have made a mistake if you make it plural.

The UPI Stylebook, though, says that *none* can be either singular or plural provided any related pronoun agrees, as in these two examples it cites:

> RIGHT   "None *are* so blind as *those* who will not see."

> RIGHT   "None *is* so blind as *he* who will not see."

The AP Stylebook's rule also recognizes that *none* can be plural but makes it singular in most instances. Since that's the stylebook you'll most likely use, we follow its advice.

Each is singular if it comes before the verb, plural if it comes after:

> *Each is* going by car.

> They *are each* going by car. [Don't write *They each are going by car.*]

Either and *neither* used by themselves are singular pronouns:

> WRONG   *Neither* of them *have* been found.

> RIGHT   *Neither* of them *has* been found.

WRONG   *Either* of the two *offer* law-enforcement experience.

RIGHT   *Either* of the two *offers* law-enforcement experience.

◯ In the constructions *either ... or* and *neither ... nor,* the words are used as conjunctions, not pronouns. The verb following them is singular or plural, depending on whether the noun or pronoun following the *or* or *nor* is singular or plural:

Neither his parents nor *John is* sure what happened next.

Neither John nor his *parents are* sure what happened next.

Intervening Nouns and Pronouns

◯ If a noun or pronoun comes between the subject and the verb, the verb still agrees with the subject, not with the intervening noun or pronoun:

Wednesday's *newspaper,* along with its supplements, *is* our biggest edition ever. [The subject is the singular noun *newspaper.* The phrase *along with its supplements* is a parenthetical modifier, so the plural noun *supplements* does not influence the number of the verb.]

No one but them *knows* the location. [The subject is *no one. Them* does not influence the verb because it is not the subject.]

Prepositional Phrases

◯ If a subject contains a prepositional phrase, remember that the noun or pronoun following the preposition is almost never the actual subject, so the verb instead agrees with the noun or pronoun before the preposition:

Three *trees* in the garden *were* blown over.

◯ But after a phrase beginning with *one of the, one of these* or *one of those* and ending with *who, which* or *that,* the real subject of the dependent clause is the noun or pronoun following *of:*

She is one of those *people* who *are* always on time.
[Of the people who are always on time, she is one.]

One of those *solutions* that *are* cheap looks good.
[Of those solutions that are cheap, one looks good.]

◯ If the *one* in such a construction is preceded by *only, one* is usually the antecedent, and the construction becomes singular again:

She is the *only one* of those people who *is* always on time.
[She's the only one who is on time.]

But there is an exception to this rule:

Only one of those solutions that *are* cheap looks good.
[Here, *solutions* remains the antecedent: This is still one solution of several that are cheap. But it is the only one of those that looks good.]

Subject and Predicate Nominative in Disagreement

When the subject is plural and the predicate nominative is singular, or vice versa, many people are unsure what the number of the verb should be.

○ **The number of the verb should always agree with the number of the subject. Both of the following sentences, therefore, are correct:**

The committee *is* Ernie Havens, Ruth Brent and Bree Oliver.

Ernie Havens, Ruth Brent and Bree Oliver *are* the committee.

Inverted Order

Although the subject precedes the verb in most sentences, the subject in some sentences follows the verb. This inverted order occurs most often in questions and causes little confusion. But here are a couple of situations in which subject-verb agreement problems arise as a result of subjects following verbs.

○ **In a sentence beginning with *here* or *there*, the verb agrees with the number of the subject, which follows the verb:**

WRONG   Here *is* the answers to Sunday's crossword.

RIGHT   Here *are* the answers to Sunday's crossword.

WRONG   There *is* no two ways about it.

RIGHT   There *are* no two ways about it.

○ **Don't write stilted sentences with inverted sentence order. They sound awkward and can sometimes result in confusion about subject-verb agreement:**

WRONG   From the mouths of fools sometimes *come* wisdom.

STILTED   From the mouths of fools sometimes *comes* wisdom.

BETTER   Wisdom sometimes *comes* from the mouths of fools.

AGREEMENT

Web Resources

CLASSIC TEXTS ONLINE

Project Gutenberg makes classic texts—those now in the public domain—available for ready access on the World Wide Web.

○ **Project Gutenberg**
   www.promo.net/pg

CHAPTER 5

Verbs

Verbs are probably the most important part of speech to master in speaking and writing. Look at any piece of good writing, and you'll see that verbs give a sentence life.

○ *Verbs* tell what a noun or its substitute is doing or being: *runs, writes, is, seems.* A verb expresses action or state of being. It can even sometimes stand alone as a complete sentence: *Go!*

○ A *predicate* is a verb used as a part of a sentence. Sometimes, it is called the *simple predicate* to distinguish it from the *complete predicate,* which is the verb and its associated words, such as modifiers, objects or complements:

> Two of the candidates *have dropped* from the race.
> [simple predicate: *have dropped;* complete predicate: *have dropped from the race*]

> Lathrop *is* the Republican expected to run in the next election.
> [simple predicate: *is;* complete predicate: *is the Republican expected to run in the next election*]

All verbs can be classified as either *helping verbs* or *main verbs* and *transitive* or *intransitive.* Verbs also have a *tense, voice* and *mood,* as well as *person* and *number.*

Helping Verbs vs. Main Verbs

Verbs are either *main verbs* or *helping verbs.*

○ A *main verb* may stand alone, or it may have helping verbs accompanying it:

> The mayor *loves* her job. [*Loves* is the main verb.]

> She *has loved* working as mayor.
> [*Loved* is the main verb, *has* the helping verb.]

○ *Helping verbs* are mainly used to make some verb forms, such as *simple future, perfects, progressives* and *conditional mood.* These verbs will be discussed later in this chapter.

The main helping verbs are *am, are, be, been, being, can, could, did, do, does, had, has, have, is, may, might, must, ought, shall, should, was, were, will* and *would.* Helping verbs that show mood are sometimes called *modal verbs* and include *can, could, may, might, shall, should, will, would* and *must.* Other words or phrases act like modals in some ways but like main verbs in others. They're called *semimodal verbs* and include *be able to, dare to, have to, have got to, like to, need to, ought to, used to* and *want to.*

Helping verbs are also sometimes used to help show emphasis. For example, we may use a form of the verb *to do* as a helping verb to show emphasis. Often, we underline or italicize the helping verb for emphasis. Less often, we change the helping verb *shall* to *will* or *will* to *shall* to show emphasis (see Page 63). Sometimes, we combine a couple of these techniques, although you should normally be consistent about using either an underline or italics for emphasis in one work. Here are a few examples:

TO DO	I do edit, he did edit
UNDERLINE OR ITALICS	I <u>have</u> edited, he *has* edited
REVERSAL OF *WILL* AND *SHALL*	I will edit, you shall edit

Helping verbs are often misused in several ways.

○ **Don't confuse the preposition *of* with the verb *have:***

WRONG	RIGHT
could of	could have
might of	might have
must of	must have
shall of	shall have
should of	should have
will of	will have
would of	would have

○ **Don't use *can, may, shall* or *will* in the past tense. Think of the conditional forms *could, might, should* and *would* as the past-tense forms:**

WRONG	He *can't* have gone far.
RIGHT	He *couldn't* have gone far.
WRONG	She said she *may* have done it differently.
RIGHT	She said she *might* have done it differently.

○ **Don't use a form of *have* in situations where it might imply volition when none is intended:**

WRONG   He *had* his arm broken.
        [implies the subject hired someone to break his arm]

RIGHT   He *broke* his arm.

● Don't use *would have* with *could have:*

WRONG   If he *would* not *have* had an operation the week before,
        he *could have* finished the race.

RIGHT   If he *had* not *had* an operation the week before, he *could
        have* finished the race.

● Don't use helping verbs such as *had* or *should* with *ought:*

WRONG   The settlers *had ought* to leave.

RIGHT   The settlers *ought* to leave.

● Don't use *might* as a helping verb to *could:*

WRONG   He said he *might could* help.

RIGHT   He said he *might be able to* help.

We don't insist, as some editors do, that the helping verb be kept next
to the main verb in *compound tenses* (tenses that require a helping verb in
their formation). For example, some editors would rewrite *She would absolutely like to excel* to keep the adverb *absolutely* from interrupting the
parts of the verb: *She absolutely would like to excel.*

We have been unable to find any grammar book that agrees with this
practice. In fact, Wilson Follett's influential book "Modern American
Usage" says of it, "The results are uniformly bad." We discourage the
practice for several reasons, including that it makes for sentences written
in a nonconversational order, that the adverb *not* must be placed between the parts of the verb regardless and that changing the order may
change the meaning of the sentence. See the discussion of adverb order
in Chapter 6.

Transitive Verbs vs. Intransitive Verbs

All verbs are either *transitive* or *intransitive* in any given sentence. Some
are transitive in one sentence but intransitive in another.

● *Transitive verbs* have a *direct object* (a receiver of the action)
  behind them to tell to what or to whom the action was done:

The legislature *passed* the bill.
[Passed what? Passed *the bill,* the direct object.]

Police *arrested* Fred Wilson.
[Arrested whom? Arrested *Fred Wilson,* the direct object.]

○ *Intransitive verbs* do not take a direct object. There are two kinds of intransitive verbs: *linking* (or *copulative*) *verbs* and *complete verbs.*

○ *Linking verbs* take a *predicate complement*—either a *predicate nominative* (noun or pronoun behind the linking verb) or a *predicate adjective* (adjective behind the linking verb):

> She is a *cabdriver.* [predicate nominative]
>
> That is *she.* [predicate nominative]
>
> He is *tall.* [predicate adjective]
>
> He is *impressed.* [predicate adjective]

A linking verb can be thought of as an equals sign indicating an equation between the subject and the complement. Linking verbs link the subject and the subject complement.

A linking verb must be followed either by a noun or pronoun or by an adjective. It may be followed by an adverb but always in combination with an adjective:

> He said he *often was* hungry. [*Was* is a linking verb, *hungry* a predicate adjective and *often* an adverb modifying *was.*]

The list of linking verbs includes the *be* verbs—*am, is, are, was, were, has been, have been, had been, shall be, will be;* verbs having to do with the five senses—*appear, feel, look, smell, sound, taste;* and these additional verbs —*act, become, continue, grow, remain, seem, stay, turn, wax.* Knowing when a verb is a linking verb helps you deal with troublesome choices between adjectives and adverbs, such as whether a person feels *good* or feels *well.* See Page 85.

○ *Complete verbs* take neither a direct object nor a predicate complement:

> The woman *hesitated.*

Don't confuse *passive-voice verbs* (discussed later in this chapter), which are always complete verbs, with linking verbs followed by a predicate adjective:

> They *were tired* by the long walk. [*Were,* the helping verb, and *tired,* the main verb, together form a complete verb in the passive voice.]
>
> They *were* tired. [*Were* is a linking verb; *tired* is a participle acting as the predicate adjective. There is no indication here that they were tired *by* anything— a requirement of passive voice—just that that's how they felt.]

Transitiveness or intransitiveness can be a useful distinction to keep in mind when trying to decide among three of the most commonly confused pairs of verbs: *sit* vs. *set, rise* vs. *raise,* and *lie* vs. *lay.* The first verb of each of those pairs—*sit, rise* and *lie*—is intransitive. You don't *sit* some-

thing down, rise something up or *lie something down.* The second of each pair
—*set, raise* and *lay*—is transitive. You do *set something down, raise something up* or *lay something down.* For the *principal parts* (main forms) of these verbs, see the list beginning on Page 64.

Tenses

○ *Verb tense* refers mainly to time—when the action or state of being the verb represents takes place.

Traditionally, it's often been said that English has six verb tenses: *past perfect, past, present perfect, present, future perfect* and *future,* in that order from furthest in the past to furthest in the future. More modern grammars, however, disagree on the number of tenses in English—anywhere from two to 12 or more—depending on how the term *verb tense* is defined.

ESL Tip

Speakers of other languages may note how much easier English verbs are to learn than those in most languages when it comes to the relative scarcity of *inflections*—changes in verb endings for different tenses and persons. But English verb forms may still be among the most difficult in the world to master because of the numerous specialized rules for their use.

The problem is that although we speak in English of *three broad time frames*—past, present and future—we have a number of ways to express those time frames with different nuances in meaning.

The Simple Tenses

To keep things simple and practical, we'll say that each of the three broad time frames has a form we'll call a *simple tense.* To demonstrate, we'll show the *conjugations* (various forms) of a typical verb—*to edit*—for these three simple tenses.

In the following list, each tense is represented by two columns of three lines. The two columns represent the *number* of the verb, with *singular* on the left and *plural* on the right. The three lines represent the *person* of the verb, in descending order: *first person, second person* and *third person.*

Another way to think of the number and person of a verb is as the form the verb takes with different pronouns. All nouns, except nouns of direct address, are considered to be in third person—singular or plural, depending on the ending—and require a verb of the same person and number.

VERBS

SIMPLE PAST

I edited	we edited
you edited	you edited
he, she, it, one edited	they edited

SIMPLE PRESENT

I edit	we edit
you edit	you edit
he, she, it, one edits	they edit

SIMPLE FUTURE

I will/shall edit	we will/shall edit
you will edit	you will edit
he, she, it, one will edit	they will edit

○ Use the simple tenses to identify a particular point of time. Some words that commonly suggest a simple tense include *ago, at, at that time, in (2002 or some other year), last (week, month, year, century), on, then* and *when* (as a question).

ESL Tip

The third-person singular of almost all English verbs in the present tense ends with *s*. The main exceptions are the modal verbs, such as *can, may, must, shall* and *will*.

The Perfect Tenses

In addition to the simple past, present and future, each of those time periods has a second form of expression called the *perfect tenses*, or *perfects*. They refer to completed (perfected) events taking place previous to other events in the same general block of time. In other words, they offer ways to form a verb indicating that something took place before another event in the past, that something in the present started and finished before right now, or that something will already have happened when another event in the future takes place:

She *had edited* that story before she *edited* the next one.

They *have edited* three stories and *are editing* another one apiece now.

You *will have edited* about 30 stories by the time your shift *is* over.

We summarize the three perfect forms of our example verb *to edit* in the following list:

VERBS

PAST PERFECT

I had edited

you had edited

he, she, it, one had edited

we had edited

you had edited

they had edited

PRESENT PERFECT

I have edited

you have edited

he, she, it, one has edited

we have edited

you have edited

they have edited

FUTURE PERFECT

I will/shall have edited

you will have edited

he, she, it, one will have edited

we will/shall have edited

you will have edited

they will have edited

The perfects refer to the same three broad time frames as the simple tenses, but sometimes with different implications than that they merely occurred earlier. For example, look at the following sentences:

RIGHT   Koch *has spent* time in Paris living among the artists. [present perfect]

RIGHT   Koch *spent* time in Paris living among the artists. [simple past]

Either sentence is correct if Koch is still alive. Often, simple past and present perfect are interchangeable in everyday use.

But what if the sentence is about someone who has died?

WRONG   George Washington *has slept* here. [present perfect]

RIGHT   George Washington *slept* here. [simple past]

If you were writing a story about a modern-day inn in New Jersey with a historic past, you wouldn't write the first sentence because it implies that George Washington is still alive. Clearly, you'd write the second sentence, in the simple past.

A useful guideline for deciding between using a simple tense and a perfect is to ask yourself whether the larger time frame referred to is completed by the action in the statement or whether it continues beyond that

VERBS

ESL Tip

The use of the perfect tenses in English can be especially troublesome for speakers of English as a second language because the perfects force distinctions many students may not be used to making in their own languages. For example, the perfects are dying in many European languages, such as German and French.

action. Words that commonly suggest that a larger time frame is continuing, thus calling for a perfect, include *already, during, for, how long, not anymore, not yet, since, still, this (week, month, year, decade), today, until,* and *up to now.*

The Progressive Tenses

There is yet a third way of writing about the past, present or future called the *progressive tenses* or *progressive aspects,* depending on whether a particular grammarian considers them to be tenses.

There are two progressive forms for each broad time frame, one corresponding to the simple tense and one to the perfect. The progressives are formed using some form of *to be* as a helping verb and the *progressive* (*ing,* or *present-participle,* form) of the main verb. We'll give just two examples for each of the progressives:

PAST-PERFECT PROGRESSIVE	I had been editing; he, she, it, one had been editing
PAST PROGRESSIVE	I was editing; he, she, it, one was editing
PRESENT-PERFECT PROGRESSIVE	I have been editing; he, she, it, one has been editing
PRESENT PROGRESSIVE	I am editing; he, she, it, one is editing
FUTURE-PERFECT PROGRESSIVE	I will/shall have been editing; he, she, it, one will have been editing
FUTURE PROGRESSIVE	I will/shall be editing; he, she, it, one will be editing

○ *Progressives,* it's often said, stress the ongoing nature of an activity. Linguists say they're more complicated than that and have to do with something continuing but of limited duration. But the progressives may be even more complicated:

PRESENT PROGRESSIVE	She *is sleeping.* [She started earlier and is still asleep now.]
SIMPLE PRESENT	She *sleeps.* [Possibly suggests this is something she does occasionally.]
PRESENT PROGRESSIVE	The town *is sitting* beside the Mississippi River. [We probably wouldn't say this. It doesn't sound right because it seems to personify the town.]
SIMPLE PRESENT	The town *sits* beside the Mississippi River. [This seems to convey the sense of continuation from the past better than does the progressive.]

VERBS

> ## ESL Tip
>
> Speakers of English as a second language should avoid the mistake of forgetting either the *to be* verb or the *ing* ending in progressives:
>
> WRONG   We learning grammar.
>
> WRONG   We are learn grammar.
>
> RIGHT   We are learning grammar.

Shall vs. Will

You might have noted the choice between *will* and *shall* in first-person singular in the simple future, future perfect, and future and future-perfect progressive. *Will* is more common in conversation, but the strictest traditional grammarians insist on *shall* rather than *will* in those places. We think *shall* sounds too pretentious and old-fashioned to most Americans, and we no longer insist on it, particularly in broadcast. *Shall* is used more often in Britain than in the United States, but it is losing ground there, as well.

If you do decide to use *shall* in the first person, you should know that the same people who insist on *shall* also usually teach that, for emphasis, you use *shall* where you would normally use *will* and vice versa:

NORMAL	EMPHATIC
I *shall* sing.	I *will* sing!
You *will* leave tomorrow.	You *shall* leave tomorrow!

It seems to us, though, that *will* and *shall* can be equally emphatic in the same places. Douglas MacArthur, for example, said, when leaving the Philippines in World War II, *"I shall return!"* not *"I will return!"* Likewise, in the 1960s, the civil rights marchers sang *"We shall overcome,"* not *"We will overcome."* In common usage, in fact, it seems more likely that *shall* will be used to show emphasis, and that's the main time you hear *shall* used.

Regular Verbs vs. Irregular Verbs

Most, but not all, verbs form their conjugations as the verb *to edit* does. *Regular verbs* distinguish the past from the present by adding *ed* or *t: edit, edited; leap, leaped* (or *leapt*). *Irregular verbs* distinguish the past from the present by changing the middle of the verb, by having a different *past-participle* form (for use with the perfects) than the simple-past form or by not changing from present to past to past participle at all:

sing, sang, sung

fall, fell, fallen

broadcast, broadcast, broadcast

VERBS

A common mistake with irregular verbs is to use an incorrect past participle, which usually ends in *ed* or *t*, like the simple past, or sometimes in *en: edited, leap, leaped* (or *leapt*), *written*. Because the past and past-participle forms are the same with regular verbs, mistaking the two forms is a problem only with irregular verbs, where the two may differ.

Here is a list of some of the irregular verbs that cause the most trouble. We have listed the *principal parts* (the most common verb forms) of each: the present, past, past-participle and present-participle forms. If you are in doubt about the principal parts of a verb, consult a dictionary.

PRINCIPAL PARTS OF COMMON IRREGULAR VERBS

awake, awoke, awaked, awaking

be, was, been, being

bear, bore, borne, bearing

bid *(offer),* bid, bid, bidding

bid *(command),* bade, bidden, (not *bidded*), bidding

bring, brought, brought, bringing

broadcast, broadcast, broadcast, broadcasting

burst, burst, burst, bursting

cling, clung, clung, clinging

come, came, come, coming

dive, dived, dived (*dove* is only a bird), diving

do, did, done, doing

drink, drank, drunk, drinking

drive, drove, driven, driving

drown, drowned, drowned (don't say a victim *was drowned* unless an assailant held the person's head under the water), drowning

eat, ate, eaten, eating

fall, fell, fallen, falling

flow, flowed, flowed, flowing

fly *(soar),* flew, flown, flying

fly *(hit a baseball high),* flied, flied, flying

forbid, forbade, forbidden, forbidding

forsake, forsook, forsaken, forsaking

get, got, got or gotten, getting

go, went, gone, going

hang *(suspend),* hung, hung, hanging

hang *(execute),* hanged, hanged, hanging

have, had, had, having

hide, hid, hidden, hiding

keep, kept, kept, keeping

kneel, knelt or kneeled, knelt or kneeled, kneeling

lay *(set down),* laid, laid, laying

lead, led, led, leading

lie *(recline)*, lay, lain, lying

make, made, made, making

pay, paid, paid, paying

plead, pleaded (not *pled*), pleaded, pleading

prove, proved, proved (*proven* is an adjective), proving

put, put, put, putting

raise, raised, raised, raising

ring, rang, rung, ringing

rise, rose, risen, rising

set (*place down;* also, *hens set, cement sets* and *the sun sets*), set, set, setting

shake, shook, shaken, shaking

shine, shone, shone, shining

show, showed, showed or shown, showing

shrink, shrank, shrunk, shrinking

sit *(seat oneself)*, sat, sat, sitting

slay, slew, slain, slaying

sleep, slept, slept, sleeping

spring, sprang, sprung, springing

steal, stole, stolen, stealing

strive, strove, striven, striving

swear, swore, sworn, swearing

swim, swam, swum, swimming

swing, swung, swung, swinging

tread, trod, trodden or trod, treading

wake, woke, waked, waking

weave, wove, woven, weaving

wring, wrung, wrung, wringing

Sequence of Tenses

To use the right verb for what you're trying to say, two things are especially important to understand:

1. The time order of the forms from furthest in the past to furthest in the future. That order, called the *sequence of tenses,* is as follows: *past perfect, past, present perfect, present, future perfect, future.* The easiest way to remember this is *past, present* and *future,* with the perfect form for each tense previous to the simple tense.

2. Special rules regarding the use of each form. Following are some of the most important guidelines for using verbs in the three broad time frames in English.

VERBS

VERBS

Past Tenses

Past Perfect.   Use for events that occurred before those described in the past tense and are now concluded. It's often used with *after, before, by, by the time, until* or *when* to show that one event occurred before another:

> *Until* he turned 50, he *had* never *tried* his hand at writing poetry.

Past-Perfect Progressive.   Use for actions continuing from one point in the past to another one closer to the present before concluding:

> The killing in Bosnia *had been going* unchecked until NATO intervened.

Simple Past.   Use for events that occurred in the past and are now concluded. Use if the sentence answers the question "How long ago?" or, often, if you can use *in* or *on* to express a time element:

> He first *exhibited* the signs of Parkinson's disease in 1975.

Simple Present for Past.   Journalists usually use the simple present to express the past in a headline:

> Governor *signs* death penalty into law

Additionally, in daily conversation, people often use the simple present to express the past:

> "So, then I *say* to him, 'What are you trying to pull?'"

Past Progressive.   Used for something that was happening in the past but has since ended:

> The band *was playing* to packed stadiums in 2002.

Present Tenses

Present Perfect.   Use for events that started in the past and have continued into the present or have some connection with the present. Usually, but not always, used when *already, ever, for, never, not yet* or *since* is used to express a time element:

> If you *have ever wondered* what makes fast-food french fries taste so good, the answer is a sugar coating.

Present-Perfect Progressive.   Use for actions that began in the past and are still continuing in the present. Use if the statement answers the question "How long has this been going on?" A sentence in the present-perfect progressive often uses the word *for* or *since:*

> The Kansas City Wizards *have been playing* well *since* opening day.

Simple Present.   Use for something happening now:

Her book *sits* prominently on the coffee table.

Present Progressive.   Use in place of the simple present for many situations in which something is happening right now:

The president *is meeting* with his advisers at this moment.

Future Tenses

Simple Present for Future.   English often permits the use of the simple present with an adverb of time to convey future action:

She *leaves tomorrow.*

Future Perfect.   Use for events that will have been completed in the future before something else happens. Future perfect is usually used with the word *by, by the time* or *when:*

By *the time* you read this column, the World Series *will have been decided.*

Future-Perfect Progressive.   Use for actions continuing from now into the future when the focus is on what will have been happening up to that point. Future perfect progressive, then, projects into the future and looks back:

This Monday, Tom Williams *will have been coaching* 30 years at Central.

Simple Future.   Use for events that will definitely occur in the future:

The statewide referendum *will decide* the issue this November.

Future Progressive.   Use for events continuing in the future with no end in sight:

A hundred years from now, parents *will* still *be shaking* their heads at their teen-agers' taste in music.

Keeping Tenses Consistent

○ Once you've selected the proper tense, for the most part you'll want to keep the verb tenses consistent.

For example, don't start out using *said* to attribute every quotation and then switch later to *says.* Pick one or the other (generally, use *says* for a feature story only) and stick to it.

○ You can, however, switch tenses for a reason—such as to go into a flashback or to mention an event that occurred at an earlier time or will occur in the future.

Journalism Tip
Special Rules for Verb Tenses

- The basic rule in journalism is that hard-news stories (see Chapter 11) are written mainly in past tense, feature stories in present tense.

- Broadcast news often uses the present progressive for its stories. But resist the temptation of many broadcasters to drop the *to be* helping verb in the broadcast version of a headline:

WRONG   Snow falling heavily in the metro area.

RIGHT   Snow is falling heavily in the metro area.

- Print headlines are normally written in present tense even when they describe actions in the past, but all conjugations of the simple present of *to be* are omitted:

> City Council approves road budget;
> mayor happy with results

When the headline needs to convey future action, an infinitive is substituted for the simple future:

> Senator to propose reduction in health funding

- Photo captions usually are written in the present tense, but sometimes the result is awkward: *Two thousand protesters gather last week in Washington, where 300 are arrested.* You could rewrite it: *Two thousand protesters gather last week in Washington, where 300 were arrested,* but now you've shifted tenses, and a reader might wonder when those 300 were arrested. Were they arrested before the 2,000 arrived or after? One solution would be to rewrite it in the past tense throughout, cut *where* and make two sentences instead of one: *Two thousand protesters gathered in Washington last week. Three hundred were arrested.*

- Many editors insist on a special rule governing the sequence of tenses in what is called *reported speech*. Under this rule, when one is paraphrasing (not directly quoting) what someone has said, simple present becomes simple past (for example, *edit* becomes *edited, can* becomes *could,* and *may* becomes *might*), simple past becomes past perfect (*edited* becomes *had edited*), and *shall* or *will* in the simple future or future perfect becomes *should* or *would* (although *should* is almost never used this way in conversation or in print, *would* being substituted):

QUOTE   "I am young, but I am wise."

REPORTED   She said she was young but she was wise.
SPEECH

The New York Times Manual of Style and Usage is one place where the reported-speech rule is spelled out and urged. But the manual allows for three exceptions:

Special Rules for Verb Tenses, continued

1. When an eternal truth is expressed:

   ACCEPTABLE   The rabbi said God *is* (*not* was) love.

2. When a time element is specified:

   ACCEPTABLE   He said he *was* (*not* had been) depressed Monday when he heard of the trade.

3. When the attribution is in the middle or at the end of the sentence rather than at the beginning:

   RIGHT   Halperin said she *would* (*not* will) vote for the amendment.

   RIGHT   She *will* vote for the amendment, Halperin said, as long as it's not changed.

   RIGHT   She *will* vote for the amendment, Halperin said.

The Reuters Handbook for Journalists allows only the third exception, and then only when the attribution is at the end of the sentence. The Los Angeles Times Stylebook allows for exceptions whenever the action expressed is habitual, customary, characteristic, a general truth or continuing. As it notes, "There are major exceptions to this rule, and a great deal of newspaper writing is in the realm of exceptions."

Indeed, the rule, if followed, applies only to hard-news stories, not features or any other writing in the present tense, where *says* is used in place of *said*.

We have a certain skepticism about using the rule at all, for these reasons:

1. It seems to be potentially confusing:

   She said she *was* in favor of the plan. [But is she still?]

   She said she *would* speak to the class. [But is that based on some condition?]

   Common usage here—*She said she is in favor of the plan* and *She said she will speak to the class*—is capable of more nuances of meaning.

2. Contrary to its supporters, who often call this the sequence-of-tense rule, it really is not a typical sequence-of-tense issue, and even if it were, it would certainly not be the only issue.

   Sequence of tense involves making the verbs in a sentence clear as to the time relationship between the events they describe. But with the reported-speech rule, the verb tense is changed in relation to what was originally said, not in relation to the attribution verb *said*. If the latter were the case, then all the verbs in the sentence would have to be previous to the simple past of *said*. Instead, the rule specifies that something someone said in simple present should become simple past.

3. The reported-speech rule is not nearly so universally urged in style and grammar books as its supporters imply. Not only do the stylebooks mentioned have different versions of the rule, but also the AP and UPI stylebooks, for example, don't have an entry for it at all. If your stylebook requires it, use it. If it doesn't, we suggest being flexible.

VERBS

If switching tenses becomes necessary, it is important to follow the correct sequence of tenses, using an earlier tense for an event that occurred earlier, a later one for something later. For example, if you've been writing in present tense and now you want to write about something that took place earlier, you would switch to the present perfect, past or past perfect.

Voice

All verbs are in either the active voice or the passive voice.

○ *Active voice* stresses the doer of an action by making the doer the subject of the sentence:

The *James Gang* robbed the bank.

○ *Passive voice* stresses the receiver of an action by making the receiver the subject of the sentence:

The *bank* was robbed by the James Gang.

The *bank* was robbed.

The direct object of the active-voice sentence *(bank)* becomes the subject of the passive-voice sentence.

The passive voice has three characteristics:

- It uses some form of the verb *to be*.
- It uses the past participle of the main verb.
- The word *by* or *for* is either present or implied.

The verb conjugations we listed earlier were all in the active voice. Here are sample conjugations in the passive voice:

PAST PERFECT	I had been edited
SIMPLE PAST	I was edited, you were edited
PRESENT PERFECT	I have been edited, he has been edited
SIMPLE PRESENT	I am edited, you are edited, he is edited
FUTURE PERFECT	I shall have been edited, you will have been edited
SIMPLE FUTURE	I shall be edited, you will be edited

○ The main thing to remember about passive voice is normally to avoid using it. It's too wordy, it does not stress the actor, and it relies on the easily dropped *by* or *for* phrase to tell who's doing the acting:

The documents were shredded.

Grammarian Richard Mitchell calls such sentences examples of "the divine passive"—only God knows who did it.

Journalism Tip
Active Voice vs. Passive Voice

Good writers rewrite passive-voice sentences in active voice unless they have a specific reason not to do so, such as when the action or the subject being acted on is more important than the actor, as is often the case in an accident or crime story.

For example, we might find this sentence in an accident story: *Renfrew was taken to St. Mary's Hospital, where he was listed in critical condition.* That sentence correctly uses the passive voice twice. Renfrew, the accident victim, is more important to the account than either the ambulance attendants who took him to the hospital or the doctor who reported his condition.

In crime stories, the passive voice lets us write about an event in which the person acting is unknown or not yet convicted of a crime: *A house on West 33rd was broken into by armed men and the residents beaten and robbed.*

Sometimes, writers waste time trying to rewrite what they think are passive-voice sentences that are not. The usual culprit is a sentence with a linking verb and a participle used as an adjective: *The cost was hidden.* At first, this sentence seems to meet all the requirements of passive voice. You can even imagine an implied *by*. But here the participle is used as an adjective, not as part of the verb. How can you tell? If you can put the word *very* in front of the participle, it's being used as an adjective, not as a verb. There's no need to rewrite the sentence.

○ **Some verbs should be used in passive voice. The verb *divorce* must always be passive voice or transitive:**

WRONG	They married then divorced.	[active]
RIGHT	They were divorced.	[passive]
RIGHT	He divorced her.	[transitive]

Many purists also insist that the verb *graduate* should be used in the passive voice, as in *She was graduated from the University of Arizona.* The AP Stylebook, however, says that the active voice, *She graduated from the University of Arizona,* is better. In the latter case, don't forget the *from*.

Mood

Verb mood is hard to define but has to do with how the speaker or writer regards the statement being made. There are four moods: *indicative, imperative, conditional* and *subjunctive.* It's easier to understand them when we see how each is used.

VERBS

Indicative Mood

We would guess 90 percent of English sentences are in the *indicative mood,* meaning that the sentence in which the verb appears either states a fact or asks a question. All of the verb conjugations we've listed earlier are in the indicative mood.

Imperative Mood

Some verbs are in the *imperative mood,* meaning that the sentence makes a command, issues instructions or entreats:

Add 1 cup of flour.

Please be careful as you pour in the boiling water.

Conjugating imperative-mood verbs is easy because there is only one verb tense (present) and only two conjugations:

Edit! [second-person singular or plural]

Let's edit! [first-person plural]

Conditional Mood

Some sentences use the *conditional mood,* which, as the name implies, expresses a condition. The conditional mood in English is usually represented by one of four helping verbs, although it can use the other modal verb *must,* as well as the *semimodal verbs* (see Page 56). In the conditional:

can becomes *could*

may becomes *might*

shall becomes *should*

will becomes *would*

The conditional mood has forms for many but not all of the indicative simple tenses, perfects and progressives, as these examples show:

PAST PERFECT	None
PAST-PERFECT PROGRESSIVE	None
PAST	I could/might/would/should edit
PAST PROGRESSIVE	I could/might/would/should have been editing
PRESENT PERFECT	I could/might/would/should have edited
PRESENT-PERFECT PROGRESSIVE	I could/might/would/should have been editing [same as past progressive]
PRESENT	I could/might/would/should edit [same as past]

PRESENT PROGRESSIVE	I could/might/would/should be editing
FUTURE PERFECT	I could/might/would/should have edited [same as present perfect]
FUTURE-PERFECT PROGRESSIVE	I could/might/would/should have been editing [same as past progressive]
FUTURE	I could/might/would/should edit [same as past]
FUTURE PROGRESSIVE	I could/might/would/should be editing [same as present progressive]

○ Use *can* and *will* to express certainty, *could* and *would* when a condition is mentioned or implied:

I *can* go. [definite]

I *could* go if I finished work early. [conditional]

The law *will* close tax loopholes. [definite]

The bill *would* close tax loopholes.
[This requires the conditional form because the bill is not yet a law—it would close tax loopholes if it were passed into law.]

The idea of the indicative form as being more certain than the conditional form is not as apparent with *may* and *might* and with *shall* and *should* because neither pair is used in everyday conversation the way traditional grammar asks us to use it in formal written language.

○ *May* and *might* are often used interchangeably in conversation, but we suggest that media writers distinguish between the indicative *may* and the conditional *might* because doing so lets you be correct while still sounding conversational, given that in conversation people usually don't distinguish between the two and won't be jarred.

○ As for *should* in the conditional in place of the indicative *shall*, we suggest *would* as a more conversational alternative, especially in broadcast.

Because few people use the formal *shall* in conversation, instead using *will,* they're more likely to use *would* for the conditional form. In conversation, *should* is usually used only to mean "ought to." This is simply a case where the language has changed except in a few phrases that have persisted, such as *I should think not!*

Subjunctive Mood

Consider the sentence *The bill would close tax loopholes if it were* (not *was*) *passed into law.* The *were* is in the subjunctive mood, which is often used after *if* in sentences in which the verb in the main clause is in the

VERBS

conditional. But the subjunctive mood doesn't have to follow *if*. It should be used to talk about any condition contrary to fact, such as a wish, doubt, prayer, desire, request or hope. Don't be confused: It may be a fact that I wish something, but what I wish for has not yet come true, or I wouldn't be wishing for it.

Nobody seems to have much trouble with the indicative and imperative moods, or with half of the conditional forms (although *may* and *might*, *shall* and *should* can cause problems). The subjunctive, however, is not used nearly so often in English, and few people know how to use it correctly.

Here are some examples of the subjunctive:

If I *were* you *(but I'm not)*, I'd quit.

I wish I *were* a cowboy *(but I'm not)*.

The hijackers demanded that 17 terrorists *be* set free *(they have not yet been freed)*.

The first two sentences may sound odd because many people use *I was*, the indicative-mood form, even when the subjunctive form is needed. As for the third example, most people would probably correctly use *be* because it sounds right and they would not even realize that they were using the subjunctive.

First, let's learn the conjugations in the subjunctive. Then, we'll look more closely at how this mood is used.

The *present tense of the subjunctive mood* is the infinitive minus the *to*. For all verbs other than *to be* (which conjugates in the subjunctive as *I be, we be; you be, you be; he, she, it, one be, they be*), this differs from the present tense of the indicative mood only in the third-person singular: *He asked that the editor <u>edit</u>* (not *edits*) *his story carefully for potential libel.*

PRESENT TENSE OF THE SUBJUNCTIVE MOOD

I edit	we edit
you edit	you edit
he, she, it, one edit	they edit

The past tense of the subjunctive mood for all verbs other than *to be* is the same as the past tense of the indicative mood (*I edited*, etc.). The past-tense subjunctive form of the verb *to be* is, in each instance, *were*.

PAST TENSE OF THE SUBJUNCTIVE MOOD FOR *TO BE*

I were	we were
you were	you were
he, she, it, one were	they were

This is important to remember because some of the most common mistakes using (or not using) the subjunctive involve the verb *to be*. Notice that in the indicative mood, the first- and third-person singular forms use *was* but the subjunctive calls for *were*: *if I <u>were</u> you; if she <u>were</u> taller.*

VERBS

Because all the other tenses are the same in the subjunctive as in the indicative, we often use the subjunctive without realizing it. But that also explains why, in the few cases in which the two moods differ, people often incorrectly use the indicative for the subjunctive: They're not used to making the distinctions anywhere else.

Following are situations in which to use the subjunctive.

○ **Use the subjunctive in most dependent clauses beginning with *if*.**

If usually introduces a condition contrary to fact, so the subjunctive is needed. Occasionally, the condition is not contrary to fact: If the condition is either true or noncommittal, as in this sentence, the indicative is required. Recognizing the difference can sometimes be tricky.

Here are some sentences that use the subjunctive because they contain an *if* that introduces a condition contrary to fact:

> If she *were* rich *(but she's not)*, she would quit her job.

> I could attend the class if it *were* offered sooner *(but it's not)*.

> If compassion *be* a crime, then judge me guilty. [The speaker does not really believe compassion should be considered a crime.]

By contrast, here are some sentences that use the indicative because they contain an *if* that introduces a condition that is true or about which the speaker is noncommittal as to truth or falsity:

> If this experiment *works*, I will be famous.
> [It may or may not work—it is not clearly false.]

> He must have found a ride home if he *is* not in his office. [A person might say this after hearing that a colleague is no longer in his office.]

○ **If the verb in the independent clause is in the indicative mood, the verb in the dependent clause is also usually in the indicative. But if the verb in the independent clause is in the conditional mood, the verb in the dependent clause is usually in the subjunctive:**

> I *can* do it if I *have* the proper tools. [*Can* and *have* are both indicative.]

> I *could* do it *were* I given the proper tools.
> [*Could* is conditional; *were* is given a passive-voice form of the subjunctive.]

Note, however, that although linguists consider *must* and the semi-modal verbs as conditional, those verbs, unlike *could, might, should* and *would,* do not take the subjunctive mood in an accompanying clause. Rather, they take the indicative:

> The speaker of the House *says* (*not* say) the president ought to sign the bill.

VERBS

Journalism Tip
Verb Moods

Journalists do most of their writing in the indicative mood, except for service journalism pieces, such as cooking or crafts articles, that tell people how to do things. Such articles use the imperative mood in their instructions. The conditional mood should be used whenever an article discusses what bills or other proposals would do if they were made into law. Editors should check for the subjunctive mood in sentences in which one of the clauses is in the conditional, as in the previous one.

Likewise, when *should* is used in its normal conversational meaning of "ought to," it doesn't take the subjunctive in another clause:

> The speaker of the House *says* (*not* say) the president should sign the bill.

○ Use the subjunctive in dependent clauses after verbs requiring *that* when the suggestion following is contrary to fact at present: *advise that, anxious that, ask that, demand that, doubt that, eager that, forbid that, hope that, insist that, move that, pray that, prefer that, propose that, recommend that, request that, require that, rule that, suggest that* and *urge that.*

> I *demand that* he *stay.*
>
> I *insist that* he *go.*
>
> It is *required that* I *be* left alone.

○ Verbs requiring *that* but not implying a condition contrary to present reality do not need the subjunctive: *believe that, conclude that, guess that, imply that, infer that, know that, notice that, say that, suppose that, think that* and *wonder that.*

> I *believe that* this *is* true.
>
> I *suppose that* he *is* tired.

○ Use the subjunctive after *as if:*

> He sings *as if* he *were* a professional.

○ Use the subjunctive in these idioms: *be it said, be that as it may, come Monday, come what may, far be it (for, from) me, God be with you, God bless, God forbid, lest we forget, long live (the king), so be it, suffice it to say* and *would that I were.*

> Suffice it to say she was mad.
>
> God bless America!

Two More Issues With Verbs

Consistency

○ Verb tenses should be consistent, except in instances such as flashbacks or flash-forwards, in which a change in time is clearly intended.

It should be noted that English has a number of special rules for what tenses go together in sentences with more than one clause in which a shift in time occurs. For example, when we want to express that something was already taking place when another action occurred, we use the past progressive in one clause and the simple past in another:

> He *was speaking* when the alarm *rang.*

If we merely dropped back in the sequence of tenses and tried to use the past perfect with the simple past in that example, the meaning would be different:

> He *had spoken* when the alarm *rang.*

The second sentence implies that he had already finished speaking before the alarm rang.

There are numerous instances like this with their own special rules that native speakers tend to use intuitively but that create difficulties for foreigners trying to master the subtleties of a language.

○ The voice of the verbs should be as consistent as possible. Don't needlessly shift from active to passive voice:

> WRONG   Stan Smith loves tennis, and his spare time is devoted to it.
> [The first clause is in the active voice, the second in the passive.]

> RIGHT   Stan Smith loves tennis and devotes his spare time to it.

○ The mood of the verbs should be as consistent as possible, with the understanding that it's normal for the conditional to accompany the subjunctive in multiclause sentences.

In addition to sentences where one has to choose between two indicative clauses and a subjunctive and conditional one, verb-mood consistency is often violated in commands:

> WRONG   Read the book, and then you should complete the exercises. [The first clause is in the imperative mood, the second in the conditional.]

> RIGHT   Read the book, then complete the exercises.

> RIGHT   You should read the book, and then you should complete the exercises.

VERBS

Journalism Tip
Verbs in Headlines

Verbs can pose special problems in headlines, where in the shorthand of big type, it's sometimes hard to tell whether a word is meant as a verb or what it means:

> Greeks Fine Hookers

> Juvenile court to try shooting defendant

A second problem can arise from the normal headline practice of dropping *to be* verbs:

> 12 on their way to cruise among dead in plane crash

> Ban on Nude Dancing on Governor's Desk

Be aware of these problems when you're writing headlines, and be careful to avoid them.

Nouns Used as Verbs

Although many nouns are also used as verbs in English, many editors object to using the following ones as verbs.

NOUN	CHANGE TO
author	write
contact	call, write, visit
critique	criticize
debut	have its debut
dialog	talk
gift	give
is headquartered	has headquarters in
host	hold
impact	affect
ink	sign
interface	meet, talk
jet	fly
parent	rear
pastor	lead a congregation
pen	write, sign
premiere	have its premiere
script	write
target	aim at

Likewise, you should avoid using these verbs as nouns:

VERB	CHANGE TO
disconnect	disconnection
win	victory

Verbals

Sometimes, a form of a verb is used as a part of speech other than a verb. A verb form used as something other than a verb is called a *verbal,* and there are three kinds: *gerunds, participles* and *infinitives.*

Gerunds

○ A *gerund* is the present- or past-participle form of a verb used as a noun. We discussed gerunds in Chapter 3.

Participles

○ A *participle* is the present-participle or past-participle form of a verb used as an adjective. We'll discuss participles in Chapter 6.

Infinitives

○ An *infinitive* is the form of a verb that normally has *to* in front of it, although sometimes *to* can be omitted:

May I help cook?

The infinitive is sometimes expanded into past-tense form: *to be read, to have been read.* It can also appear as part of a verb phrase: *He was supposed to leave today.*

Although *to* usually is considered a preposition, it isn't when the word is part of an infinitive. When *to* is followed by a verb, the construction is an infinitive, not a prepositional phrase.

Infinitives may be used as nouns *(To eat is to live),* adjectives *(The issue to be argued is a complex one)* or adverbs *(He went to visit his mother).*

○ Try to avoid *split infinitives*—putting an adverb between *to* and the verb following it:

SPLIT INFINITIVE: She would like *to quickly make* her mark.

NONSPLIT INFINITIVE: She would like *to make* her mark *quickly.*

SPLIT INFINITIVE: She wants *to not be* disturbed.

NONSPLIT INFINITIVE: She wants *not to be* disturbed.

Because Latin infinitives are one word, the grammarians who wrote the first English grammars in the 18th century decided that English

VERBS

infinitives should not be split. Most editors today still follow the rule not to split infinitives. Actually, however, people split infinitives all the time in conversation, and split infinitives had long been a feature of the language when grammarians invented the rule.

Sometimes, it's almost impossible to say what we want without splitting an infinitive. Humorist James Thurber was adamant on this point: *"When I split an infinitive, it's going to damn well stay split."* Many grammarians now agree and allow latitude when the writer cannot find an acceptable alternative, wants *to strongly stress* a point or is imitating a conversation.

In most instances, a conversational alternative can be found to keep the traditionalists happy. But if not, it's better to break this rule than to create an awkward sentence.

○ Avoid *dangling infinitives*—infinitive phrases at the beginning of a sentence but not next to the words they modify:

>   WRONG   *To get ahead in this business, the audience* must be kept in mind.
>   [The phrase *to get ahead in this business* modifies *the audience,* but no doubt the writer meant it to modify *you,* a word that never appears in the sentence. A reader may be able to figure it out, but a dangling infinitive makes the going tougher.]

>   RIGHT   *To get ahead in this business, you* must keep the audience in mind.

○ Don't confuse the conjunction *and* with the word *to* in an infinitive in American English.

Many people substitute *and* for *to* in an infinitive preceded by *try* or *come.* For example, they might write, *I'll try and do it* or *He'll come and work.* Although the English poet John Milton used the idiom *try and* in the 17th century, most editors seem to think the phrase a modern illiteracy and insist that you write *try to.* By the way, *try and* is also the way it's said today in England, but you should avoid it in American media writing.

○ When the infinitive *to be* is part of a linking verb, as in *believed to be* or *thought to be,* a pronoun behind it should be in the nominative case:

>   The benefactor *was believed to be* she.

Web Resources

REFERENCE MATERIALS

Several World Wide Web sites provide reference material, including dictionaries and a thesaurus.

- **Bartlett's Familiar Quotations**
  www.bartleby.com/100

- **Hypertext Webster Gateway**
  www.fin.gov.nt.ca/webster.htm

- **Merriam WWWebster Dictionary**
  www.m-w.com/netdict.htm

- **Thesaurus**
  www.thesaurus.com

VERBS

CHAPTER 6

Modifiers

Modifiers are words that describe or limit subjects, objects or verbs. They provide details.

- An *adjective* modifies a noun or its substitute by telling how many, what kind, which or whose:

    red balloon, *short* dog, *superior* medicine, *good* girl

- An *adverb* typically modifies a verb, adjective or other adverb, generally by telling how, when, where, to what degree or extent, or how much:

    turning *slowly, extremely* stupid, *quite rarely* seen

    In addition to these main uses, an adverb may sometimes modify a verbal, preposition, conjunction or clause.

- An *interjection* expresses an emotional outburst:

    Gee! Wow! Darn!

    An interjection is used to modify an entire sentence.

- A *participle* is a form of a verb, usually ending in *ing, ed, t* or *en,* that is used as an adjective:

    Add one *beaten* egg. [adjective modifying *egg*]

    Finishing a doctoral degree, she found she had little time for her personal life. [participial phrase acting as an adjective modifying *she*]

    Participles also are used in making verb tenses and progressive forms of the verb. When they do so, they function as part of the verb itself:

    The president is *considering* a veto of the bill.

- An *infinitive* is a form of a verb preceded by *to.* It may be used in place of a noun, adjective or adverb:

MODIFIERS

To get to the finals would be a longshot. [noun]

It was a good day *to run.* [adjective modifying noun *day*]

That's unlikely *to happen,* she said. [adverb modifying adjective *unlikely*]

○ A *predicate adjective* is an adjective that follows a linking verb and describes the subject:

The bridge seems *unsafe.* [linking verb: *seems*]

He felt *small,* he said, in the presence of the basketball stars. [linking verb: *felt*]

○ A *noun of direct address* names the person to whom a statement is addressed:

Tom, can you hear me?

Here it is, *Shirley.*

○ An *appositive* is a word or phrase that follows a noun or one of its substitutes and renames it. Although appositives act as adjectives, an appositive could grammatically take the place of the noun it modifies:

The runner, *Gustav,* sat on the ground doing yoga stretches to warm up.

His house, *the one without a roof,* is for sale.

Comparative Forms of Adjectives and Adverbs

Most adjectives and adverbs have three kinds of comparison—the positive, the comparative and the superlative forms—although some have only one, the positive. The *positive* is the basic form of an adjective or adverb and implies no comparison. The *comparative* is used in comparisons of two items or groups. The *superlative* is used in comparisons involving more than two items or groups.

○ For most short adjectives, to make the comparative form, add *er* to the end of the positive form or *less* as a separate word in front of the positive form. To make the superlative form, add *est* to the end of the positive form or *least* as a separate word in front of the positive form:

tall [positive]

taller or less tall [comparative]

tallest or least tall [superlative]

MODIFIERS

○ For most longer adjectives, add the word *more* or *less* in front of the positive form to make the comparative and *most* or *least* in front of the positive to make the superlative:

> beautiful [positive]
>
> more beautiful or less beautiful [comparative]
>
> most beautiful or least beautiful [superlative]

Two main exceptions are *good, better* and *best; bad, worse* and *worst.*

○ To form most adverbs, add *ly* to the end of the positive form of an adjective. This *ly* form is then the positive form of the adverb. Form the comparative by putting the word *more* or *less* in front of the positive form, and the superlative by putting the word *most* or *least* in front of the positive form:

> quick [adjective]
>
> quickly [positive form of the adverb]
>
> more or less quickly [comparative form of the adverb]
>
> most or least quickly [superlative form of the adverb]

○ **Don't confuse the comparative and superlative forms.**

For example, many writers list several items, then refer to *the latter one.* But *latter,* like *former,* should be used only when two items have been listed. That's because they are comparative, not superlative, forms. *Last* and *first* are called for, instead, in such cases. Similarly, don't say someone is *the oldest of the two brothers.* If there are only two, he's *the older.*

○ **Don't include more items in a comparison than intended:**

> **WRONG**   The new reporter is *faster than anyone* on the staff.
> [Assuming the new reporter is also on the staff, he or she cannot be faster than anyone on the staff because the staff includes this reporter.]
>
> **RIGHT**   The new reporter is *faster than anyone else* on the staff.

○ **Don't use comparative or superlative forms with modifiers referring to something absolute.**

Something cannot be *more unique* than something else because *unique* means "one of a kind." Something is either one of a kind or it isn't. Likewise, something cannot be *most unique, rather unique, somewhat unique* or *very unique.* Another word that should not be used with comparatives is *perfect,* contrary to the famous phrase in the Preamble to the Constitution "in order to form a more perfect union."

Adjectives vs. Adverbs

- Use adjectives to modify nouns or pronouns. Use adverbs to modify verbs, adjectives or other adverbs.

- Don't mistakenly use an adjective when an adverb is required to describe the manner in which something happens:

    WRONG   The microbrew is noted for going down *smooth.*

    RIGHT   The microbrew is noted for going down *smoothly.*
    [describes the manner in which it goes down]

    WRONG   The sports car brakes *quicker* than the sedan.

    RIGHT   The sports car brakes *more quickly* than the sedan.
    [describes the manner in which the cars brake]

- Don't confuse a predicate adjective with an adverb. Linking verbs—such as *appear, be, become, feel, grow, look, seem, smell, sound* and *taste*—take a predicate adjective rather than an adverb as a modifier. The predicate adjective follows the linking verb and refers back to the subject:

    The man is *handsome.*

- Some intransitive verbs in some uses may be linking verbs and take a predicate adjective, but in other uses they may be complete verbs and be followed by an adverb:

    He feels *good* to be alive. [*Feels* is a linking verb and is followed by the predicate adjective *good* modifying the subject *he.* The word *good* is an adjective, so you use it after a linking verb to describe the spirits of the subject.]

    The sculptor said her hands cannot feel the clay *well* with heavy gloves on. [*Well* is an adverb modifying the complete verb *feel.* If you want to describe the action of feeling (touching), the verb rather than the subject, you should use the adverb *well.*]

    The patient feels *well* enough to be discharged. [*Feels* here is a linking verb, and the predicate adjective *well* modifies the subject *patient.* When *well* describes someone's health, it's an adjective.]

Consider this sentence: *The thunder sounded (loud or loudly).* To decide between an adjective and an adverb, ask yourself whether the subject is acting. If the sentence means the thunder *clapped* (acted), then it sounded *loudly* (adverb). If it means the thunder *was* (being) loud, then it sounded *loud* (adjective).

So, a flower smells *sweet,* not *sweetly,* because the flower is not acting, just being—it has no nose with which to smell. Likewise, you wax (linking verb) *poetic,* but you wax (transitive verb) *carefully* your car.

MODIFIERS

> ### ESL Tip
>
> Speakers of English as a second language should note that English modifiers other than predicate adjectives and appositives usually come before the word modified. This is not the case in a number of other languages, of course, and there are sentences in English where the modifier may follow what it describes. But when in doubt, try putting the modifier before the word modified.

Coordinate Adjectives vs. Compound Modifiers

Many times, a pair of modifiers precedes a noun or pronoun. Such modifiers usually work either as *coordinate adjectives* or as *compound modifiers*.

○ *Coordinate adjectives* are adjectives that are equal in importance and just happen to be placed next to each other. You can recognize them by this test: You can reverse their order and put *and* between them, and they'll still sound right.

> The *long, narrow* passage was hard to navigate. [*Long* and *narrow* are coordinate adjectives because you could write them as *narrow and long.*]

Notice that coordinate adjectives are punctuated with a comma between them if the *and* is omitted.

○ We suggest systematically *not* placing a comma between adjectives when one or more of them refers to number, color, age, material, ethnicity, nationality or race:

> three pink flamingos [number and color]
>
> old silk dress [age and material]
>
> tall Hispanic male [ethnicity]
>
> healthy Italian man [nationality]
>
> intelligent African-American woman [race]

These exceptions are based on common professional usage in the cases of number, ethnicity, nationality and race. In the cases of color, age and material, we suggest these exceptions because people tend to disagree about the results of the test of reversing the adjectives and putting *and* between them when one of these is in the phrase in question. It's better just to agree not to put the comma there than to argue about it.

Also, note that although these categories are exceptions to putting a comma between modifiers, they do not necessarily imply that no hyphen might be required:

light-blue sky

Polish-American hero

○ *Compound modifiers* are pairs of words in which the first word, no matter what part of speech it normally is, acts as an adverb modifying the second word, which acts as an adjective. Together, the two then modify the noun or pronoun that follows:

well-intentioned friend

oil-depletion allowance

birth-control measures

less-interesting applicants

○ Use a hyphen between compound modifiers that precede the word they modify:

Price is an *out-of-state* athlete.

Remember that this rule applies only to modifiers that precede the word modified. Compare:

She was a *part-time* worker.
[*Part-time* precedes the word it modifies, the noun *worker.*]

She worked *part time*.
[*Part time* follows the word it modifies, the verb *worked.*]

○ The hyphen is usually retained, however, in a compound adjective that follows a linking verb—in other words, if the compound is a predicate adjective:

The work was *part-time*.

The object floating in the sky appeared *saucer-shaped*.

○ Sometimes, however, the hyphen will be dropped, especially if the sentence continues past the predicate adjective. Compare:

The *better-qualified* candidate was Sally. [This clearly needs the hyphen.]

Sally was *better-qualified*.
[Some would drop the hyphen here, but we suggest retaining it for consistency.]

Sally was *better qualified* than the other applicant.
[This clearly makes more sense without the hyphen.]

○ Do not use a hyphen after *very* or an adverb ending in *ly:*

They had a *very enjoyable* trip.

This is an *easily remembered* rule.

Journalism Tip
Compound Modifiers Without Hyphens

Of course, there are always exceptions to rules. In this case, there are some modifying phrases that the AP Stylebook lists without hyphens. Journalists should take care to follow the rules set forth in the stylebook.

○ According to AP style, the following modifying phrases should not be hyphenated:

administrative law judge	*standing room* only
air force base	*stock index* futures
blue chip stock	*stock market* prices
data processing entry	*wholesale price* index
full faith and credit bond	*winter storm* warning
general obligation bond	*winter storm* watch
moral obligation bond	*word processing* program
savings and loan association	

Sometimes there are "unlisted exceptions" where common professional usage takes precedence.

○ The following modifying phrases are not listed in stylebooks or dictionaries, but it is common practice to use them without a hyphen:

high school cheerleader   [but *middle-school* teacher]

income tax relief

gasoline tax increase

○ But do use a hyphen in a compound modifier after any word ending in *ly* other than an adverb, such as the adjectives *friendly, likely, manly, seemly, surly, timely* and *ugly* or the noun *family:*

> He described it as a *"friendly-service"* company.

> Doctorian's is a *family-owned* business.

○ Ages are not hyphenated in a predicate adjective:

> He is *4 years old.* [The predicate adjective *4 years old* modifies the subject of the sentence, *he.* Therefore, there are no hyphens.]

> He is a *4-year-old boy.* [The compound adjective *4-year-old* modifies the predicate nominative, *boy,* which it precedes. Therefore, *4-year-old boy* is hyphenated.]

○ The hyphen is retained in a compound word not preceding the word it modifies if the compound form is found in the stylebook or dictionary as always hyphenated, such as *old-fashioned* and words beginning with *well:*

> He took pride in being *old-fashioned.*

> Henry, *well-dressed* as always, caught everyone's attention.

Articles

○ *Articles* are the adjectives *the, a* and *an. The* is called the *definite article* and indicates a particular, unique item. *A* and *an* are called *indefinite articles* and indicate a particular item from a number of similar items. *A* is used before a word that begins with a consonant sound; *an* is used before a word beginning with a vowel sound.

Many people mistakenly think all words beginning with *h* take *an,* but only those with a silent *h* do. Others take *a: a historical play* (not *an historical play*). If an indefinite article precedes an abbreviation, remember to choose between *a* and *an* by the first sound of the abbreviation, not the letter itself: *a UFO,* not *an UFO,* because the first sound is of a consonant: *yoo-eff-oh.*

The articles do not have comparative forms, and for that reason, some grammarians treat them as a separate part of speech. We'll go with the more common list of parts of speech and call them adjectives.

Sentence Adverbs

○ *Sentence adverbs (frankly, hopefully, personally, regrettably, sincerely, strictly speaking, to be honest)* modify the whole sentence of which they are a part rather than a particular word.

The most controversial sentence adverb is *hopefully.* Although most experts think it is ungrammatical to begin a sentence with *hopefully,* others, such as Geoffrey Nunberg and Jim Quinn, have defended it as a sentence adverb no better or worse than any other.

One common objection to the use of the word is that it is not clear who is doing the hoping in a sentence such as *Hopefully, it won't snow today.* But nobody seems to be bothered by that with any sentence adverb other than *hopefully: Strictly speaking, you shouldn't misuse hopefully.*

Perhaps a better argument against *hopefully* used in this way is that the word means "in a hopeful manner." Obviously, a sentence such as *Hopefully, it won't snow today* doesn't mean *It won't snow today in a hopeful manner* but rather *I hope it won't snow today.* So, using *hopefully* in this way results in writing that does not reflect what is meant.

But language changes, and as words are used more often in certain ways, they often become more acceptable to language experts, who at some point decide they're fighting a losing battle. The American Heritage Dictionary's usage panel has accepted, in theory, the use of *hopefully,* so we may eventually see more tolerance for this word in stylebooks.

○ For now, however, avoid using *hopefully* except to mean "in a hopeful manner" because most editors and usage guides, including the AP Stylebook, object to using the word to mean "I hope."

Participles

We've already seen how *participles* (a verb form usually ending in *ing, ed, t* or *en*) are used in making verb tenses and progressive forms. (See Chapter 5.)

○ The other major use for participles is as adjectives:

Talking, they reached an agreement. [*Talking* describes *they.*]

The *frightened* victim was *hurt.* [*Frightened* and *hurt* describe *victim.*]

Lawyers gathered *written* statements from the witnesses. [*Written* describes *statements.*]

○ Participles are also used occasionally as prepositions or conjunctions, as in the case of *regarding* and *excepting.*

All were right, *excepting* the last one.

Regarding that, we'll have to wait.

The main problem with using participles as adjectives is misplacing them, which we discuss next.

Misplaced Modifiers

○ Modifiers should be placed as close as possible to the word they modify. When this doesn't happen, we call the often confusing and sometimes comical result a *misplaced modifier.*

Jim Quinn cites this example: *"Lincoln wrote the Gettysburg Address while riding on a train on the back of an envelope."* Because everyone would probably understand that the train was not on the back of the envelope, that sentence is more humorous than confusing.

Journalism Tip
Misplaced Modifiers in Headlines

Dangling participles and other misplaced modifiers can be especially funny in headlines.

Aging Expert Joins University Faculty
[Is this an expert on aging or an expert who is aging?]

Beating Witness Provides Names
[Is this about a witness to a beating or about beating a witness?]

Complaints about NBA referees growing ugly
[What's growing ugly—the referees or the complaints?]

Bond issue is readied for city incinerator
[*For city incinerator* should follow *Bond issue*, not *readied.*]

Service for man who refused to hate Thursday in Atlanta
[Did the man refuse to hate Thursday, or is that when the service is?]

Kontakis found guilty of murdering wife after brief deliberation
[Did the brief deliberation precede the murder or the verdict?]

Dr. Ruth Talks About Sex With Newspaper Editors
[Did she address or undress them?]

By the way, most of the examples of mangled headlines we cite in this book were actual headlines collected in the pages of the Columbia Journalism Review in the section called "The Lower Case." This is a regular feature of each issue of the magazine and is alone worth the cover price. Gloria Cooper has put together two books culled from those pages, and we highly recommend them, as well.

But misplaced modifiers don't just result in harmless laughs. Readers might genuinely be confused by the following sentence: *Facing an indictment on a tax-evasion charge, the City Council fired the public works director.* Who was facing an indictment? The City Council or the director?

The story is probably apocryphal, but it's said that the federal government once sent out a form to businesses asking them to list their number of "employees broken down by sex." One confused (or smart-aleck) manager replied, "We don't have anyone broken down by sex, but we do have a few alcoholics."

The *dangling participle* is a kind of misplaced modifier that's so common it has its own name.

○ A *participial phrase* (a group of related words beginning with a participle) should immediately precede the word it's modifying. When that doesn't happen, we have what's called a *dangling participle*—the participle is left dangling in front of the wrong word as though it modifies that word instead of the one it should.

In the sentence *Marching down the street, he watched the parade,* the placement of the participial phrase suggests that the person watching the parade was marching down the street. Probably, however, he was standing still, and the parade was moving. Note these further examples of dangling participles:

> *Running down the street,* his hat flew off.
> [Literally, that sentence says his hat was running down the street.]
>
> *Taking our seats,* the meeting began. [The meeting took our seats?]

○ Don't confuse a dangling participle with a *nominative absolute,* which is a noun or its substitute followed by a participial phrase. A nominative absolute modifies the whole sentence rather than a noun or its substitute, so it acts as a *sentence adverb:*

> The computer having gone down, the paper was late.
> [*Computer* is a noun, *having* a participle.]
>
> The Tigers lost, *poor hitting being to blame.*
> [*Hitting* is a gerund, *being* a participle.]

Sometimes, the participial phrase is only implied:

> The dog dead, the boy cried inconsolably.
> [*Dog* is a noun. The participle *being* is implied between *dog* and *dead.*]

Unlike dangling participles, nominative absolutes are not considered ungrammatical, but if you have trouble distinguishing between the two, you should probably avoid both of them.

Adverb Placement

○ Adverbs, like adjectives, should be as close as possible to the words they modify:

UNCLEAR   Donald *just* has *one* car.

CLEAR   Donald has *just one* car.

The word *only* poses a particular problem with placement, not only because it's often misplaced but also because writers are seldom aware of how confusing the result can be. Look at this sentence, for example: *Ostroushko only has one of the handmade instruments.* Does that mean he has *only one* or that *only Ostroushko* has one? The sentence should be rewritten to express more clearly whichever meaning is intended.

MODIFIERS

○ It's OK to put an adverb in the middle of a verb phrase.

Some writers and editors mistakenly think that an adverb should never be placed in the middle of the parts of a compound-tense verb. For example, they would rewrite *The watch was consistently gaining time* as *The watch consistently was gaining time* or *The watch was gaining time consistently.* But Wilson Follett, whose "Modern American Usage" is one of the most-quoted usage guides, says the placement of the adverb in such sentences should normally be between the two parts of the verb. He also offers this advice on alternative placement of adverbs:

○ For emphasis, put the adverb at the start of the sentence:

Really, I don't want any.

○ If the adverb is not needed for emphasis, put it in front of a single-word verb, between the helping verb and the main verb, or after the first helping verb if there is more than one:

I *really want* some.

I *don't really want* any.

I *had really been wanting* some.

○ If the adverb modifies the participle part of the verb alone, put it after the helping verbs:

Smoking *has been positively linked* to higher rates of cancer.

○ If the adverb is a phrase, put it after the whole verb:

We *have heard again and again* the same thing from the city.

Double Negatives

○ Avoid double negatives such as *not never, not no, not none* and *not nothing.*

○ The adverbs *hardly, rarely* and *scarcely* are also considered negative and do not take a *not:*

WRONG   He *can't hardly* write.

RIGHT   He *can hardly* write.

○ The word *but,* which is normally a conjunction, is sometimes used as an adverb, and it, too, is considered negative and doesn't take a *not:*

WRONG   She *doesn't have but* one friend, she said.

RIGHT   She *has but* one friend, she said.

○ The prefixes *im, in, ir, non* and *un* make adjectives negative. Negative adjectives may be used with negative adverbs, but it is often clearer to rewrite them more positively:

ACCEPTABLE   It is *not improbable* that Margaret Thatcher will go down in the history books as one of the greatest British prime ministers.

CLEARER   Margaret Thatcher may go down in the history books as one of the greatest British prime ministers.

Interjections

○ An *interjection* is an exclamation expressing strong emotion: *Ah! Ouch! Gee!* Interjections can stand alone or be used to modify entire sentences: *Darn, that hurts!*

Not all grammarians consider interjections to be modifiers. In fact, many books say interjections don't have a grammatical connection to other words in a sentence. We disagree.

Although often set off from the rest of the sentence by an exclamation mark, interjections also may be connected to the beginning of the sentence by a comma. Written this way—which is common because editors don't like to use exclamation points—they work as sentence adverbs, modifying the entire sentence. Grammarians who consider them adverbs rather than a separate part of speech note, however, that interjections don't have the comparative forms of other adverbs.

We think that interjections could be considered parts of a sentence rather than parts of speech and that other parts of speech, such as the verb *Darn!* or phrases like *Heavens to Betsy!* or even whole sentences such as *Darn it all!* can be used as interjections.

In general, the interjection is the part of speech that gives us the least trouble. But a couple of rules are worth noting:

○ Never use more than one exclamation point with an interjection (or anywhere else for that matter).

○ Avoid profanity or off-color slang in family publications such as newspapers, unless, as the AP Stylebook says, the words "are part of direct quotations and there is a compelling reason for them."

For example, the following headline, which ran in a newspaper in the Philippines, would not be printed in most American newspapers: *"Pissing policeman loses handgun to 2 holdup men."*

Web Resources

PROFESSIONAL DEVELOPMENT

Two excellent organizations that provide seminars to midcareer professionals are the American Press Institute and the Poynter Institute. Information about their many programs can be found at their Web sites.

- **American Press Institute**
  www.newspaper.org

- **Poynter Institute**
  www.poynter.org

MODIFIERS

CHAPTER 7

Connecting Words

Prepositions, conjunctions and *conjunctive adverbs* are the glue that holds sentences together and makes transitions between ideas possible.

Prepositions

○ A *preposition* shows the relationship between the noun or noun substitute following it and something else in the sentence:

> *to* school, *after* the fall, *toward* the future, *in spite of* it all

○ The preposition, the noun or noun substitute following it (the *object of the preposition*) and any words modifying the object form a *prepositional phrase*, which usually acts as either an adjective or adverb:

> The computer *with a CD-ROM drive* is more expensive.
> [acts as an adjective modifying *computer*]

> The suspect was seen running *from the scene* of the crime.
> [acts as an adverb modifying *running*]

Prepositions usually indicate direction *(to, toward, over, under, from)* or location *(on, at, beside, near)*. Here's an easy way to spot most of these types of prepositions: Imagine a bird and some trees. Prepositions are those words that describe the relationship the bird could have with the trees as it flies. It could fly *between* the trees, *toward* the trees, *in* the trees, *at* the trees, *from* the trees, *under* the trees, *over* the trees and so on. Other prepositions show time *(in, at, during, until)*; indicate possession *(of, with)*; show responsibility *(for)* or agency *(by)*; exclude *(except, without)*; or show similarity *(like)*.

In form, prepositions may be single words *(at, to, from)*, compound words *(into, upon)* or phrases *(according to, because of, in accordance with, in spite of, on top of)*. Sometimes, participles are also used as prepositions *(excepting, regarding)*.

○ Most editors prefer that you not end a sentence with a preposition unless moving it would make the sentence awkward.

The best-known rule about prepositions is not to end a sentence with one. The rule seems to go back to the 18th-century English grammar books that based their rules on Latin grammar rather than on how the English language actually works. Because Latin words have different endings depending on the role they play in a sentence, words in Latin sentences can be moved around without changing the meaning of the sentence. An exception is the rule that a Latin sentence cannot end with a preposition.

Almost as famous as the rule, however, is Winston Churchill's rejoinder, beloved by all who hate learning silly rules: *"That is the type of arrant pedantry up with which I will not put."* The fact is that English speakers have ended sentences with prepositions for hundreds of years, and some sentences, such as Churchill's, sound awkward when they don't end with a preposition. For example: *What are you waiting for?* It just doesn't sound right to turn it around: *For what are you waiting?*

Further, the most prominent 18th-century grammarian, Robert Lowth, wrote that ending a sentence with a preposition "is an idiom, which our language is strongly inclined to: it prevails in common conversation and suits very well with the familiar style in writing."

Still, it's a good idea to avoid the wrath of your editor and try to rewrite a sentence that ends with a preposition whenever you can do so in a way that sounds conversational. This is usually easy, although some sentences require more effort. For example, *They're fun to add your own touches to* may be a puzzler at first, but some thought might yield, *It's fun to add your own touches to them.*

○ Repeat the preposition in parallel prepositional phrases if that helps avoid confusion.

Some editors insist that parallel prepositional phrases repeat the preposition. For example: *The protesters said they were concerned about pollution and about road congestion.* We, however, wouldn't insist on the second *about* in that sentence because it's clear without it.

Sometimes, though, parallel prepositions help avoid confusion: *The protesters said they were concerned about pollution from the plant and about road congestion.* If we drop the second *about* in that sentence, it isn't clear whether the protesters are concerned about pollution and road congestion or about pollution that comes from the plant and from road congestion.

Here's another sentence that is confusing for its lack of parallel prepositions: *Obscurantism means opposition to progress or enlightenment.* Does this mean *obscurantism* is enlightenment or opposition to it? If the former, reverse the sentence order: *Obscurantism means enlightenment or opposition to progress.* If it's the latter, add *to* before enlightenment: *Obscurantism means opposition to progress or to enlightenment.* (By the way, it's the latter.)

Journalism Tip
Prepositions in Headlines

○ Don't end a line of a headline with a preposition unless it is part of the verb.

Except in a one-column headline, it is not normally acceptable to end a line of a headline with a preposition and to have its object on the next line. But some prepositions are actually part of the verb rather than part of a prepositional phrase. We don't just mean the *to* at the start of an infinitive. Sometimes a preposition after a verb is part of that verb. You can spot such instances by asking whether leaving off the preposition changes the meaning of the verb. Here are some examples:

carry out	head off	look up to
come about	look after	pick up
come by	look for	put on
come into	look in on	take off
come through	look into	think up
come to	look on	try out
come upon	look up	work out

It's probably advisable to end a line of a headline with such a verb-preposition combination, rather than moving the preposition to the next line, because the preposition makes more sense grouped with the verb.

A more serious problem with prepositional phrases in headlines occurs with the word *for*. Sometimes it's unclear how the phrase it introduces should be read in relation to the rest of the sentence:

Life means caring for hospital director
[Or is caring what life means for the hospital director?]

U.S. approves right to vote for released Texas felons
[They may not be any worse than current politicians.]

○ **Use prepositions to separate items that might otherwise run together confusingly.**

Usually, this involves proper nouns next to each other: *Ted Winston Sunday said …* . In such cases, either put *on* between *Winston* and *Sunday* or rewrite: *Ted Winston said Sunday …* .

Conjunctions

○ **A *conjunction* connects words, phrases or clauses.**

this *and* that

Either the city cleans up the water *or* the state has said it will intervene.

It's been two years *since* the war in the region ended.

That was then. *But* today, he had a different story.

Coordinate Conjunctions

○ *Coordinate conjunctions*—such as *and, but, for, nor, or* and *yet*
—are used when the words, phrases or clauses they connect are
of equal rank.

How do we know when they're of equal rank? The rule is that a word
equals another word *(wine and roses)*; a phrase equals another phrase *(to
be or not to be)*; an independent clause equals an independent clause *(I'm
going, and I'm not coming back)*; and a dependent clause equals another
dependent clause *(He said school desegregation would follow if the court ruled
in the group's favor or if the group won enough seats on the board)*.

○ If a coordinate conjunction connects two independent clauses,
put a comma before the conjunction:

The judge said he would open the hearing to the press, but he didn't.

Teachers and editors used to tell you not to start a sentence with a
conjunction. This old rule has been loosened, and it is now generally permissible to begin a sentence with a coordinate conjunction—most often
but. So, for emphasis, you could write *The judge said she would open the
hearing to the press. But she didn't.*

Correlative Conjunctions

○ *Correlative conjunctions* are similar to coordinate conjunctions
in that they connect words, phrases or clauses of equal rank. The
difference is that correlative conjunctions are used in pairs:

as ... as	neither ... nor
as well ... as	not only ... but also
both ... and	not so ... as
either ... or	since ... therefore
if ... then	whether ... or

Most writers have long since mastered the fact that *either* and *or* go
together, as do *neither* and *nor*—although editors occasionally find spots
where someone has mistakenly written *neither ... or*. Not many media
writers, however, seem to know the following:

○ The negative form of *as ... as* is *not so ... as.*

It is *as* long *as* it is wide.

It is *not so* long *as* it is wide.

○ *Not only* must be followed by *but also* or sometimes a colon or semicolon.

> *Not only* blacks *but also* many whites voted for Jackson in the South.

> *Not only* blacks voted for Jackson in the South; many whites did, *also*.

Subordinate Conjunctions

○ *Subordinate conjunctions*—such as *although, as, because, if, since, until, whether* and *while*—connect two unequal parts of a sentence.

Most often, these unequal parts are independent and dependent clauses. Subordinate conjunctions typically introduce dependent clauses that modify the independent clause by explaining cause, contrast, reason or time. (See Chapter 2.)

○ **Don't put a comma before a subordinate conjunction, including** *because*.

Generally speaking, you don't put a comma before a subordinate conjunction because it introduces a dependent clause. The main dispute is over *because*. Some composition books insist that a clause introduced by *because* is always preceded by a comma, but media writers put a comma before a conjunction only if it introduces an independent clause. Conclusion: Don't put a comma before *because*. (See Chapter 9.)

Conjunctive Adverbs

○ *Conjunctive adverbs* are good transition words because they show a strong logical relationship between the sentences they connect. Here are some of the most common conjunctive adverbs:

accordingly	henceforth	nevertheless
also	however	on the contrary
anyhow	in addition	on the other hand
at the same time	indeed	otherwise
besides	instead	so
consequently	in the first place	still
first, second, etc.	likewise	then
for example	meanwhile	therefore
for this reason	moreover	thus
furthermore	most important	
hence	namely	

Unlike conjunctions, which always come at the beginning of the clauses they introduce, conjunctive adverbs often can be placed at the beginning, in the middle or at the end of a clause. Another way conjunctive adverbs differ from conjunctions is that, unlike conjunctions, conjunctive adverbs may be used at the beginning of a clause after a semicolon: *The battle was over; however, all was not still.* Media writers generally avoid this use, however, because they prefer, as a rule, to minimize the use of semicolons, especially in newspapers and broadcast.

Web Resources

PHOTOJOURNALISM

The professional organization for news photographers is the National Press Photographers Association. Photojournalists also will be interested in the annual Pictures of the Year competition, the nation's largest and most prestigious photography contest.

- **National Press Photographers Association**
  www.nppa.org

- **Pictures of the Year International**
  www.poy.gov.org

CHAPTER 8

Usage

Mark Twain said finding the right word is the difference between writing *lightning* and *lightning bug*. You need to use the correct word to convey clearly and accurately what you mean.

The writer best known for finding just the right word was the French novelist Gustave Flaubert, who spoke of the importance of *le mot juste,* or the exact word. Canadian media theorist Marshall McLuhan, punning on Flaubert's French, said *le mot juste* is the word that gives your writing "the most juice."

This chapter looks at *usage*—using the right word in a phrase and making proper distinctions among words that are often confused. Using the right word helps you make your point more clearly so that the reader doesn't have to stop and try to puzzle out whether you really meant, for example, *killing* rather than *murder*.

Most people associate usage with grammar, but we see usage more as a matter of vocabulary and familiarity with idiomatic expressions. People tend to use the wrong word either because they don't really know what the word they're using means or because they're using a word in a phrase that's not what native or educated speakers would normally use there.

An example of the first would be when people use *bemused* ("confused") when they really mean *amused*. Many people have apparently heard the word *bemused*, thought they understood it but didn't and then proceeded to misuse it.

An example of the second problem, that of a distorted idiom, would be when people write, for example, *heart-rendering* instead of *heart-rending*, when they're speaking of something that causes grief. They've misheard or misremembered the expression and replaced *rending*, a verb meaning "pulling"—as in "pulling at one's heart"—with *rendering*, a noun meaning an "interpretation" or an adjective referring to a plant where animal fat is melted down or other byproducts salvaged.

Errors such as *heart-rendering* seem to many writers, editors and teachers to be clear-cut. That is, they see the situation as a word having a clear meaning or a phrase a clear wording that a writer or speaker is violating. And, indeed, it is often that simple.

ESL Tip

The main reason the English language is difficult for speakers of other languages to master is English's huge vocabulary. We have a number of *homonyms* (words that sound alike), *synonyms* (words that mean the same thing) and near synonyms with different shades of meaning, as well as a wealth of *idioms* that require a particular word in a phrase rather than a synonym. Of course, vocabulary and idioms often pose problems for native speakers of English, as well.

But the matter is complicated at other times by the fact that when enough people ignorantly make such errors, the language changes and what was once wrong now becomes right. All you have to do is browse through the entries in the Oxford English Dictionary to see what we mean. That dictionary is the best source for the history of how the meanings of words have changed in English usage over time.

It's sometimes funny, and more than a little humbling, to see how usage experts of years ago railed against words to which no one now objects. For example, Jonathan Swift in the 18th century thought *communication* and *mob* were horrible new words that should be resisted.

We think it's fine for people who care about language to resist *neologisms* — newly invented words — or new uses for older words when such changes seem ugly or awkward. So, for example, some people resisted the term *senior citizens* because it seemed to them a euphemistic and wordy replacement for *the elderly*. But now the term finds little opposition, although the AP Stylebook still suggests that it be used sparingly.

There's a time to voice your concerns when a change you don't like is just a possibility in the air and a time to acknowledge the reality of a change after it's solidified. It's not always easy, however, to tell which situation we're in right now. And sometimes, the evidence of our experience tells us one thing and the stylebook another.

Philosophy aside, following are two lists of words and phrases that are often misused. The first list is composed of single entries of words and phrases that many people misunderstand or get muddled in their minds. The second list consists of multiple-entry listings, primarily pairs of words and phrases, but sometimes three or more that either sound alike or seem enough alike in meaning that people confuse them.

Unfortunately, there's not much we can say by way of rules to help you remember all this material. Instead, browse these lists to become familiar with what's here. The more you look over the entries, the more points will stick, and the more you'll think to look something up later when you want to use it. Mark the entries that contain distinctions you didn't know, then concentrate on learning them, perhaps a few a day.

Also, invent associations that can help you remember one item of every pair. For example, if you want to remember the difference between

Journalism Tip
Conservative Stylebook Rules

That people often ignorantly misuse words is a fact. So what was yesterday's error is sometimes today's accepted wording. The problem lies in trying to figure out where we are in the process with any given "error." It's easy to label an individual's idiosyncratic variations from the norm as mistakes, but most of the errors listed in any stylebook or usage dictionary are variations that are widely practiced, or they wouldn't find their way into the book.

So, for example, almost no native speaker of English "correctly" uses *lie* to mean "rest." Instead, people tend to use *lay* in daily conversation. Yet, this is widely pointed out in book after book as an error, even though it's almost universally used except in print, where writers either know to use *lie* or editors correct it.

Of course, if we never updated our rules when the language changed, we'd be left ridiculously insisting to this day that every department of communication has a usage error in its own name. So, when we're confronted by near universal "misuse" of certain words and phrases and still the majority of stylebooks and usage guides insist on older rules, we have to admit that something else is entering the picture: a conservative strain among the arbiters making the policies.

Logical or not, agree with them or not, such rules are a fact of life we live with when we are told to make our copy conform to a particular stylebook. A wise writer or editor should be informed enough both to know the rules and to see through them. As a newer employee, you may not be able to change them, and, in fact, your job might depend on your following them for now. But when you have decision-making power, make rules that make sense as much as your knowledge permits.

premier and *premiere,* you might associate the one that ends with an *e* with *entertainment*—an opening of a movie or play. If the word needed in a certain passage doesn't have to do with an opening, you know it should be *premier*—the word without the *e* at the end.

Misused Words and Mistaken Phrases

The word or phrase in boldface is a frequent misuse. What follows is what should be written instead or, in some cases, a brief explanation of the problem.

A

a half   half a
above   This preposition is often misused as an adjective.

WRONG   The statement *above* should appear as a warning.

RIGHT   The plane flew *above* the clouds.

accident   To be an accident, an occurrence must be unforeseen, unexpected and unintended. In a legal sense, it must also be the result of no one's fault or negligence. It is not an accident, in other words, when, for example, a drunken driver's car hits another vehicle.

acquiesce (in, with)   acquiesce to

administer a blow   deal a blow

adopted an ordinance   passed an ordinance

affinity   This noun may be followed by the prepositions *between, of* and *with* but not *for*. But *penchant for* is correct.

aghast   Use only if you mean paralysis of action in addition to being appalled.

ain't   isn't, aren't, am not

alas   Avoid this archaic word.

all   Don't use this redundantly.

WRONG   Fife, Griffith and Smith were *all* released.

RIGHT   Fife, Griffith and Smith were released.

all-around   all-round. *Around* refers to position regarding a circle; *round* means full or complete.

allegedly   Never use; the word itself offers little or no legal protection and may actually get you into trouble. Instead, give the charge and identify the person making it.

all-important   An overblown and overused phrase. Whether it's correct depends on the word being modified, but few things, if any, are worthy of it.

anchors away   anchors aweigh

and   Many books tell you not to begin a sentence with *and*. Some editors will let you, but most won't, although they are more likely to let you begin a sentence with *but*. Technically, either can begin a sentence because both are coordinating conjunctions, which by definition can start a sentence or independent clause.

aren't I?   am I not?

as compared with   compared with

as for   as to

as though   as if (although some authorities, including AP, now accept either). *As if* is generally preferred when introducing a subjunctive-mood verb.

as to   Do not use in place of *or* or *for*. *About* or *on* is preferable.

as yet   yet

awesome   Something evoking awe, an emotion of mingled reverence, wonder and dread; often misused for lesser feelings.

awful   An adjective; do not use in place of adverbs such as *very, really* and *extremely*.

USAGE

B

bankrupt   Should not be used to describe a company reorganizing under bankruptcy laws. A person or company is bankrupt only if declared to be by a court.

be sure and   be sure to

begs the question   This does not mean requires asking but rather to assume something without proof that's being questioned.

belittle   Use to mean disparage, not merely ridicule.

bemused   Means confused, not slightly amused, as many people think.

bomb   It's not a bomb if it doesn't have an explosive charge. A tear-gas canister is, therefore, not a bomb.

bosoms   bosom. A woman has a bosom, not bosoms.

C

cannot help but   can only, cannot help

centers around   Use *centers on* or *revolves around* because the center is the middle of a circle—the point around which things circle.

chomping at the bit   champing at the bit

city   An area isn't a city unless incorporated.

commandeer   Use to mean seize something for use by the government, especially the military. Using it merely to mean take something by force is colloquial. Using it to mean take charge of is incorrect.

comply to   comply with

comprised of   composed of

condone   Use to mean excuse, forgive, pardon or overlook. Do not use to mean accept, approve, certify, endorse or sanction.

contiguous with   contiguous to

contrast with   contrast to

controversial   The widely cited usage expert Wilson Follett says incorrectly that the word originally meant engaging in controversy, not merely disputed. Consequently, he argues that it should not be used in the second sense, although the Oxford English Dictionary shows that he has the history backward. Better yet, don't use this buzzword at all. Instead, show why the person or thing is controversial rather than merely labeling it so.

convince to   convince (of, that)

could care less   couldn't care less

couldn't help but   couldn't help

crescendo   Because a crescendo is a gradual rise in sound volume or intensity, it is redundant to write *rose to a crescendo.*

D

decide if   decide whether

decimate   The word, originally meaning to kill every tenth person, has come to mean destroy, and most authorities now find that acceptable.

déjà vu   Use to refer only to the *illusion* that something has been experienced before. If it actually was experienced, the feeling isn't déjà vu.

depart   *Depart* always should be followed by *from* except in the phrase *depart this life.*

deserted island   desert island. *Desert* as an adjective means barren and uninhabited.

devaluated   devalued

diagnose   Doctors diagnose a patient's *condition,* not the patient.

dialogue   Language columnist William Safire says that although many insist that the word be used only as a noun to mean a conversation between two people, it may also be used as a verb and as a noun to mean a conversation among more than two people. The word is derived from the Greek *dia,* meaning across, not from *di,* meaning two, he points out. The use of the word as a verb is not a recent invention but dates back to 1597.

die (from, with)   die of

different than   different from. The AP Stylebook says never to write *different than,* so know that most editors will insist on that. But H.W. Fowler, author of a classic usage guide, says that such a rule is a superstition, and the Oxford English Dictionary lists uses of *different than* by the English writers Joseph Addison, Richard Steele, Daniel Defoe, Samuel Taylor Coleridge and William Thackeray. The Washington Post Deskbook probably is correct when it says either is correct but *different from* is preferred.

dilemma   Often misused to mean merely an unpleasant situation or a quandary, the word means a choice between two (and only two) bad alternatives, although it can also mean (but rarely does) a hard choice between two good alternatives. It should not be used to mean a choice between a good alternative and a bad one. Also note that there is no *n* in *dilemma,* contrary to many people's misperception.

dissent with   dissent from

doubt if   doubt that

(E)

either of the three   any of the three

epitome   Not merely a high point, an epitome is the ideal embodiment of something.

equally good as   as good as

erstwhile   Means former, not earnest.

estimate   Because an estimate is an approximation, it is redundant to follow it with *about.* So, instead of writing that a crowd was *estimated at about 500,* write that it was *estimated at 500.*

exploded   Avoid the hyperbolic expression that someone exploded when what you mean is that he or she became angry.

extended illness   long illness

extra bases   A double is only an *extra-base* hit.

USAGE

F

famed   The English writers William Shakespeare and John Dryden used *famed* in place of *famous,* but most editors reject it because they think it's journalese.

fire   A legally dangerous word too often used loosely, *fired* should not be used to describe someone who was laid off or quit.

first annual   first. Something isn't annual until the second time.

floppy disk   diskette or disk

following   Don't use as a preposition; change to *after.*

forbid to   *Forbid* takes *to; prohibit* takes *from.*

free of disease   free from disease

G

gay   Many editors formerly complained about the use of the word to mean homosexual, but now The New York Times, The Associated Press and popular usage condone it.

genius   Avoid this overused noun.

H

heart-rendering   heart-rending

hew and cry   hue and cry

hike   Do not use as a verb to mean increase.

Hobson's choice   This is not a dilemma; it means no choice at all.

holocaust   A bad fire or accident is not a holocaust unless many people are killed or there is great destruction. Have enough respect for the Holocaust in World War II not to use this word lightly.

I

I would hope   I hope

identical to   identical with

imbecilic   The word is *imbecile* as either an adjective or a noun, although now its use should be considered offensive.

in behalf of   Means in formal support of.

in half   (in, into) halves

inasmuch as   Means in view of the fact that.

inculcate with   inculcate (in, into)

independent from   independent of

inflict with   inflict on

insofar as   Means to the degree that.

instill with   instill into

integrate into   integrate with

into (something)   interested in

intriguing   Do not use as a synonym for *fascinating.*

investigation into   investigation of

(**J**)

jerry-built   Means built poorly of cheap materials; compare with *jury-rigged*.

jury-rigged   Means rigged for temporary use; compare with *jerry-built*.

just desserts   just deserts

(**K**)

killed (after, following) a wreck   killed in a wreck

kind of a   a kind of

(**L**)

legendary   An overused adjective.

like each other   Use only if two are being compared.

like one another   Use only if more than two are being compared.

lion's share   Means all, not just most. In Aesop's fable, the lion got the whole thing, not just most of it.

livid   Use to mean furious or black-and-blue. It is often misused to mean vivid or red.

(**M**)

meeting occurred   meeting took place. Planned events take place; unplanned events occur.

momentarily   Like the adjective *momentary,* this adverb means lasting only a moment. Some usage guides suggest it should not be used to mean in a moment, although most consider that acceptable.

moot point   A moot point is an arguable point, not one that isn't worth arguing because it's been settled.

more importantly   more important

mutual   Because it applies to a relationship between two, this adjective should not be used in the broader sense to mean shared or common, which may refer to a relationship among more than two. Exception *mutual fund*

(**N**)

nab   Use to mean grab, steal or snatch; don't use if something was earned.

neither are   neither is

nohow   anyway

nor   Some people use *nor* instead of *or* after any negative expression, but most grammarians say this is an overcorrection. *Nor* can be used after *neither.*

USAGE

O

obsolete   Do not use this adjective as a verb.

on either side   on each side

once removed   First cousins, once removed, are a generation apart; for example, your cousin's child is your first cousin, once removed; your cousin's child and your child are second cousins.

ongoing   This adjective usually says nothing because the use of a present-tense verb alone means still in existence.

other   Required in comparisons of the same class: *My car breaks down more than any other car I've owned.* Otherwise, omit.

over and over   again and again

overly   Don't use. *Over* is already an adverb and should be used instead. Say someone is *overqualified*, not *overly qualified*.

own   Often redundant, as in *do your own thing*.

P

passed a resolution   adopted a resolution

persuade (of, that)   persuade to

pinch hitter   Do not use except in baseball; it's not a mere substitute but someone put in to do a better job than the regular batter.

pivotal   Use to mean crucial, not merely important. A crucial vote is not an important election but rather a vote on which an election depends.

plan on attending   plan to attend

plead guilty to   plead guilty of (a crime)

pleased with a gift   pleased (at, by) a gift

police   Need not be preceded by *the*.

poorly   Do not use for *badly*.

practically   This adverb means for all practical purposes. It should not be used to mean almost.

presently   Despite widespread use to mean now, many editors prefer using it only to mean soon.

prevaricate   Use to mean to evade the truth or stray from it, not necessarily to lie. For example, an equivocation is a prevarication because it misleads, even though the statement may be literally true.

prohibit from   *Prohibit* takes *from; forbid* takes *to.*

put in words   put into words

Q

quite   Avoid whenever possible. The word means entirely or all the way and should not be used to mean considerably, rather or somewhat. It should never be followed by a noun.

R

range of action   range of actions

reaction   Don't use in place of *opinion*.

real good Grammatically, this idiom should be *really good*. Better still, just say *good*.

receive injuries suffer or sustain injuries

redhead AP accepts this for a red-haired person, but many people would object to being reduced to a hair color.

refute Use to mean disprove, not merely answer, dispute or rebut.

reportedly Avoid. This is an excuse for laziness about looking up the facts and a way to try to avoid responsibility for a statement.

reverend This adjective always takes the article *the* in front of it except when directly addressing a member of the clergy. Someone should never be called *a reverend*. The word *reverend* is an adjective, not a noun.

roaring to go raring to go. Means eager, enthusiastic.

run a gauntlet run a gantlet

S

safari Use for a hunting expedition, not merely a trip.

safety-deposit box safe-deposit box

same difference same thing

short ways short way

similar with similar to

some Do not substitute this adjective for the adverb *rather* or *somewhat*.

sometime Use to mean former, not occasional.

sort of a sort of

speak to speak with

stomping grounds stamping grounds

straight is the gate strait is the gate. *Strait* here means narrow.

strikebreaker Use to mean someone hired to take the place of a striker, not just anyone who crosses a picket line, such as a manager or a union member who decides to work anyway.

superior than superior to

supposed to Note the *d*.

sustain a fatal injury An injury is not sustained if it is fatal.

T

talk to talk with

temperatures They should be described as *higher* or *lower* but not as *warmer* or *cooler*.

terrified More than simply scared, *terrified* means paralyzed by fear.

that The AP Stylebook says journalists should use *that* following these verbs: *advocate, assert, contend, declare, estimate, make clear, point out, propose* and *state*. It also says to use *that* rather than *as* after the verbs *feel, say* and *think;* other books add *know* to that list.

there's no admission There's no admission charge. Better yet, just say it's free. (*There's no admission* means that nobody will be allowed to attend.)

thus Change this conjunctive adverb to *so*, which is less pompous.

USAGE

tinker's dam   tinker's damn

to the manor born   to the manner born. *Manner* is the spelling in Shakespeare's First Folio at the Folger Library.

too   Do not use to begin a sentence; instead use *also*. Do not use as a synonym for *very*. *Too* should be set off by commas, and when used with a past participle, it requires an intervening word such as *greatly, highly, little* or *much*.

tow the line   toe the line

transpire   Use to mean leak out or become known, not merely happen.

trek   Don't use as a synonym for *trip* or *journey*. A trek is a slow journey filled with hardships.

U

under way   Generally used as two words. *Underway* (one word) is correct only in nautical use before a noun, as in *underway convoy*. Often better than the two-word version is to rewrite the sentence using *started* or *began*.

unthawed   There is no such adjective; use *frozen*.

up   Do not use as a verb.

used to   Note the *d*.

V

very   Cut whenever possible. If you use it with a past participle, it requires an intervening word such as *greatly, highly, little* or *much*.

viewpoint   *Point of view* is better.

virtually   Use to mean in effect, not in fact. In most cases, *almost* or *nearly* is better.

W

well-healed   well-heeled

wet your appetite   whet your appetite. Means to stimulate the appetite, not moisten it.

when   Do not use to mean by the time that. For example, rewrite *Most of the house was destroyed when firefighters arrived* as *Most of the house was destroyed by the time firefighters arrived*. Also, clauses introduced by an adverb should not be used in place of a noun or pronoun: Rewrite *Sinning is when you separate yourself from God* as *Sinning is the act of separating yourself from God*.

where   Do not use for *that*. Rewrite *I saw on the news where the vice president is coming to town* as *I saw on the news that the vice president is coming to town*.

whet your whistle   wet your whistle. Means to moisten your mouth, not stimulate it.

while   Some experts say that *while* should be used only to mean simultaneously, not and, but, though or although. If it's the first word in a sen-

USAGE

tence and it's meant to show contrast, change it to *although*. If it's meant to show contrast later in the sentence, use *though* or *but*.

whose   This possessive pronoun should be used only with people or animals, according to some editors. They would rewrite *The door, whose lock was broken, had to be replaced* as *The door, the lock of which was broken, had to be replaced.* But because there is no possessive form of *that* or *which*, we say go ahead and use *whose* if the sentence would be awkward the other way.

worst way   Do not use to mean very much.

(wrapped, wrapt) in thought   rapt in thought

wreak and ruin   wrack and ruin

wreck havoc   wreak havoc. Considered by some a cliché, though.

Y

yet   Some say this word should always have a comma after it, but we say *consider* using a comma—we've seen plenty of places where we wouldn't put one. At the end of a sentence, it takes one before it.

Z

zoom   This word refers only to upward motion. Do not say, for example, that someone *zoomed down the highway*.

Confused Words

This is a list of words that sound alike or that have meanings that people confuse. The words are listed in groups—the words in each group are listed alphabetically, and each group is listed alphabetically by the first word in the group.

A

a while   Use as the object of a preposition: *It's been going on for quite a while.* Also used in expressions such as *a while ago* and *a while back.*

awhile   the general adverb form: *It's been going on awhile.*

abjure   to renounce
adjure   to entreat earnestly

abrogate   to annul
arrogate   to claim unduly

abstruse   hard to understand
obtuse   slow at understanding

abundant   plentiful
fulsome   excessive

accede   to agree reluctantly
exceed   to surpass

accelerate   to speed up
exhilarate   to stimulate

accept   to receive
except   but for

access   to enter
assess   to evaluate
excess   surplus

acetic   sour; acidic
aesthetic   artistic
ascetic   austere

act   a single thing that's done
action   something done that's made up of more than one act

acute   critical, intense, crucial
chronic   persistent, recurring, prolonged

ad   advertisement
add   to derive a sum

adapt   to adjust
adopt, approve   to accept. You adopt or approve a resolution.
assume   You assume a role.
decide upon   You decide upon a course.
pass   You pass a bill.

addition   something added on; the arithmetic process of making sums
edition   version of a published work

adherence   support for
adherents   supporters

adventuresome   willing to take risks
adventurous   fond of adventure

adverse   unfavorable. Things are adverse.
averse   opposed. People are averse to things.

advice   noun
advise   verb

affect   avoid as noun, except in psychology to describe an emotion; v., to
    influence or produce a change in
effect   n., result; v., to cause or accomplish

affluence   abundance
effluence   the process of flowing out
effluents   things that have flowed out, especially sewage

USAGE

after following. A driver was not killed after his car hit another unless someone went up to him and slayed him following the accident.
when at the time

aggravate to make worse. Only existing conditions are aggravated.
annoy to bother
irritate to make the skin itch

aggregate collection
total sum

agree to You agree to something.
agree with You agree with someone.

aid help
aide an assistant

ail to be sick; to make sick
ale malt beverage

air gas, atmosphere
e'er ever (poetic)
ere before (poetic)
err to make a mistake
heir an inheritor

aisle row
I'll contraction for I will
isle island

alibi legal defense that one was somewhere else when a crime was committed
excuse reason put forward to request forgiveness. Except in a legal sense, this is generally the word you want.

all ready everyone prepared
already by now

all together everyone grouped
altogether thoroughly

all ways all methods
always constantly

allowed permitted
aloud audibly

allude not mention directly
elude evade
refer mention directly

allusion casual mention
delusion mistaken belief, especially one caused by a mental disorder
elusion an escape

illusion   erroneous perception or belief
reference   specific mention

almost   nearly, as in *almost all*
most   greatest amount, degree or size, as in *most dangerous game* or *most people*

altar   sacred platform at the front of a church
alter   to change

alternate   the verb form; n., proxy
alternative   n., choice; adj., substitute. Note that this is the only form to use as an adjective.

although   the preferred form at the start of a sentence or clause; the one to use as a subordinate conjunction
though   the only correct form at the end of a sentence; the one to use as a simple adverb

alumna   woman who has attended a school. (At some schools, graduation is implied.)
alumnae   women who have attended a school
alumni   men and women who have attended a school
alumnus   man who has attended a school

amateur   nonprofessional
novice   beginner

amend   to make a formal change
emend   to correct

amid   in the middle of something larger: *amid all that confusion*
among   surrounded by three or more separate things: *among the hungry of the world*
between   relationship involving only two or a number of things compared two at a time

amoral   outside of morality
immoral   in opposition to a moral code

amount   how much (weight or money)
number   how many (individual items)

ancestors, forebears   from whom you are descended
descendants   those descended from you

anecdote   short, amusing story
antidote   cure for a poison

angel   heavenly being
angle   degree measurement between two lines or planes; a slant

ant   a kind of insect
aunt   sister of mother or father

anticipate   to foresee with the possibility of forestalling
expect   to foresee without necessarily being able to forestall

antiseptic   something that prevents bacteria from growing
disinfectant   something that destroys or neutralizes bacteria

anxious   experiencing desire mixed with dread. One is anxious *about* or
   for.
eager   marked by enthusiasm and impatience. One is eager *to.*

any   used with a choice among more than two
either   used with a choice between two

any more   something additional: *I don't have any more.*
anymore   adv., now, nowadays

any one   any single person or thing
anyone   any person at all

any way   in any manner
anyway   in any event

apparent   appears to be real
evident   evidence makes clear
obvious   unquestionable

appose   to put side by side
oppose   to set against

appraise   to evaluate
apprise   to inform

apt   implies possibility
liable   implies an unpleasant probability
libel   written slander
likely   implies probability

arbitrate   to judge
mediate   to serve as a person who conciliates or reconciles

arc   a curve; something in that shape
ark   something offering protection

are   v., form of *to be*
hour   n., 60 minutes
our   pro., possessive form of *us*

area   amount of space
aria   operatic song for one singer

aroma   pleasant smell
stench   foul smell

arouse   to excite or stimulate
rouse   to stir or waken

arrant   downright
errant   straying

as   conj., introduces clauses
like   prep., introduces words or phrases; noninclusive
such as   prep., conj.; introduces inclusive words, phrases or clauses: *A book like this* means not this one but another; *a book such as this* means this one or one like it.

ascent   climb
assent   agreement

aside   n., digression; adv., to one side, out of the way, apart from
beside   prep., alongside
besides   in addition to

assay   to test
essay   n., short prose composition; v., to try

assert   to state as true
claim   legal right; justified demand

assignation   appointment
assignment   allotted task

assistance   help
assistants   helpers

assume   to hold a hypothesis without proof
presume   to believe without proof

assure   to remove worry or uncertainty. People are assured.
ensure   to make an outcome inevitable. Events are ensured.
insure   to provide insurance. Objects or lives are insured.

astride   prep., with a leg on each side
bestride   v., when you bestride a motorcycle, you are sitting astride it

attendance   number attending; act of attending
attendants   people who attend

attorney   transacts business for you, legal or not; not a profession; a person can have "power of attorney" without being a lawyer
lawyer   professional attorney in legal matters

auditions   are heard
trials or tryouts   are watched

auger   tool for boring
augur   to be an omen

aught   n., zero; adv., at all
ought   v., should

aural   pertains to the ear
oral   pertains to the mouth; spoken
verbal   pertains to language, spoken or written

autarchy   totalitarian government
autarky   policy of economic nationalism

avenge   to right a wrong
revenge   retaliation for satisfaction, not justice

average, mean   the sum divided by the number of parts
median   the number with as many scores above as below
range   the high minus the low

avert   to turn away from
avoid   to keep away from
evade   to avoid by cleverness
prevent   to forestall, anticipate or keep from occurring

avocation   hobby
vocation   job, profession

B

bail   money forfeited to a court if an accused person fails to appear at the trial
bale   bundle, as of hay
bond   bail as a form of bond. To be specific, say *someone posted bail* or *bail was set at* instead of referring to *bond*.

baited   A hook, witness or bear is baited.
bated   Breath is bated, meaning abated.

balance   the credits minus the debits
remainder   small part left over

ball   sphere
bawl   to cry

baloney   nonsense
bologna   lunch meat

band   combo; something that encircles and constricts
banned   barred

barbell   has adjustable weight
dumbbell   has fixed weight

bare   adj., nude
bear   n., the animal; v., to carry

baron   nobleman
barren   infertile

base   n., foundation, military headquarters, bag in baseball; adj., lacking quality
bass   adj., low-voiced; n., a type of fish

bases   plural of *base* and *basis*
basis   main support

bazaar   marketplace
bizarre   odd

beach   n., sandy area; v., to run aground
beech   a kind of nut tree

beat   n., rhythm; v., to strike
beet   a kind of vegetable

because   preferred word for direct causal relationship
due to   Avoid using to mean because. If you do, the phrase should follow a form of *to be* and must modify a noun: Instead of *He resigned due to ill health,* write *His resignation was due to ill health.*
since   a temporal relationship

bellow   to shout
billow   to surge in waves

bemuse   v., to confuse
bemused   adj., engrossed in thought; does not mean amused or slightly confused
confuse   to muddle or stupefy

berry   small fruit
bury   to put under something

berth   place of rest
birth   the emergence of something, especially living

beside   at the side of
besides   in addition to

best   for comparisons of three or more
better   for comparisons of two
bettor   one who gambles

bi   prefix normally meaning every two: *Biweekly* means every two weeks.
semi   prefix meaning every half: *Semiweekly* means twice a week.

biannual   twice a year
biennial   once in two years

bibulous   given to convivial drinking
bilious   ill-natured; suffering from liver problems

bight   inward curve in a coast; slack part of a rope loop
bite   v., action involving the teeth; n., teeth wound, mouthful
byte   computer term for one group of binary digits

bimonthly   every two months
semimonthly   twice a month; every two weeks

blatant   conspicuous
flagrant   too obvious to ignore

bloc   coalition with joint purpose or goal
block   cube; obstruction

blond   adjective for either sex; noun for male
blonde   noun for female

boar   male hog
boor   insensitive person
bore   n., someone who causes boredom; v., to drill

board   v., to get on a ship; n., plank
bored   v., made a hole in; adj., experiencing ennui

boarder   lodger who takes meals
border   boundary

boat   small, open vessel. Exception: *U-boat*, a submarine.
ship   seagoing vessel larger than a boat

bold   fearless
bowled   past tense of *bowl*

bolder   more bold than
boulder   big rock

bole   tree trunk
boll   seedpod

born   to have been given birth
borne   to have given birth to; to have put up with; to have carried

borough   walled town
borrow   to be lent something
burro   ass
burrow   n., hole in the ground; v., to dig

bough   n., branch
bow   n., forward part of a boat, a loop, an archer's weapon; v., to bend in
    respect

bouillon   broth
bullion   gold or silver ingots

boy   young male
buoy   n., floating marker; v., to lift up

Brahman   Hindu caste; cattle breed
Brahmin   aristocrat

brake   v., to stop; n., stopping mechanism
break   v., to shatter; n., interval

bravery   what someone has within
courage   what someone shows when tested

breach   violation, opening or tear
breech   bottom, rear or back

bread   food
bred   raised

breadth   width
breath   n., air taken into the lungs
breathe   v., to take air into the lungs

briar   pipe
brier   thorned plant; root used for making pipes

bridal   pertains to a bride or marriage ceremony
bridle   what you put on a horse's head to restrain it; rigging on a kite

bring   to carry toward
take   to carry away

Britain   country
Briton   inhabitant

broach   to make a hole; to start a discussion
brooch   ornament

brunet   adjective for male or female; noun for male
brunette   noun for female

bunch   a number of inanimate objects
crowd   a number of people

burger   hamburger
burgher   person who lives in a town

burglary   involves entering a building with the intent of committing a crime
robbery   stealing involving violence or the threat of violence
theft   stealing without violence or threat of violence

bus   n., vehicle; v., to move by means of a bus (present participle: busing)
buss   kiss (present participle: bussing)

C

calendar   chart that records dates
calender   machine for pressing cloth or paper
colander   strainer

calk   cleat
caulk   to make watertight

callous   adj., hardened emotionally
callus   n., hardened skin

Calvary   where Jesus was crucified (near Jerusalem); often part of church names
cavalry   soldiers on horseback

can, could   *could* is the past and conditional form of *can;* is able
may, might   has permission, will possibly. *Might* is the past and conditional form of *may.* Some say *may* implies that uncertainty still persists,

while *might* refers to a possibility in the past; others say *might* is less definite than *may*.

canapé   appetizer
canopy   awning

cannon   gun
canon   church law

canvas   cloth used for tents
canvass   to cover a district to seek support or opinions

capital   city
Capitol   building (note capital letter in all cases)

carat   unit of weight; used with diamonds and other gems
caret   editing mark inserting something
carrot   vegetable
karat   measure for the purity of gold (24 being pure)
karate   martial art

careen   to sway (especially a boat or ship)
career   v., to move quickly, especially at full speed; n., course or profession
carom   to rebound after striking

carousal   drunken revel
carousel   merry-go-round

cast   n., group of actors; v., to throw
caste   social class

caster   little wheel under furniture
castor   ingredient in perfume; name of a laxative oil: *castor oil*

casual   not formal
causal   pertaining to a cause

celebrant   participant or presiding official in a religious service
celebrator   participant in a nonreligious celebration

celibate   unmarried; abstaining from sexual intercourse
chaste   morally pure; abstaining from sexual intercourse

cement   the powder in concrete
concrete   the rocklike substance of which roads, sidewalks and walls are made

censer   incense burner
censor   n., one who previews things to prevent others from seeing material deemed harmful; v., to preview things to prevent others from seeing potentially harmful items
censure   official reprimand

centenarian   person older than 100
centurion   Roman military commander

ceremonial   formal
ceremonious   overly concerned with formalities

cession   an act of granting, surrendering or transferring something
session   the term of a meeting

chafe   to rub; to wear away by rubbing
chaff   husks

champagne   bubbly wine made in the Champagne province in France or in imitation of it
Champaign   city in Illinois

chaperon   n., a man or woman who accompanies as a guardian; v., to accompany as a guardian
chaperone   n., a woman guardian; should be excluded from modern usage

character   what a person is
reputation   what others think a person is

cheap   inexpensive
cheep   to chirp

childish   immature; pejorative term
childlike   maintaining the positive qualities of childhood

choose   present tense
chose   past tense

choral   adj., written for a choir or chorus
chorale   n., choral composition or choir
coral   n., substance built by sea creatures that forms a reef; adj., reddish pink
corral   n., fenced-off area for horses

chord   harmonizing notes
cord   string or rope; unit of wood; part of the body: *spinal cord, vocal cord*

cite   to quote in support
sight   something seen; the sense
site   a place

citizen   one who shares in the political rights of a nation. A person is a citizen only of a nation, not of a city, county, region or state.
resident   a person who lives in an area

civic   pertains to a city
civil   pertains to polite society, laws other than military or criminal, or internal war

classic   n., something of the highest rank; adj., recognized for many years as a model
classical   adj., pertaining to a certain historical period, especially ancient Greece and Rome, or to serious music

clew   ball of thread or yarn
clue   piece of evidence; hint

client   person who uses the services of a professional
customer   person who buys something

climactic   refers to a climax
climatic   refers to the weather

close   to shut; to end
clothes   garments
cloths   fabrics

coarse   rough or crude
course   class; series; division of a meal; field for a sport

collaborate   to work together
collude   to cooperate secretly to deceive
connive   to provide secret help or indulgence

collision   when two moving objects hit
crash   when a moving object hits something else that is mobile or stationary

comic   n., funny person
comical   adj., funny

commensurate   corresponding to
commiserate   to feel sympathy for
corroborate   to verify

common   shared; belonging to jointly
mutual   reciprocal; having the same relationship

compare to   to point out similarities
compare with   to point out similarities and differences
contrast   to point out differences and, perhaps, similarities, as well

complacent   satisfied
complaisant   obliging

complement   v., to complete by supplementing; n., that which supplements and completes
compliment   v., n., (to) praise

complementary   supplying needs
complimentary   free; praising

compose   to create or put together: The whole is composed of the parts. Some editors insist that *compose* be used only in passive voice, but others permit it to be used actively to mean constitute.
comprise   to contain: The whole comprises the parts.
constitute   to form or make up: The parts constitute the whole.

comprehensible   understandable
comprehensive   complete

compulsive　obsessive
impulsive　spontaneous; based on whim rather than thought

concerned about　preoccupied
concerned with　engaged in

concert　requires two or more performers
recital　given by one performer

connotation　implied meaning or emotional flavor of a word or phrase
denotation　actual or literal meaning of a word or phrase

conscience　n., a moral sense
conscious　adj., awake
consciousness　n., awareness

consecutive　one after another without a break
successive　one after another

consequent　following as a natural result; used when the events are related
subsequent　following; used when the events are not related

consul　diplomat
council　deliberative body; assembly of advisers
counsel　n., legal adviser or advice; v., to advise

contagious　transmitted by contact
infectious　transmitted by water, air, and the like

contemptible　deserving of scorn
contemptuous　showing or feeling scorn

continual　repeated
continuous　uninterrupted

convince　AP says you convince *that* or *of;* some editors say you convince *yourself;* The Washington Post Deskbook says *convince* is "to win over by argument."
persuade　AP says you persuade *to;* some editors say you persuade *others;* The Washington Post Deskbook says *persuade* is "to win over by appeal to reason or emotion."

core　center
corps　group of people
corpse　dead body

co-respondent　a person in a divorce suit charged by the complainant with committing adultery with the person from whom the complainant is seeking a divorce
correspondent　one who writes; that which matches with something else

council　see *consul*
councilor　member of a council
counselor　adviser; lawyer; aide at an embassy

country　the geographical territory
nation　the political entity

courage   see *bravery*

courteous   kind beyond politeness
polite   having good manners

creak   to squeak
creek   a stream

credible   believable
creditable   worthy of approval, credit or praise

credulity, credulousness   synonyms meaning a tendency to believe too
   readily
credulous   gullible

criteria   plural
criterion   singular

crochet   a kind of knitting
crotchet   an odd fancy

croquet   lawn game
croquette   meat patty

cue   signal; billiard stick
quay   wharf
queue   lineup

currant   n., a kind of berry
current   n., flow; adj., present

customary   set by custom
habitual   set by habit
usual   ordinary

cymbal   percussive musical instrument
symbol   something that stands for something else

cypress   tree
Cyprus   country

(**D**)

dais   see *lectern*

damage   harm done to something
damages   compensation a court awards someone for a loss or injury

damaged   means partially harmed. Do not say *partially damaged* or *completely damaged.*
destroyed   means completely harmed. Do not say *partially destroyed* or
   completely destroyed.

data   usually takes a plural verb: *The data have been gathered* (many separate items); occasionally takes a singular verb: *The data is sound* (viewed
   as unit).
datum   singular

decease   to die
disease   illness

defective   faulty
deficient   lacking

definite   certain, clear, or fixed
definitive   thorough; authoritative

defuse   to stop
diffuse   v., to scatter; adj., scattered

delude   to deceive
dilute   to water down

democracy   rule by the people directly
republic   rule by representatives of the people. In the strictest sense, the United States is a republic rather than a democracy.

demur   v., to raise objections; n., an objection raised
demure   adj., quiet and serious

deny   to say something is false
dispute   v., to argue; n., an argument
rebuff   v., to snub; n., a snub
rebuke   v., to condemn for an offense; n., a reproof
rebut   to argue to the contrary
refute   to prove something is false

depositary   person you entrust with keeping something safe
depository   place where things are kept safe

depraved   corrupted
deprived   underprivileged

deprecate   to disapprove of
depreciate   to belittle or devalue

desert   n., barren region, also used in phrase *just deserts;* v., to abandon
dessert   n., sweet course in a meal; remember the two *s*'s by this hint, "If it's *dessert,* I'll take two!"

detract   to lessen; to take from
distract   to divert attention

device   noun
devise   verb

die   to lose life or to cut with a die; forms: *died, has died, is dying* (losing life), *is dieing* (cutting a die)
dye   to change color with a chemical; forms: *dyed, has dyed, is dyeing*

differs from   is different
differs with   disagrees

dinghy   boat
dingy   drab

disapprove   to express disfavor
disprove   to show something to be false

disassemble   to take apart
dissemble   to conceal true feelings

disburse   to pay money
dispense   to deal out
disperse   to scatter or vanish

disc   phonograph record or compact disc; part of a plow
disk   any round, flat object; computer disk; anatomical structure

discover   to find something that was not seen before
invent   to create something

discredit   to destroy confidence in
disparage   to belittle

discreet   prudent
discrete   separate

disinterested   impartial (may be interested but neutral)
uninterested   indifferent (lacking interest)

distinct   unmistakable
distinctive   unique
distinguished   excellent

divers   adj., several; n., people who dive in the water
diverse   different

dock   large excavated basin used for receiving ships between voyages
pier   platform extending from shore over water
wharf   platform parallel to shore

doff   to take off (a garment)
don   to put on (a garment)

done   past participle of *do*
dun   v., to annoy, as for payment of a debt; adj., grayish brown

dose   amount of medicine
doze   to nap

doubt that   used in negative statements and questions; *I don't doubt that* ... .
doubt whether   used in positive statements indicating uncertainty as to options; *I doubt whether* ... .

dribble   to bounce a ball
drivel   nonsense

drier   less moist
dryer   device for drying things

drunk   adj., used after the verb *to be*
drunken   adj., used before nouns

USAGE

dual   composed of two
duel   fight between two people

due to   see *because*

E

each other   involving two
one another   involving more than two

eclectic   drawing on a variety of sources
electric   operated by electricity: *electric can opener*
electrical   pertains to electricity but not necessarily operated by it: *electrical engineer*
electronic   produced by a flow of electrons in vacuum tubes, transistors or microchips

ecology   the science of the relationship between organisms and environment
environment   surroundings

economic   pertains to finances
economical   thrifty

eek   an exclamation
eke   to get with difficulty

effective   having an effect
effectual   true to its purpose
efficacious   produces the desired effect
efficient   competent; productive

egoistic   self-centered
egotistic   boastful

elder, eldest   used with people
older, oldest   used with things or people

electric   see *eclectic*

elegy   sad song or poem
eulogy   funeral oration

elicit   to draw out
illicit   prohibited

eligible   open to be chosen
illegible   indecipherable

elongated   increased in space
extended   increased in range
prolonged   beyond normal limits
protracted   extended needlessly to the point of boredom

emanate   to emit
eminent   prominent

immanent   inherent in; present throughout the universe
imminent   about to happen

emerge   to come into view
immerge   to plunge into
immerse   to put completely into liquid

emigrant   one who leaves a country
immigrant   one who enters a country

emigrate   to leave a country
immigrate   to enter a country

endemic   native
epidemic   rapidly spread

engine   large vehicles (ships, airplanes, rockets) have engines
motor   small vehicles (including boats) and appliances have motors. A car may be said to have either an engine or a motor.

enormity   great wickedness
enormousness   vastness

entitled   deserving (of); gave a title to (active voice)
titled   designated by a title (passive voice); gave a title to (active voice)

entitlement   benefit
right   just claim; protection from government overreaching

entomology   study of insects
etymology   study of word origins

envelop   to surround; to cover
envelope   container for a letter

envisage   to imagine; to visualize
envision   to foresee; to visualize

epigram   concise, clever statement or poem
epitaph   statement or inscription in memory of someone dead
epithet   term characterizing someone or something

equable   uniform
equitable   fair

equivalent   of equal value
equivocate   to use ambiguous terms to hide the truth

erasable   capable of being erased
irascible   quick-tempered

errant   misbehaving; traveling to seek adventure (see also *arrant*)
erring   sinning; making mistakes

error   a deviation from the truth
mistake   an inaccuracy resulting from a misunderstanding or carelessness

eruption   sudden, violent outbreak
irruption   forcible entry; sudden increase in animal population

eschatology   branch of theology dealing with death and judgment
scatology   obsession with excrement

especially   particularly; notably
specially   for a special purpose or occasion

ever so often   frequently
every so often   occasionally

every day   adverb: *editing every day*
everyday   adjective: *everyday editing*

every one   each single one
everyone   everybody

evoke   to call up or inspire emotions, memories or responses
invoke   to call for the help of, as in prayer

exalt   to raise in rank; to praise
exult   to rejoice

exceedingly   extremely
excessively   too much

exceptionable   objectionable
exceptional   unusual

excite   to arouse emotionally
incite   to stir to action

exercise   to work out physically
exorcise   to drive out (as in driving out demons)

exhume   to dig up a corpse
exude   to radiate

expatiate   to elaborate
expiate   to atone for

expatriate   someone who has left a country to live elsewhere
ex-patriot   former patriot

extant   still existing
extent   range

F

facetious   merely amusing
factious   creating dissent
factitious   not genuine
fictitious   imaginary

faint   adj., weak; v., to swoon
feign   to pretend
feint   fake attack

fair   n., periodical exhibition; adj., just
fare   n., price to travel; passenger or food provided; v., to progress

faker   someone who engages in fraud
fakir   holy man, especially a Muslim or Hindu who performs magic feats

farther   used for literal distance
further   used for figurative distance

fatal   resulting in death
fateful   deciding the fate of

faze   to disturb
phase   stage of development

feat   deed
feet   appendages on which shoes are worn
fete   lavish party

feel   should be reserved for physical or emotional sensations
think   the proper term to use for mental activity

ferment   to undergo chemical conversion after adding a yeast
foment   to cause trouble

fewer   smaller in number; used for plural items
less   smaller in amount; used for singular items
under   used for spatial comparisons only

figuratively   in a metaphorical sense
literally   actually; often confused with *figuratively*

figurine   representation, up to 2 feet tall, of a person or animal
sculptor   artist who creates three-dimensional art
sculpture   any three-dimensional work of art
statue   big representation of a person or animal
statuette   representation, from 1 to 2 feet tall, of a person or animal

filet   net or lace with a pattern of squares; filet mignon (other boneless strips of meat may be spelled either way)
fillet   a narrow strip (as of ribbon or meat)

find   to discover
fined   penalized

fine   penalty of money
sentence   penalty of time. A convict is sentenced to five years and fined $5,000, not sentenced to five years and a $5,000 fine.

fir   a kind of evergreen tree
for   preposition
fur   the hair of an animal; garment made from the hair of an animal

fiscal   financial
physical   pertaining to the body

USAGE

flack   pejorative term for a press agent
flak   anti-aircraft shells; strong criticism

flagrant   glaringly evident
fragrant   having a pleasant smell

flair   talent
flare   n., light; v., to start suddenly

flammable   preferred over *inflammable* by The Washington Post. Many other editors consider this an illiteracy.
inflammable   Use this rather than *flammable* when speaking of temperaments.
inflammation   medical condition
inflammatory   arouses emotions

flaunt   to show off
flout   to defy; to disdain

flea   a kind of insect
flee   to leave

flew   past tense of *fly*
flu   influenza
flue   smoke duct in a chimney

flier   airman; handbill
Flyer   used in the proper names of some trains and buses

flotsam   wreckage of a ship or its cargo floating at sea
jetsam   things jettisoned from a ship to lighten the load
lagan (ligan)   jetsam attached to a buoy to make recovery easier

flounder   v., to struggle helplessly; n., a fish
founder   to sink or become disabled. First you flounder, then you founder.

flour   ground grain
flower   blossom

flowed   past tense of *flow*
flown   past participle of *fly;* often mistakenly used for *flowed*

forbear   to cease; to refrain from
forebear   ancestor or forefather

forbid   you forbid *to*
prohibit   you prohibit *from*

forbidding   difficult
foreboding   n., prediction or portent; adj., ominous

forced   compulsory; strained
forceful   effective; full of force
forcible   involves use of brute force

forego   to precede
forgo   to go without; to relinquish

foregoing preceding
forgoing giving up; abstaining from

foreword introduction
forward onward

formally in a formal manner
formerly previously

fort enclosure for defense
forte n., strength; adj., loud (Italian)

forth onward
fourth place after third

forthcoming about to take place; willing to give information
forthright frank

fortuitous accidental; by chance
fortunate lucky

foul adj., rotten
fowl n., bird

freeze to form ice
frieze decorative band

fullness abundance
fulsome disgusting; insincerely excessive

furl to roll up
furrow n., wrinkle, rut in the soil; v., to wrinkle

G

gaff hook
gaffe blunder

gait a way of walking
gate entrance

gamble to wager
gambol to frolic

gantlet flogging, as in *running a gantlet*
gauntlet glove, as in *throwing down a gauntlet*

gender grammatical term for whether a word is masculine, feminine or neuter; sex-based role assigned by society (used when distinction is sociological rather than biological)
sex describes whether a being is male or female (used when distinction is biological rather than sociological)

genteel affectedly elegant
gentile to Jews, anyone not Jewish; to Mormons, anyone not Mormon
gentle not rough

gibe   to taunt
jibe   to conform; to change course
jive   to kid; to talk lingo

gild   to cover with gold
guild   union

glacier   ice field
glazier   person who puts glass in windows

glutinous   like glue
gluttonous   pertaining to overeating

gorilla   ape
guerrilla   fighter

gothic   gloomy or fantastic, as in *gothic novel*
Gothic   all other uses

gourmand   big eater
gourmet   connoisseur of food

grate   grill for holding wood in a fireplace
great   larger than normal

grill   n., metal bars for cooking meat or fish; v., to broil meat or fish, to question harshly
grille   screen or grating, such as on the front of a car

grisly   gruesome
gristly   having gristles

grizzled   gray-streaked
grizzly   n., brown bear; adj., gray

guarantee   n., pledge to replace the product or refund the money if the product doesn't work; v., to make such a pledge
guaranty   n., warranty; pledge to assume someone else's responsibility; a financial security

---

(**H**)

hail   v., to greet, to acclaim after the fact; n., ice from the sky
hale   v., to take into court, to drag; adj., healthy

half brothers, half sisters   children with only one parent in common
stepbrothers, stepsisters   children related by the remarriage of parents

half-mast   flags are lowered (not raised) to half-mast on ships and at naval stations only
half-staff   flags are lowered (not raised) to half-staff everywhere else

hall   large room
haul   to drag forcibly, to carry; n., booty, distance to be traveled

USAGE

handmade   made by hand
self-made   made by itself. A millionaire may be self-made, but an antique is handmade.

hangar   aircraft shelter
hanger   someone or something that suspends something else: *paper hanger, coat hanger*

hanged   executed
hung   put up

hapless   unfortunate
hopeless   lacking hope

hardy   bold, rugged. A plant that can survive under unfavorable conditions is hardy.
hearty   jovial; nourishing

Harold   name
herald   to announce before the fact

heal   to recover from injury
heel   back of the foot; bottom of the shoe; crust of bread

healthful   giving health. Foods are healthful.
healthy   having health. Living things are healthy.

hear   to listen
here   at this place

heard   past tense of *hear*
herd   group of animals

helix   three-dimensional design
spiral   two-dimensional design. Exception: *spiral staircase.*

heroin   drug
heroine   female hero

hew   to chop
hue   color

hippie   1960s term for a flower child
hippy   having big hips

hire   to employ; to gain use of
lease   to grant or gain by contract, especially property
let   to grant by contract, especially property

historic   having importance in history
historical   concerned with history. A historic book made history, but a historical book is about it.

hoard   n., storehouse; v., to store
horde   n., swarm

holey   full of holes
holly   a kind of plant popular at Christmas
holy   sacred
wholly   entirely

home   place where a person or family lives. A home cannot be sold.
house   building occupied by a person or family. A house can be sold.

homicide   slaying or killing
manslaughter   homicide without premeditation or malice
murder   malicious, premeditated homicide (or, in some states, a homicide done while committing another felony). Do not call a killing a murder until someone has been convicted.

homogeneous   having similar structure: *Mayan and Egyptian pyramids are homogeneous.*
homogenize   to make homogenous
homogenous   having similar structure because of common descent: *Mayan and Egyptian pyramids are not thought to be homogenous in that they seem to have developed independently.*

human   pertaining to people
humane   compassionate

hurdle   to jump
hurtle   to throw

hypercritical   too severe
hypocritical   pretending to be something you're not

I

ideal   model or goal
idle   not busy
idol   worshipped image
idyll   scene, poem or event of rural simplicity; romantic interlude

if   introduces a conditional clause: *if a, then b*
whether   introduces a noun clause involving two choices (the *or not* is redundant). Although most authorities say *if* and *whether* may be used interchangeably, many editors still insist on the distinction. See also *weather.*

imaginary   existing only in the imagination
imaginative   showing a high degree of imagination

immigrate   see *emigrate*

impassable   not capable of being passed
impassible   incapable of suffering or showing emotion

imperial   pertaining to an empire or emperor
imperious   domineering or proud

imply   to hint. Writers or speakers imply.
infer   to deduce. Readers or listeners infer.

imposter   one who levies a tax
impostor   one who pretends to be someone else

impracticable   said of a plan that's unworkable or a person who's unmanageable
impractical   said of an unwise plan or a person who can't handle practical matters

impugn   to challenge
impute   to attribute

impulsive   see *compulsive*

in behalf of   in formal support of
on behalf of   in formal representation of

in to   in and toward; preposition followed by an infinitive: *She went in to vote.*
into   in and within; preposition only: *She went into the building.*

inapt   inappropriate
inept   incompetent

inasmuch as   in view of the fact that
insofar as   to the degree that

incidence   rate at which something occurs
incidents   things that occur

incite   to arouse; see also *excite*
insight   clear understanding

incredible   unbelievable
incredulous   skeptical

indeterminable   can't be determined
indeterminate   not fixed

indict   to charge with a crime
indite   to put into words

indoor   adjective
indoors   adverb

industrial   pertaining to industry
industrious   hard-working

inequity   unfairness
iniquity   wickedness

inert   lifeless; lacking motion
innate   inborn; inherent; natural

infectious   see *contagious*
inflammable   see *flammable*

ingenious   inventive
ingenuous   honest; forthright, perhaps to the point of naiveté

insistent   demanding
persistent   continuing firmly

insoluble   can't be dissolved
insolvable   can't be solved
insolvent   can't pay debts

instinct   nonthinking, automatic response of animals
intuition   knowledge gained without conscious reasoning

interment   burial
internment   detention

interstate   between states
intestate   not having a will
intrastate   within a state

it's   contraction for *it is*. Some editors also permit it as a contraction for *it has*.
its   possessive form of *it*

J

jail   where suspects and people convicted of misdemeanors are kept; cities and countries have them
prison   where felons are kept; states and the federal government have them

jam   made from the whole fruit (usually not citrus fruit)
jamb   side of a doorway or window frame
marmalade   made from the pulp and rinds of citrus fruit
preserves   fruit preserved by cooking with sugar

judicial   pertaining to a judge or court
judicious   sound in judgment
juridical   pertaining to the administration of justice

juggler   person who juggles
jugular   neck vein

K

knave   rogue
nave   part of the interior of a church

knead   to mold
kneed   past tense of *knee*
need   to require

knew   past tense of *know*
new   recent

knight   medieval soldier
night   part of the day after the sun has set

knit   to loop yarn to make a fabric
nit   louse

know   to comprehend
no   adj., not any; adv., opposite of *yes*

⊂   L   ⊃

lam   an escape, as in *on the lam*
lamb   baby sheep

lama   Tibetan monk
llama   animal found in the Andes

languid   weak or sluggish
limpid   clear or calm

last   final. Exceptions: *last week, last month, last year.*
latest   most recent, as in *latest letter* (not the final one)
past   most recent, as in *past three years* (not the final ones)

laudable   praiseworthy
laudatory   expressing praise

lay   transitive v., to set down; principal parts: *lay, laid, have laid, is laying*
lie   intransitive v., to recline; principal parts: *lie, lay, have lain, is lying*
lye   a strong alkaline solution

leach   to separate a solid from its solution by percolation
leech   n., bloodsucker; v., to suck blood

lead   n., metal; v., present tense of *lead*
led   past tense of *lead*

leak   v., to go through an opening; n., hole
leek   n., vegetable related to the onion

lean   to stand diagonally, as in resting against something
lien   the right to take or sell a debtor's property as security or payment on a loan

leased   past tense of *lease*
least   smallest

leave alone   to depart from by oneself; to allow someone to stay by himself or herself
let alone   to allow to be undisturbed

lectern   the stand behind which a speaker stands
podium, dais   a platform to stand on while speaking

legislator   lawmaker
legislature   body of lawmakers

lend   verb; past tense is *lent,* not *loaned*

loan   noun. Some authorities permit this to be used as a verb if what is lent is money, but you should avoid that usage to be on the safe side.

lone   adj., by oneself

less   see *fewer*

lessee   tenant

lessor   landlord or one who grants a lease

lessen   to make less

lesson   instruction

lesser   smaller

lessor   landlord

let's   contraction for *let us*

lets   allows

levee   riverbank

levy   n., an imposed tax; v., to impose a tax

liable   legally responsible; should not be used to mean likely (see *apt*)

libel   v., defame; n., defamation

likely   probable or probably

lichen   funguslike plant that grows on trees and roots

liken   to compare

lightening   making less heavy or dark

lightning   flash of light in the sky

like each other   two are alike

like one another   more than two are alike

linage   number of lines of printed material

lineage   descent from an ancestor

lineament   facial contour

liniment   salve

liqueur   sweet, flavored alcoholic drink

liquor   distilled alcoholic drink

literal   actual

littoral   pertaining to a shore

literally   see *figuratively*

load   v., to pack; n., a pack

lode   deposit of ore

loath   reluctant; is followed by *to*

loathe   to dislike greatly

local   nearby

locale   site

located   set

situated   set on a significant site

loose   v., to unfasten; adj., not tight
lose   v., to fail to win; to fail to keep

luxuriant   abundant
luxurious   comfortable or self-indulgent

(**M**)

made   past tense of *make*
maid   female servant

magnate   powerful person in business
magnet   metal object that attracts iron

mail   n., letters; v., to post
male   adj., masculine; n., man

majority   more than half
plurality   largest number but less than half

mall   shopping area
maul   to handle roughly

-mania   abnormally intense enthusiasm for something
-philia   tendency toward or abnormal attraction to something
-phobia   abnormal fear of something

manikin   model of a human body with parts that detach
mannequin   clothes dummy

manner   way
manor   estate

manslaughter   see *homicide*

mantel   wood or marble structure above a fireplace
mantle   sleeveless cloak; region between Earth's core and crust

margin   the difference between two figures
ratio   the relation between two figures. If a committee votes 4-2, the margin is two votes and the ratio is 2-to-1.

marital   pertaining to marriage

marshal   v., to direct; n., title of an official in the military, or in a police or fire department; the person leading a parade; sometimes, used capitalized as a name
Marshall   word as name only: *Marshall McLuhan, Marshall Islands*
martial   warlike; pertaining to the military, as in *martial law.*

mask   n., a disguise; v., to disguise
masque   masquerade; amateur musical drama

masseur   man who gives massages; preferred term: massage therapist
masseuse   woman who gives massages; preferred term: massage therapist

masterful   powerful; fit to command
masterly   expertly

material   thing out of which something is made
materiel   supplies of a military force

may, might   see *can, could*

may be   v., as in *it may be late*
maybe   adv., perhaps

meat   flesh of an animal
meet   v., to get together or be introduced; n., a gathering; adj., proper
mete   v., to distribute; n., a measure or boundary

medal   award
meddle   to interfere
metal   class of elements including gold, iron, copper and so on
mettle   character

media   plural: *The media are wolves.*
medium   singular: *The medium is the message.*

meretricious   deceptive; attracting attention in a gaudy way
meritorious   deserving merit

might   conditional form of *may;* see *can, could*
mite   small arachnid; small object; small amount

mil   measure of wire
mill   a property tax unit representing $1 per $1,000 of assessed valuation

militate   to work against
mitigate   to lessen

miner   one who mines
minor   adj., underage, lesser; n., one who is underage

minks   plural for the furry animal
minx   mischievous girl

mislead   present tense
misled   past tense

misogamy   hatred of marriage
misogyny   hatred of women

mistake   see *error*

moat   ditch filled with water for protection
mote   speck, as of dust

mold   n., fungus, form; v., to form
molt   to shed

momentary   short-lived
momentous   important

moot   open to argument
mute   speechless

moral   adj., virtuous; n., lesson
morale   confidence or spirits of a person or group

more than   used with figures: *more than 60 people*
over   usually spatial; however, the AP Stylebook allows such constructions as *He is over 40* and *I gave over $100*. It's probably best to use *over*
only in the spatial sense to avoid confusion.

morning   early part of the day
mourning   grieving

motif   main theme or repeated figure
motive   inner drive

motor   see *engine*

mucous   adj., secreting mucus
mucus   n., liquid secreted

murder   see *homicide*

mutual   shared
reciprocal   interacting

N

nation   see *country*

nauseated   how you feel when your stomach turns
nauseous   what something is if it makes your stomach turn

naval   pertaining to the navy
navel   n., bellybutton or depression resembling a bellybutton, as in *navel
orange* (an orange with such a depression)

negligent   careless
negligible   unimportant; small

neither   not either
nether   below

new   recent
novel   unusual

noisome   offensive
noisy   clamorous

none   not any; not one
nun   female member of a religious order

notable, noteworthy   worth noting
noted   famous
noticeable   capable of being seen; prominent
notoriety   a bad reputation
notorious   having a bad reputation

USAGE

O   *O* is not followed by a comma and is used in addressing someone: *O Father, I have something to tell you.*

Oh   *Oh* is followed by a comma or an exclamation point and is used for exclamation rather than address: *Oh, my!*

oar   long paddle
o'er   over (poetic)
or   conjunction
ore   mineral deposit

obsequies   funeral rites
obsequious   sickeningly respectful

observance   the act of paying heed to a custom or ritual
observation   the act of viewing

obtuse   see *abstruse*

ocean   water between continents, the floor of which is made of dense basaltic rock
sea   narrower body of water than an ocean, the floor of which is made of lighter granitic rock of the continent

oculist   may be either an ophthalmologist or an optometrist
ophthalmologist   physician treating illnesses of the eyes
optician   makes eyeglasses (need not be a physician)
optometrist   measures vision (need not be a physician)

ode   lyric poem
owed   past tense of *owe*

odious   hateful
odorous   fragrant

official   authorized
officious   meddlesome

older, oldest   see *elder, eldest*

omnifarious   of all kinds
omnivorous   eating any kind of food

one another   see *each other*

opaque   cannot be seen through
translucent   can be seen through but not clearly
transparent   can be seen through clearly

oral   see *aural*

ordinance   law
ordnance   weapons and ammunition

other   adjective: *Turn the other cheek.*
otherwise   adverb: *He's 50, but she thinks otherwise.*

over   see *more than*

overdo   to do to excess
overdue   tardy

(**P**)

packed   past tense of *pack*
pact   an agreement

paddy   swamp
patty   flat, usually fried, cake

pail   bucket
pale   adj., light

pain   n., v., (to) hurt
pane   sheet of glass

pained   receiving pain
painful   giving pain

pair   couple
pare   to trim
pear   a kind of fruit

palate   roof of the mouth
palette   board on which paint is mixed
pallet   small, hard bed; small platform for moving and storing cargo; tool
    for mixing clay; tool for applying gold leaf

parameter   a constant used for determining the value of variables
perimeter   the curved, outer boundary of an area

pardon   to release a person from further punishment for a crime
parole   early release of someone imprisoned
probation   the punishment received by one who is sentenced for a crime
    but not sent to prison

parity   equality
parody   comic imitation

parlay   to increase
parley   to talk

part   piece
portion   allotment

partake of   to share
participate in   to take part in

partially   to a limited degree; in a biased way
partly   part of the whole

passed   v., past tense of *pass*
past   n., history; adj., most recent (see *last*)

patience endurance
patients people receiving treatment

pause a break
paws animal feet

peace opposite of *war;* calm
piece part

peaceable disposed to peace; promoting calm
peaceful tranquil; not characterized by strife. Suspects surrender peace-
  fully, not peaceably (unless they are anti-war demonstrators).

peak n., high point; v., to reach a high point
peek n., brief look; v., to look briefly
pique n., transient feeling of wounded vanity; v., to provoke

peal to ring or resound
peel to pare

pedal lever operated by the foot
peddle to sell
petal part of a flower

pediatrician children's doctor
podiatrist foot doctor

peer an equal
pier platform extending from shore over water (see *dock*)

penal pertaining to punishment
penile pertaining to the penis

penance act of repentance
pennants flags

pendant ornament worn around the neck
pendent hanging

penitence feeling of remorse
penitents people showing remorse

people The AP Stylebook prefers this as the plural for *person* in all
  instances.
persons Many usage experts argue that this should be used as the plural
  of *person* when an exact or small number of people is defined and that
  people should be used to refer to masses. The AP Stylebook prefers *people* for both meanings.

peremptory decisive
pre-emptory prior

perquisite privilege
prerequisite requirement

persecute to oppress
prosecute to take to court

personal   private; individual
personnel   employees; staff

perspective   view
prospective   expected

perspicacious   having great insight
perspicuous   easily understood

persuade   see *convince*

petroglyph   carving in stone
pictograph   painting on stone

phenomena   plural
phenomenon   singular

physical   see *fiscal*

pidgin   combination of languages
pigeon   a kind of bird

pistil   part of a flower
pistol   handgun

pitfall   danger not easily anticipated
pratfall   fall on the rump; humiliating blunder

plain   n., flat country; adj., not fancy
plane   n., airplane, type of tool; v., to shave level

plaintiff   person who sues
plaintive   mournful

plurality   see *majority*

podium   see *lectern*

pole   n., stick
poll   n., survey, voting place; v., to conduct a survey

polite   see *courteous*

pom-pom   weapon
pompom   ornamental tuft carried by cheerleaders
pompon   a type of flower or the flower head
pomposity, pompousness   synonyms meaning self-importance

poor   lacking
pore   n., opening in the skin; v., to study carefully
pour   to make a liquid flow

poplar   a kind of tree
popular   well-liked

populace   the common people
populous   full of people

poring over   looking over
pouring over   emptying a liquid on

portend   to foreshadow
portent   omen

practicable   describes a thing that's possible
practical   describes a sensible person or thing

pray   to worship
prey   n., a hunted animal; v., to plunder or hunt

precede   to go before
proceed   to continue

precipitant   adj., rash
precipitate   to hasten, to bring on ahead of expectations
precipitous   adj., steep

predominant   adj., prevailing
predominate   v., to prevail

premier   n., prime minister; adj., outstanding
premiere   n., first presentation of a movie or play. Do not use as a verb or adjective, although many authorities permit it.

prescribe   to order
proscribe   to prohibit or condemn

presence   act of being present; bearing
presents   gifts

presentiment   premonition
presentment   presentation

presumptive   founded on presumption
presumptuous   taking too many liberties

pretense   false or unsupported claim of distinction
pretext   what is put forward to conceal the truth

primer   elementary textbook; substance used to prepare a surface for painting
primmer   more prim

principal   n., someone or something first in rank; adj., most important
principle   basic rule or guide

prodigy   something or someone extraordinary
protégé   someone guided or helped by someone more influential

profit   money made on a transaction
prophet   one who foresees

prohibit   see *forbid*

prone   lying face downward
supine   lying face upward

prophecy   noun
prophesy   verb

proposal   plan offered for acceptance or rejection

proposition   n., assertion set forth for argument, improper proposal; v., to make an improper proposal

prostate   male gland

prostrate   to lie prone

proved   v., past tense of *prove*

proven   adj., tested and found effective

purposefully   aiming at a goal

purposely   intentionally

purposively   psychological term for opposite of *aimlessly*

Q

quarts   plural of *quart,* the measurement

quartz   a kind of mineral

quash   to annul

squash   to crush

quaver   to be tremulous (said of the voice)

quiver   to shake

quell   to suppress

quench   to satisfy thirst; to douse

queue   see *cue*

quiet   silent

quite   very

quote   v.; also acceptable as a noun in informal usage and in referring to quotations in journalism

quotation   n.; preferred noun form in more formal writing, especially when what's quoted is famous

R

rack   n., stretching frame used for torture; v., to torture or strain

reek   to give off a strong, bad odor

wrack   damage brought about by violence, as in *wrack and ruin;* best avoided as a verb

wreak   to inflict, as in *wreak havoc* or *wreak vengeance*

wreck   to damage or destroy

rain   precipitation

reign   term of a sovereign's power

reins   straps to control a horse; used in *free rein,* meaning loosened control

raise   transitive v.: *raise, raised, has raised*

raze   to destroy

rise   intransitive v.: *rise, rose, has risen*

rappel   a descent by a mountain climber
repel   to drive back

rare   in short supply all the time
scarce   in short supply temporarily

ravage   to destroy
ravish   to rape and carry away by force; to enrapture

real   adjective: *The clock is real.*
really   adverb: *She is really tired.*

reapportion   applies to state legislatures
redistrict   applies to congressional districts

rebound   to spring back
redound   to have a result

reciprocal   see *mutual*

recourse   a resort; that to which one turns for help
resource   a supply

re-cover   to cover again
recover   to regain health or possession

re-create   to create again
recreate   to take leisure

recur   to happen again often
reoccur   to happen again once

relaid   laid again
relayed   transmitted

reluctant   unwilling to act
reticent   unwilling to speak

remediable   capable of being fixed
remedial   intended as a remedy

rend   to split apart; to distress
render   to submit; to extract by melting

repairable   used with something physical that can be repaired
reparable   used with something not physical that can be repaired, such as a mistake

repellent   n., something that repels; adj., repulsive
repulse   to rebuff by discourtesy; to disgust
repulsive   offensive; disgusting

replica   a copy made by the original artist or under that person's supervision

reproduction   a copy made by someone else

re-sign   to sign again
resign   to quit; to give up a job or office

respectable   worthy of respect
respectful   showing respect
respective   in order

resume   to start again
résumé   a summing up, especially of a career

review   critical examination; scholarly journal
revue   theatrical production with skits, music and dancing

right   correct
rite   religious ceremony
wright   worker
write   to put down in words

robbery   see *burglary*

role   an assumed part
roll   n., a kind of bread or pastry; v., to tumble

round   single shot
salvo   succession of shots
volley   number of simultaneous shots

rout   overwhelming defeat resulting in confusion
route   a way traveled

rye   a kind of grass
wry   twisted

S

sac   pouch in a plant or animal
sack   bag for carrying goods

salary   fixed compensation for a nonhourly worker
wages   pay to an hourly worker

sanguinary   bloody
sanguine   ruddy; cheerful

saving   bargain
savings   money in the bank

sculpture   see *figurine*

seasonable   suitable to the occasion
seasonal   occurring during a particular season

sensual   licentious
sensuous   pertaining to the senses

sentence   see *fine*

serf   person in feudal servitude
surf   n., edge of the sea that breaks when it hits shore; v., to ride the
   waves on a board

settler   one who settles down
settlor   one who makes a legal property settlement

sewage   human waste
sewerage   system that carries away sewage

sex   see *gender*

shear   to shave or cut
sheer   v., to swerve; adj., steep, transparent or thin

since   see *because*

skew   to distort; to place at an angle
skewer   n., long pin; v., to pierce with a skewer

slatternly   in the manner of a disorderly, unkempt woman
slovenly   in the manner of a disorderly, unkempt person

sleight   skill, especially at deceiving
slight   adj., meager; v., to neglect

sniffle   to sniff repeatedly
snivel   to whine

sociable   enjoying company
social   pertaining to society

solecism   violation of grammar, usage or property
solipsism   belief that nothing is real but the self

solidarity   show of support
solidity   firm, stable

soluble   capable of being dissolved; capable of being solved
solvable   capable of being solved

spade   shovel
spayed   past tense of *spay*, to sterilize a female animal by removing its
   ovaries

specially   see *especially*

specie   coin
species   the biological term for a grouping more distinct than a genus

specious   deceptive; used to describe abstract things
spurious   counterfeit; used to describe concrete things

stable   n., animal shelter; adj., sturdy
staple   constantly used commodity

staid   sedate
stayed   past tense of *stay*

stanch   to restrain
staunch   firm in opinion

stationary   not moving
stationery   writing paper

statue   a kind of sculpture (see *figurine*)
statute   law

stimulant   alcohol or drugs
stimulus   incentive

straight   not crooked
strait   singular. Geographers prefer this term for a narrow passage connecting two bodies of water.
straits   plural. This term is accurate when there is more than one strait, as in *Straits of Mackinac*.

straight-laced   strict; severe
strait-laced   pertaining to confinement, as with a corset

successive   see *consecutive*

suit   n., set of clothes, lawsuit; v., to please
suite   set of furniture, rooms or dance pieces

summon   verb: *Summon him to court.*
summons   singular noun: *Give her a summons.* Also, third-person singular verb: *She summons a cab.*
summonses   plural noun: *Give them summonses.*

superficial   on or near the surface
superfluous   more than is needed

sure   adjective: *He is sure to attend.*
surely   adverb: *Surely she knows better.*

systematic   systemlike
systemic   affecting the whole system

T

tack   course of action
tact   ability to do the kind thing in a delicate situation

talesman   person summoned to fill a jury
talisman   a charm

taught   past tense of *teach*
taunt   to mock
taut   tight
tout   to praise or solicit

team   squad
teem   to abound

tempera   a method of painting
tempura   a method of cooking

temporal   transitory; worldly
temporary   not permanent

tenant   person who lives in a rented house
tenet   doctrine

terminable   able to be ended
terminal   at the end

theft   see *burglary*

therefor   for it; for that; for them
therefore   for that reason

think   see *feel*

thorough   complete
threw   past tense of *throw*
through   preposition
thru   misspelling

thrash   to beat an opponent. *To thrash something out* means to settle something with a detailed discussion.
thresh   to tramp grain

throne   seat
thrown   past participle of *throw*

tic   twitch
tick   bloodsucking arachnid

til   sesame plant used in India for food and oil
'til   prep., acceptable but not preferred shortened form of *until*
till   prep., preferred shortened form of *until;* v., to plow; n., money tray

tocsin   disaster signal
toxin   poisonous substance of animal or plant origin

toe   one of five appendages on the foot
tow   to pull

tort   legal name for a wrongful act
torte   a kind of round layer cake

tortuous   twisting; complex; deceitful
torturous   pertaining to torture

tread   v., to trample; n., the outer layer of a tire or the sound of someone walking.
trod   past tense of *tread*

troop   group of soldiers, police, highway patrol officers, scouts, people or animals
trope   figure of speech
troupe   company of actors, dancers or singers

trooper   cavalry soldier, mounted police officer or highway patrol officer
trouper   member of a theatrical company; veteran performer

turbid   dense
turgid   bloated

U

under   see *fewer*

unexceptionable   beyond reproach
unexceptional   common

uninterested   see *disinterested*

unquestionable   indisputable
unquestioned   something that has not been questioned

V

vain   possessing vanity
vane   device for showing wind direction
vein   blood vessel; streak

valance   short curtain
valence   an atom's capacity to combine

varmint   regional variation of *vermin;* plural: *varmints*
vermin   disease-carrying pest; plural: *vermin*

venal   corruptible
venerable   worthy of respect
venial   minor

veracious   truthful
voracious   tremendously hungry

verbal   see *aural*

verbiage   excess words
wording   how something is said

vertex   highest point
vortex   whirlpool

vial   small bottle
vile   evil
viol   a kind of stringed instrument

vice   corruption
vise   tool for gripping

viral   pertaining to a virus
virile   having masculine strength

viscose   solution used to make rayon
viscous   resembling a sticky fluid

visible   able to be seen
visual   received through sight

USAGE

W

waive   to give up or no longer require
waiver   the giving up of a claim
wave   n., a curve of something; v., to move back and forth
waver   to falter

wangle   to get by contrivance
wrangle   to bicker

war horse   horse used in battle
warhorse   veteran of battle

warranty   guaranty (see *guarantee*)

way   manner
weigh   to check for weight

weather   atmospheric conditions
whether   introduces a noun clause involving two choices (the *or not* is redundant); see *if*

wench   serving girl; peasant girl; wanton woman
winch   machine used in hoisting

we're   contraction for *we are*
were   past tense of *to be*
where   adverb

wet   v., to moisten; adj., moist
whet   to sharpen, as in *whet your appetite*

wharf   see *dock*

when   at a particular time
whenever   at any time

whether   see *if* and *weather*

whither   where
wither   to dry up

who's   contraction for *who is*
whose   possessive of *who*

wrack   see *rack*

Y

yoga   a kind of religious and physical discipline
yogi   one who practices yoga

yoke   device or symbol for subjugation
yolk   the yellow part of an egg

your   possessive of *you*
you're   contraction for *you are*

youth   boy or girl age 13 to 18; singular
youths   plural

Web Resources

MAGAZINES

The professional association for magazine journalists is the Magazine Publishers of America.

- **Magazine Publishers of America**
  www.magazine.org

- **Media Finder**
  www.mediafinder.com

PART TWO

Mechanics

CHAPTER 9

Punctuation

Punctuation has been around longer than traditional grammar. English punctuation grew out of Gregorian chant notations, but traditional English grammar wasn't codified until the 18th century.

And yet, the rules are different not only among various countries but also within the same country among different grammar books and stylebooks. Luckily, most American journalists accept the AP Stylebook as an arbiter of punctuation. But sometimes, learning the stylebook's rules is one thing, and applying them is something else. We've found that a knowledge of phrases, clauses and sentence structure is a key to using correct punctuation. It helps you to remember and understand the rules and to figure out solutions when the rules in the stylebook don't go far enough.

ESL Tip

Punctuation differs in different countries. Non-American speakers of English should note differences between the rules of punctuation in their countries and the rules followed in the United States. For example, in some countries, a dash is used to indicate a quotation rather than quotation marks:

—Don't quote me, said Bartlett.

In Britain, single quotation marks are used where Americans would use double ones, and vice versa. Also, commas and periods in Britain are put outside the quotation marks if the quotation is not a complete sentence, rather than inside, as we do in the United States:

| BRITISH | He called her 'brilliant but wrong'. |
| AMERICAN | He called her "brilliant but wrong." |

Also in Britain, periods aren't used at the end of some common abbreviations:

BRITISH	AMERICAN
Dr	Dr.
Mr	Mr.
Mrs	Mrs.

The two most common sources of punctuation problems are the use of commas and the handling of quotations, so we'll start with those.

Commas

Always Use a Comma

○ Use a comma after *said* when introducing a direct quotation that is one sentence long:

> Cooper said, "To leave out premarital testing from this bill is like taking a Missouri census and leaving out Kansas City."

○ Use a comma before and after the abbreviation for a state following a city, and before and after a year following a month and date:

> Roberto and Carmen met in Pulaski, Tenn., at the Butter Bowl.

> On May 2, 2002, the two giants in the field met.

○ Use a comma after words in a series but not before the conjunction unless the meaning would be unclear. (This rule may be contrary to what you learned in English class, but it is the way journalists do it.)

> The new budget proposals would cut spending for student loans, building repairs, road improvements and farm subsidies.

What would be an example of a series that would be unclear without a comma before the conjunction? One in which the same conjunction appears earlier in the series as part of an item:

> He went to town to buy a can of corn, a can of peas and carrots, and a can of beans.

○ Use a comma before the word *etc.* at the end of a series:

> Send us what you've got: the books, the tapes, etc.

○ Use a comma after introductory clauses, phrases or words:

> The House approved the measure, and so did the Senate. [The comma follows an introductory independent clause in a compound sentence.]

> Because his mother insisted, he gave college a second chance. [The comma follows an introductory dependent clause in a complex sentence.]

> Listening to the band, he decided to audition. [The comma follows an introductory participial phrase.]

PUNCTUATION

In July, Taylor was born. [The comma follows an introductory preposi- tional phrase.]

Often, she was without shelter. [Most writers and editors are inconsistent about commas after introductory adverbs such as this one. Sometimes, they put them in; sometimes, they don't, depending on whether they would pause there when saying the sentence. But such a subjective approach wastes time and money because a writer may put in a comma that an editor will take out and a proofreader put back. We suggest always putting a comma after intro- ductory words, phrases or clauses, even when they're only one word long.]

Gee, the rain smells good. [The comma follows an introductory interjec- tion. For added emphasis, you could use an exclamation point either after the interjection or after *good*. If after the interjection, you would capitalize *the*.]

Through the door into the building, the SWAT team charged. [If there is more than one prepositional phrase at the beginning of a sentence, put a comma after the last one only.]

○ **If a gerund or gerund phrase or an infinitive or infinitive phrase is the subject of the sentence, it is not considered an introductory word, phrase or clause, so it should not be followed by a comma:**

Jogging is fun. [*Jogging* is a gerund used as the subject.]

Jogging five miles is something she did every morning. [*Jogging five miles* is a gerund phrase used as the subject.]

To live is to be. [*To live* is an infinitive used as the subject.]

To live well is to live a good life. [*To live well* is an infinitive phrase used as the subject.]

Compare the previous examples to the following sentences with in- troductory phrases that would take commas:

Jogging five miles, she tired. [*Jogging five miles* is a participial phrase, not a gerund phrase. Participial phrases can never be the subject of a sentence and must always be followed by a comma at the start of a sentence.]

To live well, one must eat well. [*To live well* is an infinitive phrase modify- ing the subject of the sentence, *one*. *To live well* here is not the subject of the sentence but an introductory phrase requiring a comma.]

○ **Use a comma between two independent clauses joined by a conjunction to form a single sentence. No comma is needed when what follows the conjunction is not an independent clause:**

A dentist and her assistant discussed tooth care with the students, and they used Mr. Gross Mouth to illustrate their points. [A comma is needed before the conjunction at the start of the second independent clause.]

A dentist and her assistant discussed tooth care with the students and used Mr. Gross Mouth to illustrate their points. [No comma is used before *and* here because *and used Mr. Gross Mouth to illustrate their points* could not stand alone as a complete sentence—it's the second half of the compound predicate *discussed … and used* and is not a clause by itself.]

○ **Use a comma between two imperative clauses linked by a conjunction, such as those often used in recipes:**

> Braise the meat for 10 minutes, and then remove it from the pan. [These are independent clauses even though the subject is implied in the imperative.]

○ **Use commas around *nonrestrictive* (nonessential) words, phrases or clauses. (See Pages 19-20.)**

> The yellow car, which was in the driveway, belongs to Jim.

○ **Use a comma between *coordinate adjectives*—that is, if you can reverse the adjectives and put *and* between them. (See Chapter 6.)**

> The sleek, spotted cat pounced on the mouse.

○ **Use a comma before the adverbs *also, as well, too* or *yet* at the end of a sentence:**

> Roberto Dumas came to the event, too.

○ **Use commas to set off a conjunctive adverb *(however, likewise, at the same time, therefore)* from the rest of the sentence. (See Pages 100-101.)**

> Nitish, however, was early.
>
> However, Nitish was early.
>
> Nitish was early, however.

○ **Use a comma after an adverbial clause beginning with *although, if, because* or *since* at the start of a sentence:**

> Although the police were criticized for the arrest, the chief defended it.
>
> Because clouds covered the sky, it was difficult to see the comet last night.

○ **Use a comma before *not* when showing contrast:**

> She said she thought independent voters preferred Stevens, not Malkowitz.

○ **Use a comma to set off a noun of direct address:**

John, could you come help me?

○ Use a comma in a headline in place of the word *and:*

City Council rejects tax increase, approves spending cuts

But beware of possible unintentional double meanings that might be created:

Officials warn clams, oysters can carry virus

Lie Detector Tests Unreliable, Unconstitutional Hearing Told

Louisiana Governor Defends His Wife, Gift From Korean

Never Use a Comma

○ Never use a comma before a subordinate clause:

The game was called because it was raining. [*Because it was raining* starts with a subordinate conjunction and could not stand as a complete sentence, so there is no comma in front of it.]

○ Never use a comma between clauses that form part of a compound direct object:

Bridges said none of the workers required medical treatment and the leak did not pose a danger to public safety. [Think of it as *He said this and that.* The clauses here are really part of a compound direct object. Putting a comma between them implies that, rather than Bridges saying the leak did not pose a danger, the reporter is editorializing about the leak.]

My face is still slightly swollen, but my doctor says that is normal and I can get my hair done next week. [Again, the doctor is saying two things: *That is normal and I can get my hair done next week.* So, do not use a comma to separate the compound.]

The poll found that nine out of 10 people believe smoking should be limited in public and that eight out of 10 believe employers should be allowed to limit smoking in workplaces. [No comma in this sentence because the poll found both opinions.]

○ Never use a comma before the conjunction at the end of a series unless it would be confusing without one:

The U.S. flag is red, white and blue.

The menu included cereal, pancakes and bacon, and omelets.

○ Never use a comma between compound adjectives—that is, two words that team up as one adjective, with one word describing the main adjective. Use a hyphen instead:

The sun beat brightly through a cloud-free sky the morning of the accident.

See the discussion of hyphens later in this chapter.

- Never use a comma between adjectives when the second adjective is closely linked with the noun:

    a new stone wall [*New* and *stone* are not coordinate adjectives here—you cannot reverse them and put *and* between them.]

- Never use a comma after a quotation mark. The comma, if needed, goes before the quotation mark:

    "The beverage-container ordinance will probably be supported by the voters," MacDonald said.

- Never use a comma after a period, exclamation point or question mark in a quotation when the sentence continues past it:

    "Swim!" her father yelled.

- Never use a comma before a partial or indirect quotation:

    Feldman said "old-age blues" set in when he turned 30.
    [No comma after *said* because the quotation is not a complete sentence.]

- Never use a comma around the abbreviation *Jr.* or *Sr.* after a name. (This is contrary to what you learned in English class, but it is the way journalists do it.)

    Martin Luther King Jr. was a civil rights leader.

- Never use a comma around the abbreviation *Inc.* in a company name. (This is another exception to your training in English class.)

    Merck & Company Inc. is a pharmaceuticals company.

Possibly Use a Comma

- You may use a comma to separate a series of three or more short independent clauses:

    "I came, I saw, I conquered."

- You may use a comma to separate the same word used consecutively:

    Whatever is, is.

Quotation Marks and Other Problems of Quoting

The handling of quotations is the second most common source of punctuation problems. Because journalists live and die by the quote, this is an especially important matter for them to master. So, we've broadened the discussion here to include both punctuation and related issues that arise concerning quotations.

What to Quote

○ Quote someone's words to add color, detail or authenticity to a news or feature story.

If the words aren't colorful, don't provide important details or don't help authenticate or back up a point being made, then don't quote them. Consider leaving them out, using a partial quote or paraphrasing them instead:

USELESS QUOTE: She said, "I'm happy to be here." [This has neither color nor an important detail.]

BETTER: She said she was happy to be here. [Even though four of these words are an exact quote, they're so common that you need not call attention to them by using quotation marks. In journalism, as opposed to research-paper writing, it is better to drop the quotation marks and simply offer a paraphrase.]

GOOD, COLORFUL QUOTE: Silber said, "It's been so dry around here that the cows are giving powdered milk."

GOOD QUOTE PROVIDING IMPORTANT DETAIL: Christiansen said, "Posicorp is looking to expand into a new market next year with a product line aimed at kids."

GOOD QUOTE BACKING UP A POINT: The grocery's owner charges that the Eversons' lawsuit threatens to drive him out of business. "Since this whole mess began, I've dropped about $150,000 in attorney fees," Mohr said, "and my business has declined 7 percent since all the bad publicity began."

○ Put quotation marks only around the exact words a speaker or writer uses, not paraphrases:

The president said the new military aircraft would be built next year. [Do not insert quotation marks here. The word *said* can be properly used with either quotes or paraphrases, so an editor should not assume that the words are a quote. Inserting quotation marks would probably create a misquotation because the writer gave no indication that the words were quoted.]

PUNCTUATION

○ Quotation marks should be a contract with the reader that these are the exact words the source used. Journalists shouldn't rewrite a quote and leave it in quotation marks.

If the quote is wordy or grammatically incorrect, consider not using it, paraphrasing it or using a partial quote. If it contains profanity, possibly use hyphens in place of some of the letters of the offending word:

ORIGINAL	"I don't give a damn what the president thinks," Stauffer said.
WRONG	"I don't care what the president thinks," Stauffer said. [These are not Stauffer's exact words, so they should not be presented as a quote.]
RIGHT	Stauffer said she didn't care what the president thought. [The statement is paraphrased, so there are no quotation marks.]
RIGHT	"I don't give a d--- what the president thinks," Stauffer said.

○ Single-word quotations generally don't need quotation marks. At that point, aren't you really paraphrasing? Sometimes, however, a single word may be so colorful that it's worth quoting by itself:

He said he felt fine. [No quotation marks needed around *fine*.]

He said he felt "wondrous." [The word is unusual enough that it could be quoted.]

○ Do not draw attention to clichés by putting quotation marks around them:

WRONG	An Ashland, Mo., youth is "sadder but wiser" after a con artist took him for $400 he had saved. [Not only is it unnecessary to quote a cliché, but also, in this case, a reader might mistakenly think the youth is being quoted. It's better to avoid using clichés altogether.]

○ Do not put quotation marks around the names of musical groups, dance companies or theater troupes:

WRONG	"The Beatles"
RIGHT	The Beatles

○ Do not use a quotation mark in place of the word *inches* or *seconds*.

WRONG	12"
RIGHT	12 inches; 12 seconds

○ Newspapers typically use quotation marks around all titles except those of magazines, newspapers, the Bible and other sacred books, reference books and descriptive titles of musical works (such as Symphony No. 1 or Opus 23). Actual titles of musical works, such as "Symphonie Fantastique" or "Visage," are set in quotation marks.

This differs, of course, from what you learned in English class, where titles of books, films and magazines, for example, were underlined or italicized.

Attribution of Quotations

○ Include attribution (who said it) every time a different source is quoted and thereafter when necessary to remind the reader:

> Fire Chief Lawrence Wong estimated damage to the warehouse at "maybe $200,000," but the owner said it could go even higher.
> "I probably lost $200,000 worth of stored equipment alone, not to mention the damage to the warehouse itself," said Bill Pendergast, who bought the building last May. [The speaker changes, so attribution is required.]

> "Unfortunately, the layoffs come at a bad time," said Fred Meyers, an assembly-line worker who escaped this round. "Santa Claus will shortchange lots of kids because Mom or Dad is out of work." [No attribution needed for the second quoted sentence because clearly the same person is speaking.]

○ Include attribution with every paraphrase, or the reader will likely think the reporter is making the statement:

> WRONG   How can people rush to a solution before the investigation is complete?

> RIGHT   "I don't understand how people can rush to a solution before they complete the investigation," Gingrich said.

○ The first time a quotation is used from a particular person, that person's full name and qualifications are usually cited:

> "We condemn all violence," said Muhammad Rashad, leader of an Islamic prayer group.

○ On second reference, the person's last name only is cited:

> "Our group supports only peaceful protest," Rashad said.

○ If the person has a title that was used on first reference, such as the *Rev., Dr., Professor,* or *Gov.,* that title is dropped on all following references, although sometimes the title—written out and without capital letters—can be used in place of the name on some of the later references:

> The governor said ...

○ Stick to one tense in attributions—either *said* or *says*—throughout. Use *said* for hard-news stories, *says* for feature stories:

WRONG	"I'm not happy with the verdict," Teresa Caruso said. She says the jury didn't take into account all the evidence.
RIGHT	"I'm not happy with the verdict," Teresa Caruso said. She said the jury didn't take into account all the evidence.

○ Don't strain for synonyms for *said* or *says*. Journalists prefer *said* and *says* to other attributions because of their brevity and neutrality:

Stated is longer.

Claimed and *according to* can imply doubt. Some editors prefer *according to* when a document is being quoted. *According to* is also correct when you mean "in accordance with rules."

Admitted implies guilt.

Refuted means "successfully answered."

Added means the statement was an afterthought.

Nobody ever *grinned, smiled* or *laughed* a statement. Somebody said it with a grin.

To say that someone *believes, feels, hopes* or *thinks* something is mind reading unless the person used these words. Thus, *David Wong said he hopes for the best.*

○ If *said* or *says* is followed by a time element, follow the time element with the word *that:*

> The president said Friday *that* he would send the proposal to Congress.

○ Although some editors prefer that attribution generally be placed after a quote, it can properly appear before or in the middle of a quote, as well:

> The senator said, "I won't comment on unfounded accusations."

> "The worst thing about the situation," Rep. Maggie Feldman said, "is that we can't find reliable information."

In fact, a more conversational approach, especially useful in broadcast, is to put the attribution before the quote. Also, attribution should not follow a multiple-sentence quote but either precede it, with the attribution followed by a colon, or follow a comma at the end of the first quoted sentence.

○ **The order of source and attribution verb should usually be** *source said,* **not** *said source:*

> "I can't believe I hit the jackpot," Mary Koch said.

The *source said* order is more conversational because usually the subject precedes the verb in English. You may want to use the *said source* order if the source and the *said* are separated by a long description, such as a title. It also may be useful as a transition, especially between quotations by different speakers.

> "This is outrageous," said Marisa Peters, president of a local citizens rights group.

○ **If the attribution precedes a quote, the punctuation at the end of the attribution should be as follows: nothing in front of a partial quote or paraphrase; a comma in front of a one-sentence quote; a colon in front of a quotation of two sentences or more:**

> The airline analyst said airfares from smaller airports stack up well against those from Detroit. [paraphrase]
>
> The airline analyst said airfares from smaller airports "compare well with those from Detroit." [partial quote]
>
> The airline analyst said, "Airfares from Toledo, Lansing and Flint compare well with those from Detroit." [one-sentence quote]
>
> The airline analyst said: "Airfares from Toledo, Lansing and Flint compare well with those from Detroit. It just depends on your destination." [multiple-sentence quote]

○ **If the attribution follows a one-sentence quote, partial quote or paraphrase, use a comma at the end of the quote:**

> "Airfares from Toledo, Lansing and Flint compare well with those from Detroit," the airline analyst said. [one-sentence quote]
>
> Airfares from smaller airports "compare well with those from Detroit," the airline analyst said. [partial quote]
>
> Airfares from smaller airports stack up well against those from Detroit, the airline analyst said. [paraphrase]

○ **Although AP often uses a comma after a multiple-sentence quote, it is better to move the attribution after the first sentence, following a comma, or in front of the first sentence, followed by a colon:**

WRONG	"Airfares from Toledo, Lansing and Flint compare well with those from Detroit. It just depends on your destination," the airline analyst said.
RIGHT	"Airfares from Toledo, Lansing and Flint compare well with those from Detroit," the airline analyst said. "It just depends on your destination."
RIGHT	The airline analyst said: "Airfares from Toledo, Lansing and Flint compare well with those from Detroit. It just depends on your destination."

Paraphrases

○ If a person is paraphrased as saying two clauses in one sentence, don't separate the clauses with a comma:

> Chung said that the road was icy and the other car was speeding.

○ If a person is paraphrased after the word *said,* many editors insist that the clause following it must be in the same tense to maintain the proper sequence of tenses. But there is some disagreement about this. (See Pages 67-70.)

> He said he was (*not* is) going.

Quotations Across Paragraphs

○ Do not put a quotation mark at the end of a *full-sentence quote* if the quote is continued at the start of the next paragraph:

> Peters said: "I'm upset by the whole situation.
>   "I didn't know what I was getting into when I came here."

○ Do put a quotation mark at the end of a *partial quote* if it's continued at the start of the next paragraph:

> Peters said he was "upset by the whole situation."
>   "I didn't know what I was getting into when I came here,"
> he said.

○ Don't go from a partial quote to a full-sentence quote within the same quotation marks:

WRONG	Jones said he was "happy to be alive. I can't believe it happened."
RIGHT	Jones said he was "happy to be alive." "I can't believe it happened," he said. [Notice the start of a new paragraph after the partial quote and the opening quotation mark before *I*.]

Other Issues With Quotes

○ Place periods and commas *inside* closing quotation marks:

"Prohibitions against doctors' advertising are unfortunate," Rhysburg said, "because we end up with uneducated patients."

○ Place semicolons—if you use them—or colons *outside* closing quotation marks:

Nixon said, "I am not a crook"; others weren't so sure.

Fredericks spoke with pride of his "future farmers": his sons, Chris and Sam, and his daughter, Jane.

AP makes an exception if the semicolon or colon is part of the quoted material, but in practice this exception never seems to be observed—probably because it would look too odd.

○ Place question marks and exclamation points *inside* closing quotation marks if they are part of the quotation, *outside* if they are not:

Have you read Ezra Pound's "Cantos"? [The question mark is outside the quotation mark because it is not part of the title.]

"Darn it!" she yelled. [The exclamation point is inside the quotation mark because it is part of the quotation; the person said the statement with strong emotion.]

○ Generally, don't use ellipses (...) to indicate words left out of quotations. Instead, use paraphrases or partial quotes to get around this issue.

○ Capitalize the first word of a quotation only when it is a complete sentence that is directly quoted:

Thomas said the conditions were "appalling."

Thomas said, "The conditions are appalling."

Semicolons

○ Use a semicolon between items in a series that has commas inside the items. Remember to put a semicolon before the final conjunction:

The American flag is red, white and blue; the Canadian flag is red and white; and the German flag is red, gold and black.

Their diet consists of juice, toast and coffee for breakfast; fruit with yogurt, cottage cheese or tofu for lunch; and lean meat, vegetables and a starch for dinner.

Journalism Tip
Punctuation in Headlines

Different publications have different rules for headlines and titles, but here are some common ones observed at many American newspapers.

○ Most newspapers write headlines in "down style," capitalizing only the first letter of the first word and any proper nouns:

President opposes Senate bill

○ Don't put a period at the end of a headline, even though, except for a label-style title, a headline should be a complete sentence.

○ If you have two sentences in one headline, separate them with a semicolon. If your publication uses "down style," do not capitalize the first word of the second sentence. A semicolon should not be used in a headline except to separate two complete sentences:

Johnson pleads guilty; family supports him

○ Use single rather than double quotation marks in headlines:

'I'm shocked,' senator says

○ Use a comma in place of the word *and*, but watch for unintentional double meanings:

RIGHT   Man is shot, stabbed in attack

DOUBLE   Victim beaten, naked police say
MEANING

○ Attribution is best shown with the word *says*, but it is often shown with a colon instead. If a colon is used, capitalize the first word that follows if it begins an independent clause:

Governor says criticism unfair

Governor: Criticism unfair

A third, less desirable, way to show attribution, is with a dash at the end of the thought, followed by the name of the person who said it. But beware of possible confusion:

Cause for AIDS found — scientists

○ Multiple-line headlines must break at logical places — at pauses between natural breath units. Don't break a headline between a modifier and the word it modifies. Don't break a prepositional phrase or an infinitive.

Some leeway is permitted in one-column heads, but only as a last resort. Typically, this would involve splitting a modifier and the word it modifies. Prepositional phrases usually would still not be split.

○ Never abbreviate a person's name, days of the week or months unless followed by a date:

WRONG   Fri., Sept., J. Jones

Punctuation in Headlines, continued

○ Many newspapers do not allow certain states or months to be abbreviated:

WRONG   Tx., Mar.

○ Many newspapers do allow abbreviations for states without a city name preceding *(Mich.)* and for some cities, such as *KC* for *Kansas City, Mo., L.A.* for *Los Angeles* and *NY* for *New York*. Many allow *U.S.* for *United States* and *U.N.* for *United Nations,* even as nouns. Most allow abbreviations for local universities *(UNH),* as well as *H.S.* at the end of a high school's name *(Oakmont H.S.).* Some, but probably not most, will let you abbreviate *county* as *Co.* and *department* as *Dept.* if the rest of the name is present.

○ Most newspapers will let you use a numeral for a number less than 10 and the percent sign *(%)* for *percent:*

Red Sox win 4 in a row

60% of voters turn out

○ A semicolon may be used between independent clauses when a conjunction is absent, but journalists would typically avoid it and instead use something else—a comma followed by a conjunction, or a dash without a conjunction, if the thoughts are closely related. If they're not, a journalist would make them two separate sentences:

RIGHT, BUT NOT COMMON IN JOURNALISM: The Padres are weak this year; they have the worst record in the league.

RIGHT: The Padres are weak this year—they have the worst record in the league.

RIGHT: The Padres are weak this year. They have the worst record in the league.

○ Use a semicolon in a headline to join two sentences together, but make sure the two sentences don't seem as absurd joined into one thought as these two examples:

5½-foot boa caught in toilet; woman relieved

Coach suspended in sexual probe; players honored

○ A semicolon can be used before a conjunctive adverb connecting two independent clauses, but journalists would usually rewrite as two sentences:

RIGHT, BUT NOT COMMON IN JOURNALISM: Frome's lawyer contended he was mentally incompetent; however, the jury decided the evidence was not so clear.

RIGHT: Frome's lawyer contended he was mentally incompetent. The jury, however, decided the evidence was not so clear.

Colons

○ **Use a colon to introduce a quotation of more than one sentence:**

> Jimenez said: "As of now, there can't be a merger. We need more co-operation first between the city and county fire departments. We have to work together more."

○ **Use a colon to introduce a list of items introduced with bullets or dashes:**

> In other action, the commission:
> —Approved Belle Kaufman's request that she be allowed to build a guesthouse in back of her home.
> —Rejected the request by Ralph Kawaski that a parcel of land he owns on Route 1 be rezoned to allow him to build a dog-race track.

○ **Use a colon after an independent clause to introduce a single-item summary or explanation with a dramatic pause:**

> He said you could summarize Jesus' message in three words: "Love thy neighbor."

If what follows the colon could stand alone as a complete sentence, as in the preceding example, capitalize it. Otherwise, do not.

○ **Use a colon to take the place of *says* in a headline:**

> Jackson: 'I want to be your president'

Some editors disapprove of this practice, but it's done in many newspapers.

○ **Use a colon to introduce a subtitle:**

> Theodore Bernstein wrote "The Careful Writer: A Modern Guide to English Usage."

○ **Use a colon to show time if it's not an even hour:**

> 7:30 p.m.

○ **Use a colon to separate chapter and verse in a Bible citation:**

> James 2:11

Dashes

○ **Use dashes to set off a list or parenthetical material containing commas in the middle of a sentence:**

The Jayhawks' defense—the linemen, the linebackers and the defensive backs—was exhausted after being pounded by the Sooner offense.

○ **Use a dash for emphasis when a pause longer than a comma is needed:**

He said he would do it—later.

Some editors say length of pause is not enough by itself and there also has to be a sharp turn of thought.

○ **Use a dash after a dateline or the wire-service credit in a newspaper story:**

LONDON—

NEW YORK (UPI)—

NEW BLOOMFIELD, Mass. (AP)—

○ **Use a dash in front of the attribution in a *blurb* or *pull quote* (material pulled from the text and highlighted in larger type for typographic purposes):**

'Let's face it: Hearst started the Spanish-American War.'
—Mayor Jonathan Richardson

Note the use of single quotation marks in such cases.

○ **A dash is used in many newspapers as a bullet introducing items in a list:**

In other business, the City Council:
—Approved a $525,000 contract with James Bros. Construction Co. to reroof City Hall.
—Refused to rezone a half-acre tract at 202 Trenton Place for construction of a neighborhood market.
—Approved the rezoning of 10 acres at Hinton and Market streets from single-family residential use to multiple-family apartments.

○ **Put a space on each side of a dash unless it is used as a bullet item.**

This is a wire-service rule, and it also keeps spell-checker programs from flagging words on each side of a dash as one unrecognized word. If your keyboard doesn't have a dash key, use two hyphens with no space between them.

Parentheses

○ **Although journalists usually avoid parentheses, you may use parentheses to set off an aside, such as nonessential information**

PUNCTUATION

or words inserted to clarify a quotation. If the aside contains at least one complete sentence, put the period at the end inside the parentheses. If not, put it outside:

She said her favorite movie was "Das Boot" ("The Boat").
[*"The Boat"* is not a complete sentence, so the period comes after the parentheses.]

Her dress was inappropriate for the funeral. (It was bright red.)
[This aside contains a complete sentence, so the period is inside the parentheses.]

Hyphens

- Use a hyphen between compound modifiers that precede the word they modify, but do not use a hyphen after *very* or an adverb ending in *ly*. (See Chapter 6.)

  high-profile case

  very high profile case

  highly publicized case

- Use a hyphen after some prefixes, especially when without one, a vowel would be doubled. (See the section on hyphenation beginning on Page 193.)

  pre-empt

  re-elect

- Use hyphens in suspensive cases involving a modifier that applies to several words:

  She most enjoyed the 3- and 4-year-old children.

- Use hyphens in place of *to* in odds, ratios, scores and some vote tabulations:

  The odds were 3-2.

  She led by a 2-1 ratio.

  The Royals beat the Cardinals 11-2 in the exhibition game.

  The Senate voted 48-2 in favor of the amendment.

- Use hyphens when fractions or numbers from 21 to 99 are written out:

  two-thirds

  eighty-seven

Apostrophes

Remember, the bottom of the apostrophe always points to the left. If it points to the right, it's not an apostrophe but a single open quotation mark.

○ Use an apostrophe to show possession with nouns.

>the dog's breath
>
>the building's grandeur

○ Use an apostrophe to show that something has been left out in contractions:

>don't
>
>I'll
>
>decade of the '90s
>
>rock 'n' roll

○ Use an apostrophe to make the plural of a single letter but not of a single numeral:

>A's
>
>1s

○ Use an apostrophe with a pronoun to form a contraction:

>it's [it is]
>
>who's [who is]

○ Do not use an apostrophe to form the possessive of any pronoun except those ending in *one* or *body:*

>one's
>
>theirs
>
>anybody's

○ Do not use an apostrophe in place of the words *feet* and *minutes:*

>WRONG   10'
>
>RIGHT   10 feet; 10 minutes

Slashes

○ Use a slash to form a fraction or mixed number if your keyboard does not have a single key for the fraction:

PUNCTUATION

1/10

2 1/2

○ Do not use slashes with expressions such as *and/or, c/o, either/or* or *his/hers* except in quoted material. Instead, it is better to avoid *and/or* and *either/or* altogether and to write out *in care of* and *his or hers*.

Periods, Exclamation Points and Question Marks

If only all punctuation were as easy as using these three symbols! Periods, exclamation points and question marks don't give writers much trouble, so we won't go into all their uses. Instead, we'll just note a few frequent problems.

○ **Don't shoehorn too many ideas into one sentence.**

Editor Kenn Finkel has said that the main problem journalists have with periods is not getting to them soon enough.

○ **Know when to use periods in abbreviations.**

This is a subject we cover in the appendix on wire-service style.

○ **Journalists typically confine the use of exclamation points to quotations in which people express strong emotion or to strong opinions expressed in editorials or personal columns.**

In other uses, exclamation points run the risk of making an article sound biased, sensational or gushy. Still, they have their place, as in the first sentence of this section.

○ **Never use two exclamation points next to each other or an exclamation point next to a question mark.**

Some writers double the exclamation points to show extra emphasis or combine an exclamation point with a question mark to indicate a question asked emotionally. Don't do either. Exclamation points and question marks are terminal punctuation marks that signal a full stop. Only one is needed or correct.

○ **Don't use question marks after indirect quotations.**

WRONG   He said he wondered how it got there?

RIGHT   He said he wondered how it got there.

○ Journalists should avoid putting a question mark in parentheses to suggest dubiousness:

> **WRONG**   The music (?) consisted of squawks and static.

Such a practice has no place in a news story, which readers expect to be as free as possible from personal opinion.

Web Resources

COPY EDITING

Newspaper copy editors have sites of their own to provide guidance on matters of style and consistency.

○ **American Copy Editors Socicty**
www.copydesk.org

○ **Copy Editor**
www.copyeditor.com

○ **The SLOT: A Spot for Copy Editors**
www.theslot.com

PUNCTUATION

CHAPTER 10

Spelling Relief

According to Andrew Jackson, "It's a damn poor mind that can think of only one way to spell a word!" Good minds or not, professional writers and editors are expected to be able to spell words correctly. And that spell-checker in your word processor only makes correct spelling even more important because people assume that now you have no excuse for misspellings.

And yet there are problems with relying too heavily on spell-checkers. Sure, they can be great for helping you catch most typos. But they won't catch *it's* when you mean *its* or *there* when you mean *their*. Also, publications require a consistent spelling of words according to their official stylebook and dictionary, but no spell-checker around will have all the same spellings. So, for example, your spell-checker is unlikely to catch *teenager*, which should be spelled with a hyphen *(teen-ager)* according to Associated Press style.

We begin with a few spelling rules that will save you time by eliminating the need to look up many spellings. A list of frequently misspelled words follows. Learn as many of these as possible to reduce the time you spend with a dictionary. We also have compiled rules of hyphenation and a useful reference list to save you time determining whether something should be one word, two words or hyphenated. Finally, for foreign students who learned British rather than American English, we provide a brief comparison of common spelling differences.

Spelling Rules

Prefixes

A *prefix* is a syllable, group of syllables or word united with or joined to the beginning of a word to alter its meaning or create a new word.

○ **Prefixes usually have no effect on the spelling of the root word:**

> legal, illegal [*Il* is a prefix meaning "not." You don't change the spelling of the root *legal* to add the prefix.]

Journalism Tip
Spelling and Your Career

If it's not enough to persuade you that a knowledge of spelling is useful because it saves you time and embarrassment, you should know that one of the most common types of tests given to prospective interns and job applicants in the professional writing and editing business is a spelling test. So, even if you're one of those people who think there's no need to learn spelling when there are spell-checkers—even though you need to learn math despite calculators—it's time to accept the fact that, like it or not, a knowledge of spelling may be important in getting that job you want.

○ If a word has the prefix *dis* or *mis,* there should be two *s*'s only if the root starts with an *s:*

disappear, disappoint, disservice, misspell

Suffixes

A *suffix* is a sound, syllable or group of syllables added to the end of a word to change its meaning, give it grammatical function or form a new word. For example, *ish* added to *small* creates *smallish; ed* added to *walk* creates *walked.* There are some instances where suffixes change the spelling of words. Here are a few basic rules.

○ Remember that *y* changes to *i* before the suffixes *er* and *est:*

happy, happier, happiest

○ Change a final *y* to *i* before adding a suffix that begins with any vowel other than *i:*

likelihood, fiftyish

○ The words *mimic, panic, picnic* and *traffic* add a *k* before the suffixes *ed, er* and *ing:*

mimicked, mimicker, mimicking

○ Words ending in *al* or *ful* form adverbs by adding *ly:*

minimally, carefully

○ Words ending in *ic* generally form adverbs by adding *ally:*

basically

An exception to this rule is *publicly*.

Vowels (the letters *a, e, i, o, u* and sometimes *y*) and consonants (the other letters of the alphabet) also may affect spelling, depending on where they fall in the word.

○ **Double a final single consonant before adding a suffix that starts with a vowel if the root word is one syllable or the last syllable is stressed. Otherwise, do not double the consonant:**

  DOUBLED CONSONANT: admitted, beginning, committed, deferred, dropped, forgettable, fulfilling, occurred, preferred, regrettable

  SINGLE CONSONANT: benefited, canceled, galloped, happening, traveled

Exceptions to this rule are words with two vowels before the final consonant *(eaten, woolen);* words ending in *x (fixing, taxed);* and four other words: *handicapped, kidnapped, programmed* and *transferred.*

○ **To decide whether a word should end in the suffix *able* or *ible*, remember that words that end in *able* generally are ones that can stand alone without the suffix and words that end in *ible* are generally ones that cannot stand alone without the suffix:**

  acceptable, adaptable, workable

  credible, divisible, flexible, horrible, permissible, tangible, terrible

○ **If a word ends in a single *e,* drop the *e* before adding *able:***

  likable, lovable, movable, salable

○ **If a word ends in two *e*'s, keep both when adding *able:***

  agreeable

○ **Add *ible* if the root ends in a soft *c* sound, but first drop the final *e:***

  forcible

Exceptions to these rules include *accessible, capable, collectible, durable, flexible, repressible, indispensable* and *responsible.*

The Silent *e*

○ **A silent *e* on the end of a word usually is kept if the suffix starts with a consonant:**

  hopeful

○ **A silent *e* is usually dropped if the suffix starts with a vowel:**

  hoping

Exceptions to this rule are *European* and *dyeing* (meaning "to color").

○ If the silent *e* follows a *c* or a *g,* the *e* is usually dropped before a suffix that starts with a consonant *(acknowledgment, judgment)* but kept before a suffix that starts with a vowel *(advantageous, enforceable, knowledgeable, manageable, noticeable, outrageous).*

An exception to this rule is *arrangement.*

Other Spelling Rules

○ Form plurals and possessives as described in Chapter 3.

○ Use *i* before *e* except after *c.* But there are some notable exceptions:

ancient, aweigh, beige, caffeine, counterfeit, financier, foreign, forfeit, heifer, height, inveigle, leisure, neighbor, neither, protein, science, seize, seizure, sleigh, sleight, sufficient, their, weigh, weight, weird

○ To decide between *ede* and *eed,* remember that one-syllable words typically are spelled with a double *e* but only four words of two syllables are. Other words take *ede:*

SINGLE-SYLLABLE WORDS WITH *eed:* bleed, deed, feed, need, peed, seed

DOUBLE-SYLLABLE WORDS WITH *eed:* exceed, indeed, proceed, succeed

WORDS WITH *ede:* concede, intercede, precede, recede

Supersede is the only word ending in *sede.*

○ To decide whether a word should be spelled with a *c* or an *s,* remember that nouns usually have a *c,* verbs an *s:*

NOUN	VERB
prophecy	prophesy
advice	advise

Exceptions that are the same for both noun and verb are *license* and *practice.*

○ Don't subtract letters when words are joined together:

overrule

withhold

○ To decide between *ary* and *ery,* remember that only seven common words end in *ery: cemetery, confectionery, distillery, millinery, monastery, periphery* and *stationery* (paper). Other than these, use *ary.*

○ To decide between *efy* and *ify*, remember that only four common words end in *efy: liquefy, putrefy, rarefy* and *stupefy*. Other than these, use *ify*.

Words Often Misspelled

A

aberration
abet
abhorrence
abridgment
abscess
acceptable
accessible
accessory
accidentally
accommodate
accumulate
achievement
acknowledge
acknowledgment
acoustics
acquaintance
acquit
acquitted
across
adherent
admissible
adviser
affidavit
aficionado
aggressor
all right
alleged
allotted
already
Alzheimer's disease
analysis

annihilate
anoint
antiquated
appalled
apparent
appearance
appellate
Arctic
argument
arrangement
ascend
asinine
assassin
assistant
athlete
attendance
auxiliary

B

baccalaureate
bachelor
backward
baker's dozen
baker's yeast
ballistic
bankruptcy
barbiturate
barrenness
battalion
beggar
beginning
bellwether

benefited
benefiting
berserk
bona fide
broccoli
brussels sprouts
business

C

caffeine
calendar
caliber
campaign
canceled
cancellation
carburetor
caress
Caribbean
categorically
caterpillar
cemetery
centennial
chaise longue (not *lounge*)
changeable
chauffeur
chief
children's play
chitterlings
Cincinnati
circuit
citizens band

coconut
coed
collectible
colossal
commemorate
commitment
committal
committee
comparable
compatible
competent
conceit
conceive
confectioners' sugar
confident
congratulations
connoisseur
conquer
conscience
conscientious
conscious
consensus
consistent
controversy
convenient
coolly
corroborate
counterfeit
criticism
criticize
cruelly

D

deceit
deductible
defendant
defensible
definitely
deity

dependent
derring-do
descendant
descent
description
desiccate
desirable
desperately
deteriorate
deterrent
development
diaphragm
diarrhea
dietitian
difference
dilapidated
dilemma
dilettante
diphtheria
dirigible
disappear
disappoint
disastrous
discernible
discipline
disillusioned
dissension
disservice
dissociate
divisive
do's and don'ts
doughnut
drought
drowned
drunkenness
duly
dumbbell
dumbfounded
durable

E

ebb
ecstasy
eerie
eighth
elegant
eligible
embarrass
emphysema
employee
endeavor
environment
equipped
erroneous
especially
espresso
exaggerate
exceed
excitable
excusable
exhibition
exhilarating
existence
exorbitant
experience
explanation
extension
extraordinary
exuberant
eyeing

F

facetious
Fahrenheit
familiar
feasible
February
fierce

SPELLING

fiery
financier
firefighter
fluorescent
fluoride
forcible
foreign
forfeit
fortunately
forty
fourth
fraudulent
fuchsia
fulfill

G

gaiety
galloped
garish
garrulous
gaudy
gauge
genealogy
glamorous
glamour
goodbye
gorilla
government
grammar
grievance
guarantee
guard
guerrilla

H

handkerchief
harass
harebrained

harelip
height
heir
hemorrhage
hierarchy
hitchhiker
homicide
hygiene
hypocrisy
hysterical

I

ifs and buts
illegibly
illegitimate
immediately
impostor
inadmissible
inadvertent
inaugurate
incidentally
inconvenience
incredible
independent
indispensable
inevitable
inflammation
inherent
innocence
innocuous
innuendo
inoculate
inseparable
insistence
insulation
intercede
Internet
interrupt
irascible

iridescent
irrelevant
irreligious
irresistible
irreverent

J

jeopardy
jewelry
judgment
judicious

K

keenness
khaki
kidnapped
kimono
kindergarten
knowledgeable

L

laboratory
laid
lambaste
legerdemain
legionnaire
legitimate
leisure
liability
liaison
license
lieutenant
lightning
likable
likelihood
liquefy
loathsome
loneliness
luscious

M

mah-jongg
maintenance
malarkey
manageable
maneuver
marijuana
marriage
marshal
mayonnaise
meander
medicine
medieval
Mediterranean
memento
menswear
merited
metallic
millionaire
mimicked
miniature
minuscule
miscellaneous
mischievous
missile
misspell
mollify
monastery
murmured
mystifying

N

naive
naphtha
necessary
neighbor
newsstand
nickel
niece
ninth
noticeable
nowadays
nuisance

O

oblige
observer
occasion
occurred
occurrence
offense
offered
OK'd
omission
omitted
opportunity
oppressive
ordinarily
original
oscillate
overrule
Oyez

P

paid
papier-mâché
paraffin
parallel
paralyzed
paraphernalia
parishioner
parliamentary
particularly
pastime
pavilion
peaceable
peculiarly
penicillin
percent
peremptory
permanent
permissible
perseverance
persistent
Philippines
physician
picnicking
pierce
pigeon
plaque
plausible
playwright
pneumonia
poinsettia
Portuguese
possession
practically
precede
predecessor
preferred
preparation
prerogative
presence
presumptuous
pretense
prevalence
preventive
primitive
privilege
procedure
proceed
prodigy
professor
profited
propeller

prosecutor
prurient
publicly
purify
pursue

Q

quandary
quantity
quantum
quarreling
querulous
query
questionnaire
queue
quotient

R

rarefy
rarity
readable
receipt
receive
recommend
reconnaissance
reconnoiter
recur
referee
reference
referred
rehearsal
reign
relevant
religious
reminiscence
renovation
renowned
repetitious

repressible
reservoir
resistance
responsibility
restaurateur
resurrection
retinue
Reye's syndrome
rheumatism
rhyme
rhythm
ridiculous
rock 'n' roll

S

sacrilegious
salable
sanatorium
sanitarium
schedule
scissors
secession
seize
seizure
separate
sergeant
sheriff
short-lived
siege
sieve
signaled
silhouette
similar
sincerely
sizable
skier
skiing
skillful
skulduggery

soldier
solicitor
soliloquy
soluble
soothe
sophomore
sovereign
spiraled
straitjacket
strictly
stupefy
subpoena
subtlety
subtly
succeed
successful
superintendent
supersede
surfeit
surprise
surveillance
susceptible
symmetry
synonymous

T

tariff
teachers college
teen-age
temperamental
tendency
tentacles
tepee
thoroughly
till
tinker's damn
tobacco
toboggan
tournament

toward
tranquillity
transferal
transmitter
traveler
truly
Tucson
tumultuous
twelfth
tying
typing
tyrannous

U

ukulele
uncontrollable
undoubtedly
upward
usable

V

vacancy
vacillate
vacuum
vengeance
verifiable
veterinary
vicious
victuals
vilify
villain
virtually
volume
voyageur
voyeur

W

Wednesday
weird

wherever
wholly
wield
wiener
willful
wiry
withhold
witticism
women's college
wondrous
woolen

X

X-ray

Z

zany
zucchini

Hyphenation as a Spelling Problem

Rules for Hyphenation

Writers and editors often are confused about whether a word is written as one word, as two words or with a hyphen. Here are some rules to remember that may help. The rules are followed by a useful reference list.

- Suffixes are not usually hyphenated unless adding one would result in three *l*'s in a row:

    catlike

    shell-less

- Sometimes, compound adjectives in which the "suffix" is really a separate word are hyphenated, and other times they're not:

    penny-wise

    streetwise

- Many compounds that use a preposition such as *down, in, off, out, over* or *up* are hyphenated, but many other compound words with prepositions at the end have dropped the hyphen:

  break-in, carry-over, close-up, fade-out

  breakup, fallout, holdover, takeoff

- These prefixes are generally not hyphenated:

  a (not, out)

  ante (before)

  anti (against)

  bi (two)

  by (near) — exception: *by-election*

  dis (opposite)

  full (complete)

  hydro (water)

  hyper (above, excessive)

  infra (below)

  inter (among, between)

  intra (within)

  mid (middle)

  mini (small)

  multi (many)

  non (not)

  pan (all)

  post (after) — exceptions: *post-bellum, post-mortem, post-obit*

  pre (before)

  re (again) — exceptions: When two different words would otherwise be spelled the same, hyphenate the one that means "again": *re-cover* (cover again), *re-creation* (a new creation).

  semi (partly)

  sub (under)

  trans (across)

  ultra (beyond)

  un (not)

  under (beneath)

  up (above)

- These prefixes generally are hyphenated:

  after (following) — exception: no hyphen if used to form a noun

  all (every)

  co (with) — exceptions: AP says to retain the hyphen when forming words that "indicate occupation or status" *(co-author, co-pilot, co-star)* but not to hyphenate other combinations *(coed, coeducation, coequal, coexist, coexistence, cooperate, cooperative, coordinate, coordination)*.

  ex (former) — exceptions: words that mean "out of," such as *excommunicate, expropriate*

  like (similar) — exceptions: *likelihood, likeness, likewise*

  odd (unusual) — exception: *oddball*

  off (away) — exceptions: *offbeat, offcast, offhand, offload, offprint, offset, offshoot, offshore, offside, offspring, offstage*

  one (single)

  pro (for) — exceptions: words that do not connote support for something, such as *produce, profile, pronoun*

  self — exceptions: *selfish, selfless, selfsame*

  well (very)

  wide (completely) — exception: *widespread*

- Words beginning with the prefixes *half* and *pre* are sometimes hyphenated, sometimes not. You'll just have to look them up. If they do not appear in Webster's New World College Dictionary, hyphenate them.

- The prefix *vice* remains a separate word:

  vice president

- When a prefix is added to a number or a word that starts with a capital letter, use a hyphen after the prefix:

  anti-American, mid-20s, pre-Columbian, trans-Atlantic

- When a prefix is added to a word that starts with the same letter, use a hyphen after the prefix:

  pre-election, pre-eminent, pre-empt, pre-establish, pre-exist, semi-invisible

Exceptions are *cooperate* and *coordinate*.

Looking Up Words for Hyphenation

Compound nouns pose spelling problems because they are so inconsistent. Some are written as two words, some are one word, and some are hyphenated. A compound noun generally starts as two words. Then, as the phrase becomes more frequently used, the two words get shoved together as one, perhaps going through a preliminary hyphenated stage. If you look through the "One Word, Two Words or Hyphenated?" list that follows, you'll see how unpredictable and inconsistent compound nouns can be.

To decide whether a word is one word, two words or hyphenated, here's the procedure for looking it up, according to the AP Stylebook:

1. Check the AP Stylebook.
2. If it's not there, check Webster's New World College Dictionary, Fourth Edition.
3. If it's not in the New World, check Webster's Third New International Dictionary.
4. If it's not in the Third, we suggest you make the word two words if it's a noun or verb, hyphenated if it's an adjective.

Make sure you follow these steps in order and not stop until you either find the word or reach the fourth step. Otherwise, there's a good chance you won't be spelling the word right. For example, it would be possible for AP to have a certain compound as two words, for Webster's New World to make it hyphenated and for Webster's Third to have it as one word. So, if you thought you'd save time by skipping straight to Webster's New World or Webster's Third, you'd be spelling the word wrong according to AP.

Following these rules, we've put together a list of commonly questioned compound words. You might want to check this list before going through the four-step procedure above because if we have the word here, it could save you some steps and time.

One Word, Two Words or Hyphenated?

A

able-bodied
about-face
aboveboard
absent-minded
accident-prone
acid test
ad hominem
ad-lib (n., v., adj.)
ad nauseam
A-frame
African-American (n., adj.)

aftereffect
after-hours
afterthought
aide-de-camp, aides-de-camp
air base
air-condition (v.)
air-conditioned
air conditioner
air conditioning
aircraft
airfare
air force base

airline, airlines (but check individual name)
air lock
airmail
airport
air show
airstrip
airtight
airtime
air traffic controller
airwaves
airways

a la carte

a la king

a la mode

all-clear

all-out

all-purpose

all ready (everyone is ready), already (by now)

all right

all-round

allspice

all-star

all time (n.), all-time (adj.)

alma mater

a lot

also-ran (n.)

anal-retentive (adj.)

anchorman

anchorwoman

anteroom

anti-aircraft

anti-bias

antibiotic

antibody

anticlimax

antidote

antifreeze

antigen

antihistamine

anti-inflation

anti-intellectual

antiknock

anti-labor

antimatter

antimony

antiparticle

antipasto

antiperspirant

antiphony

antiproton

antiseptic

antiserum

anti-slavery

anti-social

antithesis

antitoxin

antitrust

antitussive

anti-war

any more (something additional: *I don't have any more*), anymore (adv.)

any one (any person at all), anyone (any single person or thing)

any way (in any event), anyway (in any manner)

apron strings

Aqua-Lung (trademark)

archbishop

arch-Democrat

archdiocese

archenemy

arch-Republican

archrival

arm-wrestling

arrowhead

art form

artifact

artwork

ashcan

ashtray

attorney general, attorneys general

autoeroticism

automaker

auto racing

autoworker

awe-struck

a while (noun as object of prep. or in phrases such as *a while ago* or *a while back*), awhile (adv.)

B

baby boomer

baby-sat

baby-sit

baby sitter

baby-sitting

backboard

backcountry

backcourt

backcourtman

back door (n.), backdoor (adj.)

backfield

backfire

backhanded

back porch (n.), back-porch (adj.)

back seat (n.), backseat (adj.)

backstabbing

backstop

back street (n.), back-street (adj.)

back-to-back

backtrack

back up (v.), backup (n., adj.)

backwoods

back yard (n.), backyard (adj.)

badman

bail out (v.), bailout (n.)

baldfaced

ball boy

ball carrier

ballclub

ballgame

ball girl

ballhandler

ballpark

ballplayer

ball point pen

ballroom

Band-Aid (trademark)

bandleader

band saw

band shell

bandwidth

bank robber

bare-bones (adj.)

barefaced

barehanded

bareheaded

barhop

barkeeper

bar mitzvah

barrel-chested

barrelhouse

barroom

barstool

baseboard heating

baseline

batboy

batgirl

bathtub

battle-ax

battlefield

battleground

battleship

battle station

beanbag chair

bedbug

bedclothes

bedpan

bed rest

bedsheet

bel canto

bell-bottom

bellboy

belles-lettres

bellhop

bellwether

bellybutton

belly dance (n.),
belly-dance (v.)

belly dancer

best seller

best-selling

big band, (n.),
big-band (adj.)

big-bang theory

big house

big-ticket

big time (n.),
big-time (adj.)

bigwig

bikeway

bilingual

bimonthly

biodegradable

biodiversity

bipartisan

bird dog (n.),
bird-dog (v.)

bird's-eye

bird-watching
(n., adj.)

birthrate

biweekly

blackboard

blackout

blackstrap molasses

blast off (v.),
blastoff (n., adj.)

blind side (n.),
blindside (v.)

blockbuster

blood bath

bloodhound

bloodstain (n., v.)

bloodstained

blow-dryer

blow up (v.),
blowup (n.)

blue blood (n.),
blue-blooded (adj.)

blue chip stock

blue collar (n.),
blue-collar (adj.)

blue line

blue-sky (adj.)

boardinghouse

boarding school

boardroom

bobsledding

bodybuilder

bodyguard

boilerplate

boldface

boll weevil

bombproof

bona fide

bonbon

boo-boo

bookcase

bookdealer

bookend

bookmobile

bookshelf

bookstore

bookworm

boomtown

bottom line (n.),
bottom-line (adj.)

bowlegged

bowl game

boxcar

box kite

box office (n.),
box-office (adj.)

box score

boyfriend

brain wave

brand name (n.),
brand-name (adj.)

brand-new

breadbox

breadwinner

break dancing (n.),
break-dancing (adj.)

breakdown

break in (v.),
break-in (n., adj.)

breakthrough

break up (v.),
breakup (n., adj.)

breast-feed

bricklayer

bridegroom

bridesmaid

broad-minded

broadside

broodmare

brother-in-law,
brothers-in-law

brown-nose (v.),
brown-noser (n.)

brownout

brush fire

build up (v.),
buildup (n., adj.)

bulldozer

bullet hole

bulletproof

bullfight

bullfighter

bullfighting

bullpen

bull's-eye

Bundt cake

bushelbasket

businesslike

businessman

businesswoman

bus line

busload

buy out (v.),
buyout (n.)

by-election

bygone

bylaw

byline

bypass

byproduct

bystreet

⌈   C   ⌉

cabdriver

cabinetmaker

cakewalk

call up (v.),
call-up (n., adj.)

camera-ready (adj.)

candleholder

candlemaker

candymaker

cannot

card maker

carefree

caretaker

carmaker

car pool

carport

carry over (v.),
carry-over (n., adj.)

car seat

carsick

carwash

caseload

cashbox

cash cow

cash flow

cast member

catch all (v.),
catchall (n., adj.)

cave in (v.),
cave-in (n, adj.)

CD-ROM

cease fire (v.),
cease-fire (n., adj.)

center field

center fielder

centerfold

cha-cha

chain saw

chairman

chairperson

chairwoman

change over (v.),
changeover (n.)

change up (v.),
change-up (n., adj.)

check up (v.),
checkup (n.)

cheese maker

chock-full

chowhound

Christmastime

churchgoer

church member

citizens band

city editor

city hall

citywide

claptrap

clean-cut

clean up (v.),
cleanup (n., adj.)

clear-cut

clearinghouse

cloak-and-dagger

closed shop

close up (v.),
close-up (n., adj.)

clubhouse

coal mine,
coal miners

coastline

coatdress

coattails

co-author

Coca-Cola
(trademark)

co-chairman

coconut

co-defendant

coed

coeducation

coequal

coexist

coexistence

coffee grinder

coffee maker

coffeepot

coffee table (n.),
coffee-table (adj.)

co-host

coleslaw

collectors' item

colorblind

commander in chief

concertgoer

congressman

congresswoman

con man

consumer price index
(generic), Consumer
Price Index (U.S.)

continentwide

cooperate

cooperative

coordinate

coordination

co-owner

co-partner

co-pilot

cop out (v.),
cop-out (n.)

copy desk

copy edit

copy editor

copyright (n, v., adj.)

co-respondent

cornstarch

co-signer

co-star

cost-effective

cost of living (n.),
cost-of-living (adj.)

cost-plus

countdown

counteract

countercharge

counterfoil

counterintelligence

counterproposal

counterspy

countertop

countryside

countrywide

courthouse

court-martial (n., v.)

courtroom

cover up (v.),
cover-up (n., adj.)

co-worker

crack up (v.),
crackup (n., adj.)

crawfish

crawl space

crew member

crisscross

Crock-Pot (trade-
mark), crockpot
(generic)

cropland

cross country (the
sport), cross-country
(other contexts)

cross-examination

cross-examine

cross-eyed (adj., adv.)

cross fire

cross over (v.),
crossover (n., adj.)

cross rate

cross section (n.),
cross-section (v.)

cure-all

curtain raiser

custom-made

cut back (v.),
cutback (n., adj.)

cut off (v.),
cutoff (n., adj.)

cutoffs

cut out (v.),
cutout (n.)

D

dark horse

database

SPELLING

data processing (n., adj.)

date line (the international one), dateline (on a news story)

daughter-in-law, daughters-in-law

daylight-saving time

daylong

daytime

day to day (adv.), day-to-day (adj.)

D-Day

dead center

dead end (n.), dead-end (adj.)

deathbed

decade-long

decision maker

decision making, decision-making (adj.)

Deepfreeze (trademark)

deep freezer

deep freeze (postpone)

deep-sea (adj.)

deep water (n.), deep-water (adj.)

degree-day

derring-do

desktop (n., adj.)

die-hard (n., adj.)

dinner table

disk operating system

ditchdigger

docudrama

dogcatcher

doghouse

dollhouse

door to door (n.), door-to-door (adj.)

double bind

double-check

double-faced

doubleheader

double-parked (n., v., adj.)

double play

downdraft

downgrade

down-home (adj.)

downside

downside risk

down-to-earth

downtown

drive in (v.), drive-in (n., adj.)

driveway

drop out (v.), dropout (n.)

dump truck

dust storm

Dutch oven

dyed-in-the-wool (adj.)

E

earmark (v.)

easygoing

editor in chief, editors in chief

electrocardiogram

e-mail

empty-handed

end line

end zone

en route

euro

Eurodollars (n.), Eurodollar (adj.)

even-steven

every day (adv.), everyday (adj.)

every one (each individual item), everyone (all people)

ex-convict

ex-governor

ex-president

extra-base hit

extra-dry

extra-large

extralegal

extramarital

extra-mild

extraterrestrial

extraterritorial

eyesore

eyestrain

eye to eye (adv.), eye-to-eye (adj.)

eyewitness

F

face-lift

face off (v.), face-off (n., adj.)

face to face (adv.), face-to-face (adj.)

fact-finding (n., adj.)

fade out (v.), fade-out (n.)

fair ball

fair catch

fairway

fall out (v.), fallout (n.)

far-fetched

far-flung

farmhouse

farmland

farmworker

far-off

far-ranging

farsighted

fastball

father-in-law, fathers-in-law

feather bedding (mattress), featherbedding (union practice)

fender bender

Ferris wheel

ferryboat

Fiberglas (trademark), fiberglass (generic)

field goal

field house

field trip

fieldwork

figure skater

figure skating

filmgoer

filmmaker

filmmaking (n., adj.)

film ratings

fingertip

firearm

fire breather

fire chief

firefighter

fireman

fireproof

firetruck

fire wagon

first baseman

first-degree (adj.)

firsthand

fistfight

flagpole

flagship

flameout

flare up (v.), flare-up (n.)

flash flood (n., adj.)

flea market

flimflam

flip-flop

floodwaters

floor leader

floor-length

floppy disk

flower girl

flyswatter

folk singer

folk song

follow-through

follow up (v.), follow-up (n., adj.)

foolproof

foot-and-mouth disease

forebrain

forecast

forefather

foregoing

foreman

foretooth

fore-topgallant

fore-topmast

fore-topsail

forewoman

fortuneteller

fortunetelling

forty-niner or '49er

foul ball line

foul line

foul shot

foul tip

foul up (v.), foul-up (n.)

four-flush

fourfold

Four-H Club or 4-H Club

4-H'er

fraidy-cat

frame up (v.), frame-up (n.)

free-for-all

free-lance (v., adj.), free-lancer (n.)

free on board

freestanding

free throw

free-throw line

freewheeling

freewill offering

freeze-dried

freeze-dry

freeze-drying

frontcourt

front line (n.), front-line (adj.)

front page (n.), front-page (adj.)

front-runner

fruit grower

fullback

full-court press

full-dress

full faith and credit bond

full-fledged

full house

full-length

full page (n.), full-page (adj.)

full-scale

full-size (adj.)

full time (n.),
full-time (adj.)

fund-raiser (n.)

fund raising (n.),
fund-raising (adj.)

furlong

<hr>

G

game plan

general obligation
bond

get away (v.),
getaway (n.)

get together (v.),
get-together (n.)

gift wrap (n.),
gift-wrap (v.)

girlfriend

give away (v.),
giveaway (n.)

go ahead (v.),
go-ahead (n.)

goal line

goal-line stand

goal post

goaltender

goaltending

gobbledygook

go between (v.),
go-between (n.)

godchild

goddaughter

go-go

goodbye

good night

goodwill (n., adj.)

goose bumps

granddad

granddaughter

grant-in-aid,
grants-in-aid

greenmail

gross national
product

groundbreaking

groundhog

ground-rule double

ground rules

groundskeeper

groundswell

ground water

grown-up (n., adj.)

G-string

guardsman

guesthouse

gunbattle

gunboat

gunfight

gunfire

gung-ho

gunpoint

gunpowder

<hr>

H

hair dryer

hairsbreadth

hairstyle

hairstyling

hairstylist

halfback

half-baked

half-blood

half brother

half-cocked

half-court pass

half dollar

halfhearted

half-hour (n., adj.)

half-life

half-mast

half-mile pole

half-moon

half note

half sister

half size (n.),
half-size (adj.)

half-staff

half tide

halftime

halftone

halftrack

half-truth

handball

hand-carved

handcrafted

hand-held

handhold

handmade

handoff

hand-painted

hand-picked

hand-set (v.),
handset (n.)

hand-sewn

hands off (n.),
hands-off (adj.)

hand-stitched

hand to hand (n.),
hand-to-hand (adj.)

hand to mouth (n.),
hand-to-mouth (adj.)

hand warmer

handwrought

hangover

hang up (v.),
hang-up (n.)

hanky-panky

hardback

hard-bound

hard copy

hardcover

hard drive

hard-line

hardworking

harebrained

harelip

has been (v.),
has-been (n.)

H-bomb

headache

headlong

head-on

health care (n.),
health-care (adj.)

health club

heartbeat

heartfelt

heart-rending

heartwarming

helter-skelter

heyday

hideaway

hide out (v.),
hide-out (n.)

hi-fi

higher-up (n.)

high jinks

high point

high-rise (n., adj.)

high-step (v.)

high-stepper

high-tech

hit and run (v.),
hit-and-run (n., adj.)

hitchhike

hitchhiker

hit man

hocus-pocus

hodgepodge

ho-hum

hold over (v.),
holdover (n.)

hold up (v.),
holdup (n., adj.)

home-baked

home builder

home buyer

homegrown

homemade

homemaker

homeowner

home page

home plate

home run

hometown

hoof-and-mouth
disease

hook shot

hook up (v.),
hookup (n.)

horsepower

horse race

horse racing

horse rider

horse-trader

hotbed

hotheaded

hot line

hot seat

hot spot

hot tub

hour-long

house call

housecleaning

household

househusband

houseplant

hurly-burly

hush-hush

hydroelectric

hydrophobia

hyperactive

hypercritical

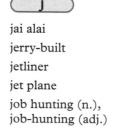

I

ice age (n., adj.)

ice storm

inasmuch

inbound

in-depth

Indochina

indoor (adj.),
indoors (adv.)

industrywide

infield

infighting

infrared

infrastructure

in-group

in-house

in-law

inpatient (n., adj.)

insofar

in spite of

inter-American

interracial

interstate

intramural

intrastate

J

jai alai

jerry-built

jetliner

jet plane

job hunting (n.),
job-hunting (adj.)

jukebox

jumbo jet

jump ball

jump shot

jury-rigged

K

keynote

kick off (v.),
kickoff (n., adj.)

kilowatt-hour

kindhearted

Kmart (trademark)

knickknack

knock off (v.), knock-
off (n.)

knock out (v.), knock-
out (n., adj.)

know-how

kowtow

L

lamebrain

lame duck (n.),
lame-duck (adj.)

last-ditch effort

latecomer

lawsuit

layup

left guard

left hand (n.)

left-handed (adj.)

left-hander

left wing (n.),
left-wing (adj.)

lengthwise

let up (v.),
letup (n., adj.)

life jacket

lifelike

lifelong

Life Saver (trademark
for candy),
lifesaver (generic)

life-size

lifestyle

lifetime

life vest

lift off (v.),
liftoff (n.)

light bulb

lighthearted

light-year

like-minded

like-natured

likewise

linebacker

line drive

lineman

line up (v.),
lineup (n.)

long distance (n.),
long-distance (adj., or
in reference to phone
calls)

long-lasting

long-lived

long-range

long run (n.),
long-run (adj.)

long shot (n.),
long-shot (adj.)

long-standing

long term (n.),
long-term (adj.)

long time (n.),
longtime (adj.)

look-alike

lovemaking

low-ball

lumberyard

lunchbox

lunch cart

lunchroom

lunchtime

M

machine gun (n.),
machine-gun
(adj., v.)

machine-gunner

machine-made

mah-jongg

major league (n.),
major-league (adj.)

major leaguer

makeshift

make up (v.),
makeup (n., adj.)

man-to-man

mapmaker

marketbasket

marketplace

meatball

meatcutter

meatloaf

menage a trois

menswear

merry-go-round

metalwork

mid-America

mid-Atlantic

midcourt

middle class (n.),
middle-class (adj.)

middleman

midnight

midsemester

midshipman

midterm

milquetoast

mind-set

mine shaft

minibus

miniseries

miniskirt

mix up (v.),
mix-up (n., adj.)

mock-up (n.)

moneymaker

money-saving

monthlong

mo-ped

mop up (v.),
mop-up (n., adj.)

moral obligation
bond

mother-in-law,
mothers-in-law

motorboat

motor home

mountain man

mousehole

moviegoer

movie house

moviemaker

moviemaking

mudslide

mudslinging

multicolored

multilateral

multimillion

multimillionaire

muscle ache

mutual field

N

nail clippers

name tag

narrow gauge (n.),
narrow-gauge (adj.)

narrow-minded

nationwide

near shore (prep.
phrase),
nearshore (adj.)

nearsighted

nerve-racking

net asset value

newfangled

newsmagazine

newsroom

newsstand

news writer

news writing

new wave (n.),
new-wave (adj.)

nickname

nightclub

night shift

nightspot

nighttime

nitpicking

nitty-gritty

no man's land

nonaligned

nonchalance

nonchalant

nondescript

nonentity

nonrestrictive

nonsense

nonsensical

nonviolent

no one

O

oceangoing

odd-looking

odd-numbered

oddsmaker

off-Broadway

off-color

off-duty

offhand

officeholder

off-off-Broadway

off-peak

off-road

off-season

offset

offshore

offside

offstage

off-white

oilman

old-fashioned

old-time

old-timer

old times

Old West

Old World

one-fourth

one-half

one-sided

one-third

one time (n.),
one-time (adj.)

ongoing

online

open-minded

outact

outargue

outbluff

outbrag

outclimb

outdated

outdistance

outdrink

outeat

outfield

outfielder

outfight

outfox

outhit

outleap

outmatch

out of bounds (adv.),
out-of-bounds (adj.)

out of court (adv.),
out-of-court (adj.)

outpatient (n., adj.)

outperform

outpitch

outpointed

outpost

outproduce

output

outquote

outrace

outscore

outshout

outstrip

outswim

outtalk

outwalk

ovenproof

overall

overbuy

overexert

overrate

override

oversize

over the counter
(adv.),
over-the-counter
(adj.)

overtime

overview

P

pacemaker

pacesetter

paddy wagon

painkiller

panchromatic

pantheism

pantsuit

pantyhose

Pap (test, smear)

paper bag

paper clip

paper towel

paperwork

pari-mutuel

parkland

part time (adv.),
part-time (adj.)

partygoer

passed ball

passer-by, passers-by

patrolman

patrolwoman

paycheck

payday

payload

peacekeeper

peacekeeping

peacemaker

peacemaking

peace offering

peacetime

pell-mell

penny-wise

pen pal

percent

pet store

petty officer

pigeonhole (n., v.)

pile up (v.),
pileup (n., adj.)

pillowcase

pinch hit (v.),
pinch-hit (n., adj.)

pinch hitter

Ping-Pong (trade-
mark), pingpong
(generic)

pin up (v.),
pinup (n.)

pipeline

pitchout (n.)

pivotman

place kick

place-kicker

place mat

play off (v.),
playoff (n., adj.)

pocketbook

pocket watch

point-blank

police officer

policyholder

policy-maker

policy-making
(n., adj.)

pom-pom (weapon),
pompom (cheer-
leader paraphernalia)

pooh-pooh

post-bellum

postcard

postdate

postdoctoral

postelection

postgraduate

post-mortem

postnuptial

post office

postoperative

SPELLING

postscript

postseason

postwar

pothole

potluck

potshot

pound-foolish

powder keg

power line

power play

power-play goal

prearrange

precondition

pre-convention

precook

precut

predate

pre-dawn

predispose

pre-election

pre-eminent

pre-empt

pre-establish

pre-exist

prefix

preflight

preheat

prehistoric

preignition

prejudge

premarital

premenstrual

prenatal

preregister

preschool

preseason

preset

pretax

pretest

pretrial

prewar

prewash

price-earnings ratio

price tag

prima-facie (adj.)

prime rate

prizewinner

prizewinning

pro-business

profit-sharing (n., adj.)

profit taking (n.), profit-taking (adj.)

pro-labor

pro-life

pro-peace

pro-war

pull back (v.), pullback (n.)

pull out (v.), pullout (n.)

punch line

purebred

push-button (n., adj.)

push up (v.), push-up (n., adj.)

put out (v.), putout (n.)

Q

Q-and-A format

QE2

quarterback

quick-witted

R

racetrack

racquetball

rainstorm

ranch house

ranchland

rangeland

rank and file (n.), rank-and-file (adj.)

rawhide

razor strop

razzle-dazzle

razzmatazz

ready-made

rearview mirror

recover (regain), re-cover (cover again)

red-haired

red-handed (adj., adv.)

redhead

redheaded

redlining

redneck

re-elect

re-election

re-emerge

re-employ

re-enact

re-engage

re-enlist

re-enter

re-entry

re-equip

re-establish

re-examine

reform (improve), re-form (form again)

rendezvous

resign (quit), re-sign (sign again)

riffraff

right guard

right hand (n.), right-handed (adj.)

right-hander (n.)

right of way

right-to-work (adj.)

right wing (n.),
right-wing (adj.)

ring bearer

rip off (v.),
rip-off (n., adj.)

riverboat

roadside

rock 'n' roll

role model

roll call (n.),
roll-call (adj.)

roller coaster

roller skate (n.),
roller-skate (v.)

roller skater (n.)

roly-poly

round table (n.),
round-table (adj.)

round trip (n.),
round-trip (adj.)

round up (v.),
roundup (n.)

rubber band

runback (n.)

run down (v.),
rundown (n.),
run-down (adj.)

runner-up,
runners-up

running back

running mate

rush hour (n.),
rush-hour (adj.)

S

safe-deposit box

sales pitch

sandbag

sandstorm

saucepan

savings and loan

association

school bus

schoolteacher

scot-free

seat belt (n.),
seat-belt (adj.)

seawater

second guess (n.),
second-guess (v.)

second-guesser

second hand (n.),
secondhand (adj.,
adv.)

second-rate

secretary-treasurer

seesaw

self-assured

self-defense

self-esteem

self-governing

self-government

sell out (v.),
sellout (adj., n.)

semiannual

semicolon

semifinal

semiofficial

semitropical

semiweekly

send off (v.),
send-off (n.)

set up (v.),
setup (n., adj.)

7-Eleven
(trademark)

Seven-Up or 7UP
(trademarks)

sewer line

shake up (v.),
shake-up (n., adj.)

shape up (v.),
shape-up (n., adj.)

Sheetrock
(trademark)

shirt sleeve (n.),
shirt-sleeve (adj.)

shoeshine

shoestring

shoot out (v.),
shootout (n.)

shopworn

shortchange

short-handed

short-lived

shortstop

shotgun

showcase

show off (v.),
showoff (n.)

showroom

showstopper

shut down (v.),
shutdown (n.)

shut in (v.),
shut-in (n.)

shut off (v.),
shut-off (n.)

shut out (v.),
shutout (n., adj.)

side by side (adv.),
side-by-side (adj.)

side dish

side effect

sidestep

side street (n.)

sidetrack

side trip

sightseeing

sightseer

sign up (v. or n.),
sign-up (adj.)

single-handed

sister-in-law,
sisters-in-law

SPELLING

sit down (v.),
sit-down (n., adj.)

sit in (v.),
sit-in (n., adj.)

skyrocketing

slantwise

slap shot

sledgehammer

sleight of hand (n.),
sleight-of-hand (adj.)

slide show

slow down (v.),
slowdown (n.)

slumlord

slush fund

small-arms fire

small-business man

smash up (v.),
smashup (n., adj.)

smoke bomb

smoke screen

snowdrift

snowfall

snowflake

snowman

snowplow

snowshoe

snowstorm

snowsuit

so called (adv.),
so-called (adj.)

softcover

soft pedal (n.),
soft-pedal (v.)

soft-spoken

software

songwriter

son-in-law,
sons-in-law

sound bite

sound effects

sound stage

soundtrack (n., adj.)

spacecraft

spaceship

space shuttle

spacewalk

speechmaker

speechmaking

speechwriter

speech writing

speed bump

speed up (v.),
speedup (n., adj.)

spin off (v.),
spinoff (n., adj.)

split end

sportswear

sportswriter

spot-check

spotlight

squeeze play

staff writer

stage fright

stained glass (n.),
stained-glass (adj.)

standard-bearer

stand in (v.),
stand-in (n., adj.)

standing room only

stand off (v.),
standoff (n., adj.)

stand out (v.),
standout (n., adj.)

stand up (v.),
stand-up (adj.)

starboard

start up (v.),
start-up (n., adj.)

statehouse

state police

states' rights

statewide

station wagon

steady-state theory

stepbrother

stepchild

stepdaughter

stepfamily

stepfather

stepmother

stepparent

steppingstone

stepsister

stepson

stockbroker

stock index futures

stockman

stock market prices

stone carver

stool pigeon

stopgap

stop off (v.),
stop-off (n.)

stop over (v.),
stopover (n.)

storm tide

story line

storyteller

stove top (n.),
stove-top (adj.)

straight-laced (strict
or severe)

straitjacket

strait-laced (pertain-
ing to confinement, as
a corset)

street dance

street gang

streetlamp

streetlight

street people

street-smart (adj.)

street smarts (n.)

street sweeper

streetwalker

streetwise

strikebreaker

strike zone

strong-arm (v., adj.)

strong-willed

subbasement

subcommittee

subculture

subdivision

submachine gun

suborbital

subtotal

subzero

summertime

sunbathe

sunbather

sunbathing

sundress

sun porch

superagency

supercarrier

supercharge

supercollider

superconducting

superhighway

superhuman

superpower

supersonic

supertanker

supragovernmental

supranational

surface-to-air missile

sweat pants

sweat shirt

sweat suit

_____T_____

tablecloth

tablespoon

table talk

table tennis

tag end

tailback

taillight

tailor-made

tailpipe

tailspin

tail wind

take charge (v.),
take-charge (adj.)

take down (v.),
takedown (n., adj.)

take-home pay

take off (v.),
takeoff (n., adj.)

take out (v.),
takeout (n., adj.)

take over (v.),
takeover (n., adj.)

take up (v.),
takeup (n., adj.)

talebearer

talk show

tap dance (n.),
tap-dance (v.)

tap dancer

tape-record (v.)

tape recording (n.)

task force

tattletale

tax-deductible

teachers college

teakettle

teammate

team teaching

tear gas (n.),
tear-gas (adj., v.)

teaspoon

teen-age (adj.)

teen-ager

teeny-weeny

telecommute

teleconference

telecourse

telemarketing

TelePrompTer
(trademark)

Telex (company),
telex (generic)

telltale

temperature-humidity
index

tenderhearted

tenfold

term paper

terror-stricken

terry cloth

Texas leaguer

thank you (v.),
thank-you (n., adj.)

theatergoer

thermonuclear

Third World

3-D

3M

three R's

threesome

throw away (v.),
throwaway (n., adj.)

thruway

thumbscrew

thumbtack

thunderbolt

thundershower

thunderstorm

thunderstruck

tick-tack-toe

ticktock

tidal wave

tidbit

tiebreaker

tie in (v.),
tie-in (n., adj.)

tie up (v.),
tie-up (n., adj.)

tight end

time-lapse

timeout (n.)

timesaver

timesaving

time share (n.)

time-shared (adj.)

time sharing (n.),
time-sharing (adj.)

timetable

Time Warner Inc.
(trademark)

tiptoe

tiptop

titleholder

tollbooth

tollhouse

Tommy gun
(trademark)

tongue-lashing

top-notch

torch singer

torch song

touchback (n.)

touchdown (n.)

touch up (v.),
touch-up (n., adj.)

town house

townspeople

toy maker

track and field

track lighting

tractor-trailer

trade in (v.),
trade-in (n., adj.)

trademark

trade off (v.),
trade-off (n., adj.)

trade route

trans-Atlantic

transcontinental

transoceanic

trans-Pacific

transsexual

transship

trapshooting

trash can

trendsetter

trigger-happy

triple play

truck driver

truck stop

trustbuster

try out (v.),
tryout (n.)

T-shirt

tune up (v.),
tuneup (n., adj.)

turboprop

turnkey (n., adj.)

turn off (v.),
turnoff (n.)

turnpike

tutti-frutti

twi-night
double-header

twofold

two-on-one break

U

U-boat

ultrahigh frequency

ultraleftist

ultramodern

ultranationalism

ultrarightist

ultrasonic

ultraviolet

un-American

underclass (n., adj.)

underdog

underfoot (adj., adv.)

undergarment

underhand

undersheriff

undersold

understudy

under way (all senses
but nautical),
underway (in nautical
sense when used as an
adj. before a word, as
in *underway flotilla*)

unidentified flying
object

upbeat

uplink

upper hand

upside down (adv.),
upside-down (adj.)

upstate

upstream

up-tempo

U-turn

V

vacationland

variable interest rate

variable rate
mortgage

V-E Day

V-8 engine

V8 juice

vice chancellor

vice consul

vice president

vice principal

vice regent

vice secretary

vice versa

videocassette
(n., adj.)

videodisc

video game

videophone

videotape (n., v.)

videotex

V-J Day

V-neck

voiceprint

voir dire

volleyball

voodoo

vote-getter

(**W**)

wagonmaker

wagon master

waistline

walkie-talkie

walk in (v.),
walk-in (n., adj.)

walk on (v.),
walk-on (n., adj.)

walk out (v.),
walkout (n.)

walk over (v.),
walkover (n.)

walk up (v.),
walk-up (n., adj.)

wallboard

wallcovering

walleye

wall hanging

wallpaper

wall-to-wall

Wal-Mart
(trademark)

war chest

war crime

warhead

war horse (horse),
warhorse (veteran)

warlike

warlord

warmhearted

warm up (n.),
warm-up (n., adj.)

wartime

washcloth

washed up (v.),
washed-up (adj.)

wash out (v.),
washout (n.)

washstand

wastebasket

wasteland

wastepaper

wastewater

watchband

water bed

watercolor

waterline

waterlogged

watermark

water polo

waterproof

watershed

water ski (n.),
water-ski (v.)

water-skier

water-skiing

waterspout

water tank

watertight

water wings

wavelength

wax paper

weak-kneed

weakside

weather-beaten

weatherman

weatherproof

weatherstripping

weather vane

weedkiller

weekend

weeklong

weeknight

weightlifting

well-being

wellhead

wellspring

well-to-do

well-wisher

westernmost

wet bar

wheelbarrow

wheelchair

wheeler-dealer

whereabouts

wherever

whirlwind

whistle-blower

whistle-stop

white collar (n.),
white-collar (adj.)

whiteout (weather
condition)

white paper

whitewash (n., v.,
adj.)

white water (n.),
white-water (adj.)

wholehearted

wholesale price index

whole-wheat

wide-angle

wide-awake

wide-brimmed

wide-eyed

wide-open
wide receiver
wide-screen
widespread
wife beater
wild card
wildfire
wildlife
wild pitch
willpower
wind chill index
wind gauge
windmill
window-dress (v.)
window dressing (n.)
windowpane
window seat
window-shop (v.)
window-shopping
wind power
wind shear
wind-swept
wind up (v.),
windup (n., adj.)
winemaker
winemaking
wine taster
wingspan
winter storm
warning
winter storm watch
wintertime

wire-rimmed
wiretap
wood-burning (as in
wood-burning stove),
woodburning (as in
woodburning kit)
woodcarver
woodcarving
woodcutter
wood heat
woodlot
woodpile
woodsmoke
woodstove (our rule)
woodwork
word-of-mouth
(n., adj.)
word processing
(n., adj.)
workday
work force
workhorse
working class (n.),
working-class (adj.)
workingman
workingwoman
workmanlike
work out (v.),
workout (n., adj.)
workplace
workweek
world-weary
worldwide

worn-out
worrywart
worthwhile
wrap around (v.),
wraparound (adj.)
wristwatch
write in (v.),
write-in (n., adj.)
wrongdoing

X

X-ray

Y

yard sale
yardstick
yardwork
year-end (adj.)
yearlong
year-round
yellow-bellied
yellow-belly
yesteryear
yo-yo
yuletide

Z

zero-base budgeting
zigzag
ZIP code
Ziploc (trademark)
zoot suit

SPELLING

American vs. British Spelling

American spellings began diverging from British ones in the 19th century when America's most famous dictionary maker, the newspaper editor Noah Webster, decided this country should show its independence by developing its own system of simplified spellings. His suggested variations, however, didn't go that far in making American spelling either simple or

ESL Tip

The playwright George Bernard Shaw once said America and England were two nations separated by a common language. He probably overstated the case, but when it comes to spelling, if you're a foreign student who learned British English or you come from another English-speaking country such as Canada, you'll notice that the preferred American spellings are sometimes different. If you're more familiar with British spellings than American, or if your country's spelling is closer to the British, this section can help you avoid problems.

logical. If you're used to British spellings, you'll find that American ones generally aren't that different.

A few generalizations will help you recognize many spelling differences.

○ Words that end in *ise* in Britain sometimes end in *ize* in America:

BRITISH	AMERICAN
baptise	baptize
civilise	civilize
criticise	criticize
organise	organize
realise	realize

A common exception to this generalization is that Americans spell *surprise* the same as the British.

○ Words ending in *our* in Britain usually end in *or* in America:

BRITISH	AMERICAN
behaviour	behavior
colour	color
honour	honor
labour	labor
neighbour	neighbor

A common exception is that Americans spell *glamour* the same as the British.

○ Words that end in *re* in Britain usually end in *er* in America:

BRITISH	AMERICAN
centre	center
litre	liter
metre	meter
theatre	theater

Many American theaters spell their names the British way, however, typically to suggest sophistication.

○ **Words that contain an *x* in Britain often are spelled with a *ct* in America:**

BRITISH	AMERICAN
connexion	connection
inflexion	inflection
reflexion	reflection

A common exception to this generalization is that Americans spell *complexion* the same as the British.

In addition to these generalizations, you should note that a number of other words are spelled differently in the two countries. Here are some common examples:

BRITISH	AMERICAN
aeon	eon
aluminium	aluminum
burnt	burned
checque	check
diarrhoea	diarrhea
draught	draft
fulfil	fulfill
gaol	jail
grey	gray
haemorrhage	hemorrhage
judgement	judgment
kerb	curb
manoevre	maneuver
mould	mold
moustache	mustache
oestrogen	estrogen
paediatrician	pediatrician
plough	plow
practise	practice
programme	program
pyjamas	pajamas
skilful	skillful
sulphur	sulfur
sunburnt	sunburned
tyre	tire
vice	vise

You should also note these common vocabulary differences between the two countries:

BRITISH	AMERICAN
afters	dessert
aubergine	eggplant
biscuit barrel	cookie jar
bonnet (of a car)	hood
boot (of a car)	trunk
braces	suspenders
call	formal visit
chips	french fries
closet (or water closet or wc)	bathroom
courgette	zucchini
crisps	potato chips
cycle	bike
davenport	desk
draughts	checkers
dummy	pacifier
dustman	garbage collector
earthing an electrical line	grounding an electrical line
estate agent	real estate agent
first floor	second floor
flat	apartment
football	soccer
French beans or runner beans	green beans or string beans
geyser	water heater
greengrocer	vegetable market
ground floor	first floor
to hoover	to vacuum
to be knocked up	to be awakened
ladder	run (in a stocking)
large sofa	davenport
lift	elevator
loo	toilet
lorry	truck
lounge	living room
macintosh	raincoat
mean	stingy
motorcar	automobile
nappy	diaper

SPELLING

BRITISH	AMERICAN
nil	nothing or zero
noughts-and-crosses	tick-tack-toe
pecker	courage
petrol	gasoline
pitch (athletic grounds)	field
porridge	hot cereal
pram	baby carriage
pullover or jumper	sweater
queue	line
rates	local property taxes
ring up	phone
roundabout or circus	traffic circle
scone	biscuit
shares	stocks
silver plate	sterling silver
smalls	underwear
spend a penny	go to the bathroom
stocks	bonds
suspenders	garters
sweet or pudding	dessert
sweet shop	candy store
telly	TV
torch	flashlight
treacle	molasses
vest	undershirt
waistcoat	vest
windscreen	windshield
wing (of a car)	fender

Web Resources

INVESTIGATIVE REPORTING

Investigative reporters and those who use advanced reporting techniques such as computer-assisted reporting can find help on the Internet.

○ Investigative Reporters and Editors
www.ire.org

○ National Institute of Computer-Assisted Reporting
www.nicar.org

PART THREE

Style

CHAPTER 11

Writing as a Journalist

"The night ambulance attendants shuffled down the long, dark corridors at the General Hospital with an inert burden on the stretcher. They turned in at the receiving ward and lifted the unconscious man to the operating table. His hands were calloused, and he was unkempt and ragged, a victim of a street brawl near the city market. No one knew who he was, but a receipt, bearing the name of George Anderson, for $10 paid on a home out in a little Nebraska town served to identify him.

"The surgeon opened the swollen eyelids. The eyes were turned to the left. 'A fracture on the left side of the skull,' he said to the attendants who stood about the table. 'Well, George, you're not going to finish paying for that home of yours.'

"'George' merely lifted a hand as though groping for something. Attendants hurriedly caught hold of him to keep him from rolling from the table. But he scratched his face in a tired, resigned way that seemed almost ridiculous and placed his hand again at his side. Four hours later he died."

—Ernest Hemingway,
The Kansas City Star, Jan. 20, 1918

Many people who choose journalism as a career dream of writing the great American novel, as Ernest Hemingway did. In the meantime, becoming a reporter or editor is a great way to earn a steady paycheck, as Hemingway was doing when he wrote this feature story on a hospital emergency room. Like Hemingway, many great authors got their start in journalism, which gives a budding writer the chance to see all sides of life while learning to write about it.

In addition to Hemingway, those who began as journalists include Willa Cather, Stephen Crane, Charles Dickens, John Dos Passos, Theodore Dreiser, William Dean Howells, Sinclair Lewis, Mario Vargas Llosa, Jack London, Gabriel García Márquez, Frank Norris, George Orwell, Katherine Anne Porter, Upton Sinclair, John Steinbeck, Mark Twain, Eudora Welty, Tom Wolfe, Richard Wright and Émile Zola.

Many great writers, of course, remain in journalism. Often, their names are not as well-known, but readers appreciate good writing when they see it, whether from Saul Pett, James J. Kilpatrick, Tom Wicker, Edna Buchanan, Jacqui Banaszynski or Tad Bartimus. Those who do stay in journalism are addicted to recording the big stories of our day—the assassination of a president, man's first walk on the moon, the pursuit of a cure for cancer, war in the desert or terrorist attacks on New York and Washington. Those, after all, are human triumphs and tragedies that are compelling partly because of their reality.

Today's journalism makes more liberal use of advanced writing techniques more often associated with novels. Despite the literary license afforded Hemingway in The Kansas City Star many years ago, never more than today have journalists enjoyed such immense freedom to strut their stuff—to chronicle the news of the day with compelling prose filled with the metaphors, similes and good old-fashioned storytelling. Journalists today often refer to that as narrative writing, but it is writing that borrows heavily from the repertoire of the novelist.

Make no mistake, however: There remain fundamental differences between writing news stories and writing novels, just as there are differences between all kinds of writing. The purpose of journalism is to convey information clearly, correctly and concisely. The literary license to invent scenarios that is permitted, or even encouraged, in fiction writing is taboo in journalism. As one form of nonfiction writing, journalism has much in common with technical writing—writing reports, manuals and instructions—especially in straightforward news stories aimed at conveying information.

Of course, some journalism, such as features, columns and reviews, has much in common with creative writing, such as novels, short stories, plays and poems. But for all of you with literary aspirations, here are some differences between journalistic writing and creative writing.

- **Clear, simple writing.** Straight-news reporting tends to stress the clear, correct and concise statement of facts, rather than an expression of imagination or vision. Creative writers take license with the language for literary effect, and ambiguity is often praised. Literary critics value writing that is *ambiguous* (which means it has multiple meanings) but usually not writing that is *obscure* (which means readers have no idea what it means). People reading the news, however, want neither obscurity to confuse them nor multiple meanings to puzzle them. Instead, they want the facts, clearly and quickly. Of course, when people read features, columns and reviews, they also expect to be entertained.

- **Quick, efficient writing.** Journalism of the hard-news variety, which we see in objective news accounts, is more formulaic than creative writing is. Other than feature writers, reviewers and columnists, journalists place less emphasis on originality of style and more on knowing story formulas that help them write quickly while covering a subject logically and thoroughly. As we'll see in Chapters 14 and 15, however, journalists often use formulas even in soft-news stories.

- **Emphasis on mechanics.** Journalism places greater emphasis on mechanics (grammar, usage, spelling, style and tight writing) than creative writing does because adherence to such rules keeps the reader from being distracted by irregularities. By contrast, the poet e.e. cummings, for example, avoided capitalization and punctuation in his poems to develop an original style that could sometimes make use of the double meanings that were created when such guideposts were missing.

  Using correct mechanics also helps maintain a journalist's credibility. If people find mistakes or inconsistencies of any kind in journalism, they start wondering whether they can trust the accuracy of the news presented.

Keys to Good Journalistic Writing

Good, tight journalistic writing demands that the writer and editor follow these guidelines.

○ **Keep paragraphs short.**

Most paragraphs should be one or two sentences long. Quotations that form a complete sentence should usually get a paragraph of their own.

○ **Keep sentences short.**

Sentences should average about 16 words. Make sure that leads are short and uncomplicated. Vary sentence lengths and patterns to provide pacing and to avoid monotony and choppiness. Avoid compound sentences, especially ones connected with semicolons. Cut out words and phrases that don't add meaning. Avoid the passive voice, which by its nature is wordy.

○ **Use short, common words.**

Short, simple, common words are the best for journalism. Avoid foreign expressions and jargon. Explain difficult or technical terms if you need to use them. Use adjectives and adverbs only when they are essential.

By the way, the shortest words are usually also the most common, but there are exceptions. Some longer words, such as *importantly,* are clear to everyone, and some shorter words, such as *fud,* are not. (A fud is a rabbit's butt. Remember how Elmer Fudd was often the butt of Bugs Bunny's jokes?) Given the choice between a short uncommon word and a longer common one, choose the more common one.

JOURNALISTIC STYLE

○ Be objective.

Particularly in hard-news stories, don't express your opinions. Don't use words that express a value judgment. Report only what you can prove to be true. Present all sides fairly.

○ Follow style rules.

Style rules, such as those established by The Associated Press, United Press International or a particular newspaper, add consistency and therefore clarity. Use Webster's New World College Dictionary or Webster's Third New International Dictionary to check the spelling of words that are not in the stylebook.

○ Know the journalism story formulas, how to use them and when to break them.

They help you know what must be included in a story of this type and in what order generally. That, in turn, helps you know what could be left out. We present in Chapters 14 and 15 some basic formulas for hard- and soft-news stories in both print and broadcast. For now, let's just mention as an example the most widely known news formula: *In hard-news stories, use the inverted-pyramid formula—the most important news at the top, the least important at the bottom.*

In far fewer words, we could summarize these six rules as *be clear, be correct* and *be concise.* In this chapter, we look at the first two rules in detail. We shall discuss the third in Chapter 12.

Clarity

"If a man were to ask me what I should suppose to be a perfect style ...
I would answer, that in which a man speaking to five hundred people, of all common and various capacities, idiots or lunatics excepted, should be understood by them all, and in the same sense in which the speaker intended to be understood."
—Daniel Defoe

Writing Levels

Journalists try to write at the eighth-grade level, using short, simple sentences. Sometimes, when people hear this, they're shocked. "Why do journalists 'write down' to people?" they ask. The answer is that writing at the eighth-grade level isn't writing down to most people.

Readability tests, such as the Gunning and Flesch indexes, are mathematical formulas for determining how hard it is to read and understand a piece of writing. Some, but not all, readability tests report the difficulty with a grade-level designation. If a piece of writing is judged to be written at the eighth-grade level, that means it should be understandable to an average student in the eighth grade or anyone else who reads at that level.

But don't think that a piece with a high grade-level rating is better written than one with a low grade-level rating. Readability tests work by determining how long or unusual the words are and how long the sentences are. A piece written on the postgraduate level would mean the words in it are so long and unusual and the sentences so long that the average reader would not understand it. That's not good writing. By contrast, something written at the first-grade level could be so simplistic that it would bore most adult readers.

The eighth-grade level is best for a publication aimed at a general audience. The Wall Street Journal is written at that level, and as magazine consultant Don Ranly says, you'll never hear an MBA complain that the Journal is too easy to read.

It's not always enough simply to be brief. Sometimes, it's necessary to say the same thing more clearly in about the same number of words, or even to include additional material. Clarity and completeness go hand in hand.

Unanswered Questions

Often, a passage is unclear not because the words are confusing but because the passage raises questions in the reader's mind. In such instances, to achieve clarity requires that you *anticipate what questions the reader might have and answer them.*

If you were an editor and a reporter handed in a story with the following passages, what questions would be raised in your mind?

> A sizable crowd turned out to see the Michigan Wolverines play their baseball opener against the Ohio State Buckeyes.

How about these questions: Who won? What was the score? What's a "sizable" crowd? Where was the game played?

Or consider this final paragraph in an auto-accident story:

> Police said the Paris Road and College Avenue intersection is the scene of many traffic accidents.

How many accidents? Why is this intersection dangerous? Is anybody doing anything about it?

Specifics

Providing readers with specifics is closely related to the idea of answering likely questions. Occasionally, writers make generalizations that need to be pinned down. Once the specifics are supplied, the generalizations sometimes appear patently false, sometimes more persuasively true. In either case, giving specifics helps clarify the issue.

Here are some examples of a few of the most common kinds of general statements and some questions to ask to draw out detail. As an editor, be on guard for these general statements. As a writer, ask yourself these questions about your own statements.

○ **When a writer makes an abstract statement, ask, "What do you mean by that?" "What's an example of that?"**

Some people can't see the forest for the trees.

Love makes the world go round.

○ **When a writer uses a vague modifier, ask, "Compared with what?" "Compared with whom?"**

He's a great singer.

Democracy is the best form of government.

○ **When someone makes a universal statement, one that applies to all members of a group, ask, "All?" "Every?" "Never?"**

Women aren't good at science.

The Irish are hotheads.

○ **When someone refers to a large, unspecified group, ask, "Who specifically?" "What specifically?" "Which specifically?"**

Scientists say … .

They say … .

Studies show … .

○ **When someone talks about *can't, must, ought* or *should* (or their opposites), ask, "Why?" "Who says so?" "What causes that?" "What prevents that?" "What would happen if somebody did?"**

You should drink six glasses of water a day.

You shouldn't swear.

○ **When people say that something does something, ask, "How specifically does it do that?" "What makes it do that?" "Why is that true?" "Could it be done in a different way?"**

Using that spray deodorant just hastens the greenhouse effect.

Opposites attract.

Awkward Constructions

Some of the most common problems that erode the clarity of writing are lack of parallelism, misplaced modifiers and dangling participles, problems we discussed in Chapters 2 and 6.

Lack of parallelism means that similar ideas are not expressed in a similar (parallel) way. That's often what's wrong when a passage "just doesn't sound right" but you don't know why. For example:

AWKWARD   My favorite sports activities are playing soccer, Australian rules football on television and to go to a baseball game.

BETTER   My favorite sports activities are playing soccer, watching Australian rules football on television and going to a baseball game.

For clarity, modifiers should be placed next to the word they describe. A *misplaced modifier* results in confusion:

AWKWARD   Lincoln wrote the Gettysburg Address while traveling on a train on the back of an envelope.

BETTER   Lincoln wrote the Gettysburg Address on the back of an envelope while traveling on a train.

One of the most frequent kinds of misplaced modifiers is the *dangling participle*. A *participle* is a word usually ending in *ing* that acts like an adjective modifying the first noun or pronoun to follow the participial phrase. If the next noun or pronoun after it is not what it's supposed to be modifying, we have a dangling participle:

DANGLING   Flying over the North Pole, an icicle was seen.

CORRECT   [He, she, we] saw an icicle while flying over the North Pole.

The first suggests that the icicle was flying over the North Pole, although that's almost certainly not what the writer intended.

Math and Clarity

Numbers should be used in stories to inform and to clarify, but too often they are used in ways that merely confuse people.

Many reporters think they have done their jobs when they pepper their stories with a few figures. But what do those figures mean to readers? Put numbers in a meaningful context—tell readers what they mean.

For example, a business-page story tells readers that the Consumer Price Index (CPI) rose 1.3 percent in June. If readers don't know enough already to equate that index loosely with the cost of living (that's not exactly what it is), the story probably means nothing to them. Furthermore, is it a good thing or a bad thing for the CPI to have risen 1.3 percent? Readers might automatically think it's a bad thing that prices have risen. But perhaps this was the smallest increase in the CPI in six months.

Big numbers especially tend to lose readers and cease to be real. As the late Sen. Everett Dirksen, R-Ill., once said during a discussion of the federal budget, "A billion here, a billion there, and soon you're talking about real money."

In addition to supplying the raw numbers, try using analogies to help readers grasp the numbers. For example:

If you could pick up a dollar a second, it would take you 32 years to pick up a billion of them.

There's a 1 in 1.5 million chance of being killed in an airplane crash. By contrast, the number of people who die from smoking each year is equivalent to the entire population of Kansas City, Mo.

Because numbers get so fuzzy for many people, they can easily mislead when thrown about unscrupulously. Former British Prime Minister Benjamin Disraeli is often quoted as having said, "There are lies, damn lies and statistics."

For example, it is extremely important for journalists to be able to calculate percentages and to understand them. Otherwise, bias tends to creep into stories, either unintentionally or as the result of some public-relations person's manipulation.

Which of these statements is correct?

1. One percent milk has half the fat of 2 percent milk.
2. One percent milk has 50 percent of the fat of 2 percent milk.
3. Two percent milk has twice the fat of 1 percent milk.
4. Two percent milk has 200 percent of the fat of 1 percent milk.
5. Two percent milk has 100 percent more fat than 1 percent milk.
6. One percent milk has 1 percent less fat than 2 percent milk.

Actually, each statement is just a different way of saying the same thing. Some of the statements, however, sound more or less shocking than others. An advocate of 1 percent milk might choose No. 4 because it makes its point dramatically. A journalist should know enough math to see the statement for what it is.

Here's another story problem to mull: A book sold twice as many copies in the United States as in Britain, but the United States has four times as many people. Which of these statements is correct?

1. The book sold twice as well in the United States.
2. The book sold half as well in the United States.

Again, each statement is correct. The choice between the two depends on what is meant by *as well*.

Although some journalists might have chosen their career partly to avoid one that entailed math, they can't escape dealing with percentages. Percentages come up in every story involving government budgets, charity fund raising and so on. You need to know how to calculate them.

The formula for calculating percentages is $a/b = p/100$, where a is the number you want to find to be what percentage p of the number b. To put that in plainer English, divide a by b, then drop the decimal. For example, 4 is what percentage of 5? Divide 4 by 5. The answer is .80. Drop the decimal, and you're left with 80 percent.

Correctness

Journalism must be correct in at least three senses.

- Your writing needs to be correct in grammar, usage, spelling and style.

- Your writing needs to be appropriate for your audience and your purpose. They are your guides for what to put in and what to leave out of a story.

They also help you know when to be formal and when to be informal. The style of writing that is proper for The Chronicle of Higher Education might not be right for the New York Daily News. Even in the same newspaper or magazine, different writing styles are permissible. A feature story may make liberal use of slang, but a more formal news story may not. A commentary piece or review might also include words that convey value judgments, but those words should be edited out of a straight-news story.

- Your writing needs to get the facts right. It must be unbiased and accurate, which is what journalists mean when they speak of *objectivity*.

Most editors will tell you that accuracy is the most important characteristic of good news writing. The rules of journalistic objectivity are intended to help us achieve accuracy. They also help us cut words and comments from our work that would be inappropriate in a news account.

Objectivity

One of the most cutting epithets the public hurls at journalists is that we are "biased" or "nonobjective." Most journalists try hard to earn public trust by being objective in their coverage. But the public's perception of objectivity and what journalists mean by it are often quite different.

Most people think their own opinions about the world are correct. They think their view of the world is "the way it is." Therefore, if a journalist writes about an issue of concern to them, such as abortion, and the story doesn't, for example, call the pro-choice people "baby killers," the pro-life people may see the story as biased and therefore incorrect. Likewise, if the story doesn't call the pro-life people "anti-women's rights," the pro-choice advocates may object.

Never mind that the journalist took pains not to present his or her own opinion but rather tried to present both sides fairly, without biased language. Black Panther leader Eldridge Cleaver said in the 1960s that if you're not for us, you're against us, and many Americans of far more conservative political beliefs would agree today, as President Bush has implied regarding the war on terrorism.

In other words, what people often mean when they say news is biased is that it doesn't conform to their own view of the world; it doesn't confirm their prejudices. By contrast, journalists typically see their role as that of a judge in a jury trial. The journalist, like the judge, is a sort of gatekeeper for the jury, or the public. The journalist, like the judge, must be objective—by which journalists mean impartial, disinterested and unprejudiced.

Journalists usually don't see their role as that of an attorney for the prosecution or the defense, presenting information to prove one side of a case rather than to get at the truth. Journalists would call playing such a role being "subjective," an activity appropriate for public relations, advertising and editorial columns but not for a presentation of the news.

Rules of Objective Writing

Here are some typical rules journalists follow in their pursuit of objectivity.

○ **Stick to the facts.**

Stick to what you know to be true. Distinguish between fact and opinion. Attribute controversial statements. Don't guess or predict. Don't bend the facts consciously or unconsciously to make a better story.

Be careful to avoid making unwarranted assumptions or writing statements you can't prove. Of course, journalists try to be accurate. But to see how easy it is to make mistakes unintentionally, read the following reporter's notes:

> Ricardo Sanchez, 10, is dead. The police have brought in three people for questioning. All three of them are known to have been near the scene of the killing. All three have police records. We've been told by a police representative that one of them, Leroi "Fingers" Washington, has now been positively cleared of guilt in this incident.

If we assume the notes are accurate and true, which of the following statements are objectively true? Consider a statement true if, from the notes, we know it to be true, false if we know it to be false and questionable if we cannot be sure based on the given information.

1. Leroi "Fingers" Washington was near the scene of the incident.
2. We don't really know anyone is dead.
3. Leroi "Fingers" Washington is probably African-American.
4. The other two suspects were also near the scene.
5. Three men have been arrested.
6. Only Leroi "Fingers" Washington has been cleared by the police.
7. This is an especially heinous murder because the victim was a juvenile.

Here are the answers:

1. *True*. He was one of three near the scene who were brought in for questioning.
2. *False*. The reporter's notes state that Ricardo Sanchez is dead.
3. *Questionable*. Someone may surmise from the name that he is African-American, but we don't know for sure from this information alone.
4. *Questionable*. The other two people brought in for questioning were near the scene, but the statement assumes they are suspects. One or more of them may merely have been witnesses.
5. *Questionable*. First, we don't know they were all men. Second, it depends on what is meant by "arrested." We know for sure of no one who has been arrested in the sense that most people would understand the term. Some attorneys say, however, that true to the root meaning of the word *arrest*—"to stop"—anytime the police stop you against your will, it is an arrest even if you are not taken in and booked.
6. *Questionable*. We know for sure that one of them, Washington, has been cleared. That does not necessarily mean that no one else has been cleared.
7. *Questionable*. We know the person dead is a juvenile, but we don't know this is a murder. Although many would associate the word *killing* with an intent to do violence, perhaps it was meant in the sense that Sanchez was "killed," maybe in an accident. Or Sanchez may have been armed, and someone may have acted in self-defense. Or it may have been manslaughter rather than murder. In fact, we don't know it was legally "murder" unless there is a trial and someone is convicted of the charge of murder. And to label this "especially heinous," even if it turns out to be murder, is a value judgment.

○ **Be neutral. In a news story that's supposed to be objective, keep your own opinions out of it.**

Either keep your opinions to yourself or save them for more personal pieces, such as commentaries and reviews.

Don't confuse an opinion you believe to be true with journalistic objectivity. Being neutral doesn't permit you to include a statement you believe to be true unless it's also an objective fact not involving a matter of belief or opinion. For example, consider the following statements:

George W. Bush is one of our most honest presidents.

The United States is the best nation on earth.

"The Spy Who Shagged Me" is a great movie.

You may believe some or all of these statements to be true. But they are not objective statements in the eyes of a journalist because they involve value judgments, opinions or beliefs. Each of them, however, could be quoted if someone other than a journalist were making the statement.

Don't use words that express a judgment or evaluation, such as calling a person *attractive* or a proposal *idiotic,* even when you think most people would agree with them. Some editors might be more permissive about allowing value judgments to go unattributed if they express generally agreed-upon, noncontroversial matters:

> Mozart was a greater composer than Salieri.

> Adolf Hitler was a madman.

Choose your words carefully, making sure they convey no *unintentional* bias. Journalists may unwittingly take sides in a controversy if they are not careful about their choice of words. For example:

- To call an official a *bureaucrat* implies the negative connotation of someone who takes joy in binding helpless victims with red tape.

- To say a candidate *refuted* an opponent's charges does not simply mean the candidate *answered* them but rather that the candidate *successfully answered* them.

- To say that the City Council *still* hasn't taken action on a proposal implies disapproval for taking so long.

- To say national health care would cost *only* a certain amount implies that the cost is insignificant—a value judgment.

- To write *She disagrees with the fact that she is wrong* is to take the side of those who say she is wrong and to contradict her in the same sentence as her denial.

- To use hedging phrases such as *appears to be guilty* or *may be guilty* or *in my opinion, he's guilty* conveys value judgments akin to saying *he's guilty.* Such phrases are not fully neutral.

- To write *Barbara Alcott—a pretty, blond legal secretary—said she has never been the victim of sexual discrimination* is to subject Alcott to sexual discrimination in print.

Sadly, newspapers often make statements such as the last one about women. If you would not say the same of a man, it is probably sexist. Besides, such descriptions express value judgments about beauty and have no place in objective news. It would be more neutral to write *Legal secretary Barbara Alcott said she has never been the victim of sexual discrimination.* (See Chapter 13.)

In addition to avoiding value judgments and advice, journalists should be careful with the use of adjectives and adverbs in hard-news reporting. Modifiers are one of the most common ways bias creeps into a news story. They also tend to clutter sentences, making them longer than they need to be. Here are some modifiers to look out for:

absolutely	extensive	reportedly
actually	fittingly	respected
alleged, allegedly	frankly	sadly
amazing	good	seriously
archconservative	grim	shocking
archliberal	honestly	special
astounding	important	spectacular
awful	inevitable	still
bad	insurmountable	stunning
best	interesting	successfully
bizarre	ironically	suspected
candid	least	tragic
certainly	luckily	troubling
completely	major	ultraconservative
complex	most	ultraliberal
controversial	mysterious	undoubtedly
crucial	obviously	unique
definitely	perfectly	unprecedented
disturbing	poignant	unquestionably
dramatic	positively	unusual
effectively	predictably	very
evil	radical (left, right)	widespread
exciting	really	worst

○ **Be fair. Present all sides as best you can, giving people a chance to respond to charges or criticism.**

If people refuse to comment when given the chance, say so in the story so readers will know you tried to be fair.

Choose your words carefully so they are fair to the people involved. Whenever you write a crime story, for example, write it in a way that does not assume the guilt of the suspect. After all, the charges may be dropped, or he or she may be found not guilty at a trial.

For example, to write *Police said Dave Jones climbed through the window and sexually assaulted the woman* is to convict the man in print before he has stood trial. Instead, write *Police said a man climbed through the window and sexually assaulted the woman. Dave Jones was arrested Monday (on a charge of rape, and charged with rape* or *in connection with the rape).*

Likewise, don't call the suspect an *alleged rapist* or say he *allegedly raped* the woman. Although many journalists don't know it, lawyers have warned for years that the words *alleged* and *allegedly* offer little legal protection from later libel action if the person isn't convicted. Who's doing the alleging? *You* are when you print the statement.

Stories with possible legal consequences are not the only ones that demand fairness to all sides. For example, although prison officials are not likely to sue you, to write *The food is so bad at the prison that inmates have begun a hunger strike* is to agree inadvertently with the inmates. A more neutral statement would be *Inmates say the food is so bad that they have begun a hunger strike.*

- **Be impersonal in a hard-news story. Don't try to sound creative or original or to write in your own "voice" unless you're taking a feature or more opinionated approach to a story.**

We're not trying to stifle your creativity. It's just that such individuality is as out of place in most straight-news stories as in the directions for assembling a bicycle. Feature stories, reviews and commentaries are a different matter.

Web Resources

WRITING HELP

Several World Wide Web sites provide answers to questions about writing. Here are two of the better ones.

- **The Elements of Style**
  www.bartleby.com/141

- **Online Writing Lab**
  owl.english.purdue.edu

JOURNALISTIC STYLE

CHAPTER 12

Conciseness

Good writing should be precise. That's the single most agreed-upon rule of good writing, whether in journalism, technical writing, business writing or creative writing. In "The Elements of Style," William Strunk Jr. and E.B. White write, "A sentence should contain no unnecessary words, a paragraph no unnecessary sentences, for the same reason that a drawing should have no unnecessary lines and a machine no unnecessary parts."

Saving words makes writing clearer and more effective, saves space and saves the reader's time. As the architect Mies van der Rohe said, "Less is more."

It's the mark of the inexperienced writer to hold every word sacred, as jealously guarded against red-penciling as a drop of holy water against spilling. But Scottish novelist Robert Louis Stevenson knew that conciseness is one of the differences between mere scribbling and art. "There is but one art," he wrote: "to omit." He added, "A man who knew how to omit would make an Iliad of a daily paper."

Of course, anyone can discard words haphazardly, especially in someone else's writing. What's harder is knowing which words are the dead limbs that need pruning. If you prune too much or the wrong parts, you may kill a plant. Sometimes, beginning writers and editors don't understand this point and try to snip away at everything, whether it needs it or not.

But writers and editors, like gardeners, need to know what they're doing. So let's be more precise than saying brevity is the sole goal. The real virtue is not so much brevity as conciseness, which is a combination of brevity and completeness. Don't use more words than you need to get your point across. But don't use fewer words than you need, either.

A story about President Calvin Coolidge, who was known as "Silent Cal," illustrates this point. One Sunday, his wife asked him what the preacher had spoken about at church. He replied, "Sin." When his wife then asked, "Well, what about it?" he answered, "He was against it." That's brevity but not conciseness. Coolidge's report is frustratingly incomplete. So, don't just be brief. Be complete—but as briefly as possible.

Tightening

Writing tightly means choosing the words that are the fewest, shortest, simplest, most exact and, if possible, freshest to express your thoughts.

Often, beginning writers think they need to use big words and round-about phrasing to try to impress their audience. Nothing could be further from the truth. The German poet Johann Wolfgang von Goethe once said a common mistake of young writers is that they try to muddy the waters to make them look deep. But good writing isn't writing that confuses people.

Think about the power of short, common words: In Lincoln's 701-word second inaugural address, 505 of the words have one syllable and 122 have two syllables. Think, too, about the power of simple phrasing: The Lord's Prayer contains 56 words, the 23rd Psalm 118 words, the Gettysburg Address 226 words and the Ten Commandments 297 words. And think about this contrast: A U.S. Department of Agriculture directive on pricing cabbage contained 15,629 words.

Here are some specific suggestions on how to tighten your writing.

Use Fewer Words

Eliminate redundant or irrelevant words, phrases, clauses, sentences, paragraphs, sections or chapters. Get rid of details, examples, quotations, facts or ideas that don't add anything, and use single words rather than phrases whenever possible.

PHRASE TO AVOID	ALTERNATIVE
a lot	many, much
all of a sudden	suddenly
as a consequence of	because
give consideration to	consider
have a need for	need
put emphasis on	stress

○ **Get rid of the helping-verb forms of *to be* whenever possible.**

Often, they just detract from a more active verb. For example, change *he is hopeful that* to *he hopes;* change *she will be a participant in* to *she will participate in;* change *it is my intention* to *I intend;* change *is productive of* to *produces.* Forms of the verb *to be* often occur in sentences starting with *there, here* or *it.* Instead of *It was Thoreau who said,* write *Thoreau said.*

○ **Use active voice instead of passive. Passive voice is wordier, less direct and less forceful.**

Write *Police shot a 13-year-old boy* not *A 13-year-old boy was shot by police.* An exception is when the person being acted upon is more important than the person doing the acting: *President Kennedy was shot today by an unknown gunman.*

○ **Avoid vague modifiers, such as** *a lot, kind of, perhaps, quite, really, somewhat, sort of* **and** *very.*

These words are sometimes called "weasel words" because they are favorites of people trying to weasel their way out of taking a clear stand. If you are trying to be honest, the use of such words appears at worst deceitful, at best wishy-washy.

○ **Avoid doubled prepositions** (*off of* for *off*) **or prepositions that aren't needed** (the *up* in *heading up*).

In the sentence *She headed up the largest company in town,* the *up* isn't necessary. (But in the following sentence, it is: *They headed up the mountain trail.*) Other examples of verbs that don't need *up* include *count, divide, drink, eat, fold, free, gather, heat, hoist, hurry, polish, raise, rest, rise* and *settle.*

○ **Avoid whenever possible phrases beginning with** *in* **or** *the* **and ending with** *of: (in) the amount of, (in) the area of, (in) the case of, the concept of, the factor of, (in) the field of, the idea of, (in) the process of, in terms of.*

○ **Cut the conjunction** *that* **if it's unnecessary.**

If getting rid of *that* doesn't change the meaning of the sentence, then get rid of it: *He said he would,* not *He said that he would.*
But *that* is necessary when:

1. A time element, such as a day, comes between the verb and the dependent clause: *He said Tuesday that he would go.*
2. It follows one of these verbs: *advocate, assert, contend, declare, estimate, make clear, point out, propose, state.*
3. It comes before a dependent clause beginning with one of the following conjunctions: *after, although, because, before, in addition to, until, while.*

○ **Cut** *which are, which is, who are* **and** *who is* **if not needed.**

Rewrite *the movie, which is a comedy* as *the movie, a comedy.* Rewrite *the students who are attending* as *the students attending.*

○ **Don't tell us what we already know.**

In phrases such as *12 noon, personal friend, sad mourners, blue in color, true fact, armed gunman* and *completely destroyed,* one word implies the other, which is therefore unnecessary. Words such as *famed, famous, renowned* and *well-known* likewise are unnecessary if the person or thing described is indeed famed, famous, renowned or well-known.

○ Cut the adjectives *both* and *different* if they add nothing.

What's the difference between *both John and Bill* and *John and Bill*? Between *three different views* and *three views*? But leave *both* in if you think it's needed for emphasis: *He said he liked <u>both</u> George W. Bush and Richard Cheney.*

○ Cut the *or not* after the conjunction *whether.*

Whether includes both possibilities.

Use Simpler Words

○ Use shorter Anglo-Saxon-derived words rather than longer Latin-derived ones whenever possible.

Say, don't *state. Drink,* don't *imbibe.*

○ Avoid vague nouns.

Substitute something more specific for the following words whenever you can: *area, aspect, concept, condition, consideration, factor, indication, infrastructure, parameter, phase, situation, thing.*

○ Avoid *ize* verbs.

They're often no more than pretentious jargon. For example, change *finalize* to *end* or *complete; institutionalize* to *put in an institution* or *make part of the institution; personalize* to *make more personal; prioritize* to *rank;* and *utilize* to *use.* As magazine consultant Don Ranly humorously says, "If we don't quit utilizing the English language, we're going to finalize it."

○ Avoid verbs that people try to turn into nouns: *activation, fabrication, maximization, optimization, rationalization, utilization.*

○ Use verbs rather than noun phrases when you have a choice.

Instead of writing *before the committee investigation,* write *before the committee investigated.*

○ Unless your editor says otherwise, go ahead and use contractions such as *can't* for *cannot* and *it's* for *it is* or *it has.*

The Associated Press permits them, provided they're not overused, and they're generally used for all but the most formal writing. Besides, they sound more conversational, and they save space.

Use Exact Words

○ Use a specific noun or verb without a modifier rather than a general noun or verb with a modifier.

WEAK   a small city in Utah

BETTER   Cedar City, Utah

○ **Use specific verbs rather than vague ones.**

For example, change *go* or *move* to *walk, run, jump, skip, hop* or *gallop.*

○ **Beware of verbs beginning with *re*.**

Something is not *reaffirmed, redoubled* or *reshuffled* unless it already has been *affirmed, doubled* or *shuffled.*

○ **In hard-news stories, avoid modifiers that could suggest bias.**

Pick words that more exactly convey the denotation (dictionary meaning) without the connotation (personal viewpoint). See Page 230 on objectivity, as well as the list of biased words not to be used in broadcast news stories on Page 233.

○ **Avoid *euphemisms*, words that say something in an indirect manner rather than confronting the truth.**

Instead of writing *The maintenance engineer met his Maker,* just say *The janitor died.* Euphemisms, by the way, are almost by definition clichés, which brings us to a fourth rule.

Be Fresh, Not Stale

○ **Avoid clichés.**

Clichés are phrases that have been used so often they've lost their freshness and power, such as *children of all ages* and *crystal clear.* Some of them are no longer even understood in their literal sense by most people who use them: *by hook or by crook* or *dead as a doornail.* Still, clichés can sometimes be succinct, and that's why they catch on. In fact, clichés are such a part of everyday conversation that sometimes it's difficult to imagine how you could express certain thoughts without them. How about this solution? Whenever you're about to write an expression you've heard before, take the opportunity to try to express your point in a fresher way. *Go for it!* No. *Just do it?* No. *Try it; you'll like it?* No, way too stale. We didn't say creativity was easy, but it can be worth the effort.

○ **Avoid stale story approaches.**

When journalists approach stories by trying to fit them into a pattern they've seen used many times before, the story not only lacks freshness but also probably misrepresents the truth. Think of these stories as built around clichés of vision. One of the more common stale story approaches is the one that starts, *Christmas came early for … .*

ESL Tip

It's especially difficult for speakers of English as a second language to tell the difference between a cliché — which should be avoided — and an idiom, which is the preferred, conversational way of saying something. For example, when someone tells you, "Have a nice day," is that a cliché or an idiom? The difference between clichés and idioms seems to be this: Clichés are expressions people are tired of, whereas idioms are expressions people still find fresh. But which people? There's obviously subjectivity involved, although you could probably find a consensus among professionals that the expressions we've labeled as clichés in the list beginning on this page have grown tiresome.

What to Tighten, A to Z

Here's a list of pompous words and wordy phrases editors typically cut or rewrite.

When a word or phrase can easily be left out without changing the meaning of a sentence, we have indicated to cut.

When a word or phrase should be rewritten in a simpler, more straightforward way, we have indicated one or more possible changes.

When a phrase is a cliché, we have labeled it as such, leaving a fresher approach to your own sense of creativity.

We have put parentheses around some words in the list. This indicates different phrases built on the same wording. For example, *absolute (guarantee, perfection)* indicates both the phrases *absolute guarantee* and *absolute perfection.*

The advice in this list should work for most writing you'll edit, but use your own judgment. For example, you shouldn't use any of this advice to rewrite quotations unless you remove the quotation marks to indicate a paraphrase. Also, the suggestions may not work in a particular sentence where the sense of the word or phrase is something other than what we assumed here.

Finally, some of the words we suggest you cut, such as *case* and *character,* are obviously useful in some contexts, but they can usually be cut and the sentence rewritten more directly without them. So, use this only as a guide; the suggestions should work more often than not, but you need to test the advice in each sentence.

A

a distance of *cut*
a great deal of much, many
a lot many, much
a period of *cut*

abandon leave
abbreviate shorten
absolute (guarantee, perfection) guarantee, perfection
absolutely (certain, complete, essential, sure) certain, complete,
     essential, sure
accelerate speed
accidentally stumbled stumbled
accompany go with
accomplish do
accord grant
achieve do
acid test *cliché*
acquire get
acres of land land
acted as (chairman, chairwoman) presided
activation start
activity *cut*
actual (experience, fact) experience, fact
acute crisis crisis
add insult to injury *cliché*
adequate enough enough
advance (planning, reservations) planning, reservations
advent arrival
adverse weather conditions bad weather
affluent rich, wealthy
aforementioned this, that, these, those
after all is said and done *cliché*
aggregate total
agree to disagree *cliché*
aired their differences *cliché*
albeit but
all in a day's work *cliché*
all of all
all of a sudden suddenly
all things considered *cliché*
all things to all people *cliché*
all throughout throughout
all too soon *cliché*
all walks of life *cliché*
all work and no play *cliché*
all-time record record
almighty dollar *cliché*
amidst amid
amorphous formless
and/or *rewrite the sentence*
announce the names of announce, identify

another additional another
anticipate in advance anticipate
any and all any, all
appeared on the scene appeared
appears seems
apple of one's eye *cliché*
appoint to the post of appoint
appreciate in value appreciate
apprehend arrest
approximately about
ardent admirers *cliché*
area *cut*
area of *cut*
arguably *cut*
arise get up
armed gunman gunman
armed to the teeth *cliché*
arrive at a decision decide
as a consequence of because
as a matter of fact *cut*
as a result of because
as already stated *cut*
as far as the eye could see *cliché*
as luck would have it *cliché*
as of this date *cut*
as per as
ascertain find out
aspect *cut*
assemble together assemble
assess a fine fine
assist help, aid
assuming that if
at a loss for words *cliché*
at a tender age *cliché*
at an earlier date previously
at first blush *cliché*
at long last *cliché*
at present now
at the conclusion of after
at the present time now
at the time when when
at this point in time now
at which time when
attach together attach
attempt try
autopsy to determine the cause of death autopsy
awkward predicament predicament

B

back in the saddle *cliché*
badly decomposed body body (if long dead)
ball is in (her, his, their) court *cliché*
ballpark guess *cliché*
(bare, basic) essentials essentials
basic fundamentals fundamentals
be acquainted with know
be associated with work with
be aware of know
be cognizant of know, notice
beat a dead horse *cliché*
beat a hasty retreat *cliché*
bed of roses *cliché*
been there, done that *cliché*
beginning of the end *cliché*
best left unsaid *cliché*
better late than never *cliché*
between a rock and a hard place *cliché*
beverage drink
bewildering array *cliché*
big in size big
biggest ever biggest
biography of (her, his) life (her, his) biography
bite the bullet *cliché*
bitter (end, dispute) *cliché*
blame it on blame
blanket of snow *cliché*
blazing inferno *cliché;* inferno, blaze
blessing in disguise *cliché*
blissfully ignorant *cliché*
blood-red *cliché*
bloodcurdling (scream, sight) *cliché*
bloody riot *cliché*
boggles the mind *cliché*
bolt from the blue *cliché*
bombshell [announcement] *cliché*
bonds of matrimony *cliché*
bone of contention *cliché*
bored to tears *cliché*
both *cut except for emphasis*
both alike alike
bouquet of flowers bouquet
breakneck speed *cliché*
breathless anticipation *cliché*
brief in duration brief

bring to a conclusion conclude, end, finish
bring (to a head, up-to-date) *cliché*
broad daylight daylight
brutal (assault, beating, murder, rape, slaying) assault, beating, murder, rape, slaying
brute force *cliché*
budding genius *cliché*
built-in safeguards *cliché*
burn the midnight oil *cliché*
burning (desire, issue, question) *cliché*
busy as a (beaver, bee) *cliché*
by hook or by crook *cliché*
by leaps and bounds *cliché*
by the name of named
by the same token likewise

C

calm before the storm *cliché*
calm down calm
came to a stop stopped
can of worms *cliché*
cancel (each other, out) cancel
can't see the forest for the trees *cliché*
case *cut*
case of *cut*
champing at the bit *cliché*
character *cut*
charmed life *cliché*
chauffeured limousine limousine
check (into, on, up on) check
checkered (career, past) *cliché*
cherished belief *cliché*
chief protagonist protagonist
children of all ages *cliché*
chip off the old block *cliché*
circle around circle
city of *cut*
clean slate *cliché*
clear as a bell *cliché*
close down close
close (proximity, scrutiny) near, scrutiny
closed-door (hearing, meeting) *cliché*
close-up look *cliché*
coequal equal
cognizant aware

cold (as ice, comfort) *cliché*
collaborate together collaborate
collect together collect
colorful (display, scene) *cliché*
combine together combine
come full circle *cliché*
come to a head *cliché*
come to an end end
coming future future
commence begin, start
commented to the effect that said
common accord accord
communication letter, memo
commute back and forth between commute between
competency competence, ability
competent able
complete fill out, finish
complete (chaos, monopoly, overhaul) chaos, monopoly, overhaul
completely (demolished, destroyed, done, eliminated, empty, finished, full, naked, surrounded, true, untrue) demolished, destroyed, done, eliminated, empty, finished, full, naked, surrounded, true, untrue
comply with follow, obey
component part
concept *cut;* idea
concept of *cut*
conceptualize think of
concerning about
concerted effort *cliché*
concrete proposals proposals
condition *cut*
conduct a poll poll
conjecture guess
connect the dots *cliché*
consensus of opinion consensus
consequent result result
consideration problem
considered opinion *cliché*
conspicuous by (his, her, its, their) absence *cliché*
constructive helpful
consult ask
consume eat
consummate finish
contingent upon depends on
continue on continue
continue to remain *cliché*
contribute give

controversial (issue, person) *cliché*
contusion bruise
cool as a cucumber *cliché*
cooperate together cooperate
costs the sum of costs
count up count
country mile *cliché*
coveted (award, trophy) *cliché*
crack of dawn *cliché*
cradled in luxury *cliché*
crazy as a loon *cliché*
cross to bear *cliché*
crying (need, shame) *cliché*
crystal clear *cliché*
current (temperature, trend) temperature, trend
currently now
customary usual
cutting edge *cliché*

(**D**)

dangerous weapon weapon
daring daylight robbery *cliché*
dark horse *cliché*
dashed the hopes *cliché*
dastardly deed *cliché*
date with destiny *cliché*
days are numbered *cliché*
dead as a (doornail, skunk) *cliché*
dead body body
deadly earnest *cliché*
deadly poison poison
debate about debate
deceased dead
decide (about, on) decide, select
deciding factor *cliché*
deem think, believe, judge
deficit shortage
definite decision decision
demonstrate show
dentifrice toothpaste
depart leave
depreciate in value depreciate
depths of despair *cliché*
descend down descend
described as called

desirable benefits benefits
desire wish, want
despite the fact that despite
determine find out
devoured by flames *cliché;* burned
devouring flames *cliché*
dialogue talk, talks, negotiations, discussion
diamond in the rough *cliché*
died of an apparent heart attack apparently died of a heart attack
died suddenly died
different *cut*
dig in (her, his, their) heels *cliché*
disclose show
discontinue stop, quit
divide up divide
do your own thing *cliché*
dog-tired *cliché*
donate give
dotted the landscape *cliché*
double-check twice double-check
downright lie lie
down-to-earth *cliché*
drastic action *cliché*
draw a blank *cliché*
draws to a close ends
dried up dried
drink (down, up) drink
dropped down dropped
drown your sorrows *cliché*
drowned to death drowned
drunk as a skunk *cliché*
ducks in a row *cliché*
due to the fact that because
duly noted noted
duplicate copy
during the time that while
dwell live

(**E**)

each and every every
earlier on earlier
early (beginnings, pioneer) beginnings, pioneer
easier said than done *cliché*
Easter Sunday Easter
eat, drink and be merry *cliché*

eat up eat
edifice building
educationist, educator teacher
effectuate cause
egg on (his, her, their) face(s) *cliché*
elect choose, pick
electrocuted to death electrocuted
eliminate altogether eliminate, cut
eloquent silence *cliché*
eminently successful *cliché*
emotional roller coaster *cliché*
employment job
empty out empty
enable to let, allow to
enclosed (herein, herewith, within) here's, enclosed
encounter meet
end (product, result) product, result
endeavor try
engage in conversation *cliché*
enhance add to, improve
ensuing following
enter a bid of bid
enter (in, into) enter
entirely (complete, new, original, spontaneous) complete, new, original,
    spontaneous
entwined together entwined
epic struggle *cliché*
errand of mercy *cliché*
essentially *cut*
ever since since
every fiber of his being *cliché*
exact (counterpart, duplicate, facsimile, replica) counterpart, duplicate,
    facsimile, replica
exactly identical identical
exceeding the speed limit speeding
exchanged wedding vows married
execute do, sign
exercise in futility *cliché*
exhibit show
expedite speed
experience (n.) *cut*
experience (v.) *cut* (Instead of *He said he was experiencing pain,* try *He
    said he was in pain.*)
experienced veteran veteran
extensively greatly

extinguish put out
eyeball to eyeball *cliché*
eyesight sight
eyewitness witness

(**F**)

fabled *cliché*
fabrication lie, making, manufacture, product, production
face up to face
facilitate ease, help
facilities buildings, space
factor *cut*
factor of *cut*
facts and figures *cliché*
faded dream *cliché*
failed to did not
fairly *cut*
false pretense pretense
falsely fabricated fabricated, made up
famed *cut*
famous *cut*
far and wide *cliché*
far be it from me *cliché*
far cry *cliché*
fat chance *cliché*
fatal (killing, murder, slaying) killing, murder, slaying
fate worse than death *cliché*
favored to win favored
feasible possible
fell down fell
fell on (bad, hard) times *cliché*
fell on deaf ears *cliché*
fell through the cracks *cliché*
festive occasion *cliché*
few and far between *cliché*
few in number few
field *cut*
field of *cut*
fiery rebuttal *cliché*
file a lawsuit against sue
filled to capacity filled
final analysis *cliché*
final (completion, conclusion, ending, outcome, result) completion,
    conclusion, ending, outcome, result

final word *cliché*
finalize finish, complete, end
finish up finish
finishing touch *cliché*
fire swept through *cliché*
first (annual, began, commenced, ever, initiated, priority, started) annual, began, commenced, first, initiated, priority, started
firstly first
flat as a board *cliché*
flatly rejected rejected
fly in the ointment *cliché*
fold up fold
follow after follow
follow in the footsteps of *cliché*
food for thought *cliché*
fools rush in *cliché*
foot the bill *cliché*
for all intents and purposes *cliché*
for openers *cliché*
for the purpose of to
for the reason that because
foregone conclusion *cliché*
foreseeable future future
forthwith *cut*
forward send
foul play *cliché*
frame of reference *cut*
freak accident *cliché*
free and open to the public free
free (gift, of charge, pass) gift, free, pass
free up free
freewill offering offering
frequently often
fresh (beginning, start) beginning, start
frisky as a (kitten, pup) *cliché*
from time immemorial *cliché*
front headlight headlight
(frown, smile) on (his, her) face frown, smile
full and complete complete
fully clothed clothed
function act, work
funeral services services (in obituary; otherwise, *funeral*)
furnish send, provide
furrowed brow *cliché*
fused together fused
future (plans, prospects) plans, prospects

G

gainfully employed employed, working
gala (event, occasion) *cliché*
game plan *cliché*
gather (together, up) gather
general (public, rule) public, rule
generally agreed agreed
generous to a fault *cliché*
get this show on the road *cliché*
getting into full swing *cliché*
give (a green light, consideration, encouragement, instruction, rise) to
    approve, consider, encourage, instruct, cause
give (a, the) nod approve
given the green light *cliché*
glass ceiling *cliché*
go walk, run, jump, skip, hop, gallop
go for broke *cliché*
go for it *cliché*
goals and objectives goals
goes without saying *cliché*
going nowhere fast *cliché*
golf-ball-size hail *cliché*
good (as gold, speed) *cliché*
gory details *cliché*
gradually (waning, wean) waning, wean
grand total total
grateful thanks thanks
grave (concern, crisis) *cliché*
great lengths *cliché*
great majority of majority of
great minds run in the same (channel, direction, gutter) *cliché*
great open spaces *cliché*
greatly *cut*
green light (n., v.) *cliché;* give the go-ahead, approve, OK
green with envy *cliché*
ground rules rules
ground to a halt *cliché*

H

had ought ought
hail of bullets *cliché*
hale and hearty *cliché*
half a hundred 50
hammer out *cliché*

hand over fist *cliché*
handsome appearance handsome
hang up hang
hanging in there *cliché*
happy as a lark *cliché*
happy camper *cliché*
hard as a rock *cliché*
hardy souls *cliché*
has got to has to, must
has the (ability, capability, skill, talent) to can
hastily summoned *cliché*
have a (need, preference) for need, prefer
have an (effect, impact) on affect
have got have
have got to have to, must
have the belief that believe
head over heels *cliché*
head up head
headache [problem] *cliché*
heap coals on the fire *cliché*
heart (of gold, of the matter) *cliché*
heartfelt thanks *cliché*
heart's (content, desire) *cliché*
hearty meal *cliché*
heat up heat
heated argument *cliché*
heave a sigh of relief *cliché*
heavens to Betsy *cliché*
heavy as lead *cliché*
Herculean effort *cliché*
hereby *cut*
herein *cut*
hereto *cut*
herewith *cut*
high as a kite *cliché*
high (noon, technology) noon, technology
hit the nail on the head *cliché*
hobbled by injury *cliché*
hoist up hoist
hook, line and sinker *cliché*
hope for the future *cliché*
hopes and fears *cliché*
hopping mad *cliché*
hostile environment *cliché*
hot (potato, pursuit) *cliché*
hot-water heater water heater

hour of noon noon, noon hour
hungry as (a bear, wolves) *cliché*
hunker down *cliché*
hurry up hurry

(I   )

idea of *cut*
if and when if, when
ignorance is bliss *cliché*
illuminated lighted
imbibe drink
immortal bard *cliché*
implement do, start, begin
important essentials essentials
in a very real sense *cut*
in fact *can often cut*
in (full swing, high gear, our midst) *cliché*
in lieu of instead of
in light of because of, considering
in my opinion *cut*
in no uncertain terms *cliché*
in order to to
in question *cut*
in terms of *cut*
in the (aftermath, final analysis, last analysis, nick of time, same boat,
    wake of) *cliché*
in the event that if
in the not-too-distant future soon
in the shape of *cut*
in this (day and age, time frame) *cliché*
in view of the fact that because
inaugurate begin, start
include among them include
inconvenience trouble
incumbent (governor, president, representative, senator) governor,
    president, representative, senator
incursion invasion
indeed *cut*
indicate show
indication sign
indignant upset
individual person, man or woman
inevitable sure
inextricably (linked, tied) *cliché*
infinite capacity *cliché*

inform tell
infrastructure basic institutions of society; power, education, transportation and communication systems
infringe (on, upon) infringe
initial first
initiate begin, start
innocent bystander *cliché*
input opinion, suggestion
inquire ask
institute start
institutionalize put in an institution, make part of the institution
insufficient not enough
interface connect, talk, meet
interim period between interim
interrogate question
inundate flood
invited guest guest
iron out (difficulties, disagreements, troubles) *cliché*
irons in the fire *cliché*
irregardless regardless
is going to will
is hopeful that (he, she, they) (hopes, hope)
is productive of produces
is reflective of reflects
is representative of represents
issue in question issue
it appears (seems) that *cut*
it goes without saying *cliché*
it is (her, his, their) contention (she, he, they) (contends, contend)
it is (her, his, their) intention (she, he, they) (says, say) (she, he, they) (intends, intend)
it is interesting to note *cut*
it should be noted *cut*
it stands to reason *cut*
it would appear that *cut*

J

Jewish rabbi rabbi
join in join
joint (cooperation, partnership) cooperation, partnership
just do it *cliché*

K

keeled over *cliché*
keeping (his, her, their) options open *cut*

kind of *cut*
knit together combined, figured out
know about know

L

labor of love *cliché*
laceration cut, gash
largest ever largest
lashed out *cliché*
last (analysis, but not least, word) *cliché*
last-ditch effort *cliché*
later on later
laundry list (of desired programs, for example) *cliché*
leaps and bounds *cliché*
learning experience experience, something to learn from, educational
leave no stone unturned *cliché*
leaves much to be desired *cliché*
left up in the air *cliché*
legal hairsplitting *cliché*
legend in (his, her) own (mind, time) *cliché*
legendary *cliché*
lend a helping hand *cliché*
level *cut* (Instead of *She teaches on the college level,* try *She teaches college.*)
level playing field *cliché*
light (as a feather, of day) *cliché*
like a bolt from the blue *cliché*
lingered on lingered
lion's share *cliché*
local residents residents, locals
locate find
lock horns *cliché*
lock, stock and barrel *cliché*
lonely (isolation, solitude) isolation, solitude
long (arm of the law, years) *cliché*
lose out lose
low ebb ebb
loyal (Democrat, Republican, supporter) *cliché;* Democrat, Republican, supporter
lucky few *cliché*

M

mad as a hornet *cliché*
made a motion moved
made a pretty picture *cliché*
made a (speech, statement, talk) spoke

made an escape escaped
made an inquiry regarding asked about
made contact with met, saw
made good an escape escaped
made mention of mentioned
made the acquaintance of met
made (up, out) of made of
main essentials essentials
maintenance upkeep
maintenance engineer janitor, custodian
major breakthrough breakthrough
make a killing *cliché*
make a list of list
make adjustments adjust
make an approximation estimate
make hay while the sun shines *cliché*
makes one's home lives
mantle of snow *cliché*
manufacture make
many and various *cliché*
many in number many
marked (contrast, improvement) *cliché*
married (her husband, his wife) married
mass exodus *cliché*
massive big, large
matinee (performance, show) matinee
matter of *cut*
matter of life and death *cliché*
maximization best, improvement
maximize increase as much as possible
maximum possible maximum
meaningful big, important
meaningful dialogue *cliché*
meet head-on *cliché*
meets the eye *cliché*
merchandise goods
merchandize sell
merge together merge
mesh together mesh
met (his, her) Maker died
method in (his, her, their) madness *cliché*
might possibly might
minimize lessen as much as possible
miraculous escape *cliché*
mix together mix
mixed blessing(s) *cliché*
modicum of some

moment of truth *cliché*
momentous (decision, occasion) *cliché*
monkey (on, off) (his, her, their) back(s) *cliché*
more preferable preferable
more than meets the eye *cliché*
most all most
most unique unique
motley crew *cliché*
mourn the loss *cliché*
move walk, run, jump, skip, hop, gallop
mutual cooperation cooperation
mutually beneficial *cliché*

N

name of the game *cliché*
narrow down narrow, reduce
narrow escape *cliché*
nature cut (Instead of *He has a serious nature,* try *He is serious.*)
neat as a pin *cliché*
necessary (requirement, requisite) requirement, necessity
necessitates calls for
need my space *cliché*
needless to say *cut*
needs no introduction *cliché*
never a dull moment *cliché*
never at any time never
new (addition, baby, beginning, bride, construction, creation, initiative, innovation, record, recruit) addition, baby, beginning, bride, construction, creation, initiative, innovation, record, recruit
newly created new
nick of time *cliché*
night of terror *cliché*
nipped in the bud *cliché*
no easy answer *cliché*
no place like home *cliché*
no sooner said than done *cliché*
none the worse (for the experience, for wear) *cliché*
not to be outdone *cliché*
numerous many

O

objective goal
obtain get
of course *can often cut*
off of off

official (capacity, protest) *cliché*
oftentimes often
old (adage, cliché, habit, legend, maxim, proverb, tradition, veteran)
    adage, cliché, habit, legend, maxim, proverb, tradition, veteran
on a few occasions occasionally
on a roll *cliché*
on account of because
on any given day on any day
on more than one occasion *cliché*
on the face of it *cliché*
on the grounds that since, because, as
on the occasion of when
one and the same identical
one fell swoop *cliché*
one of life's little ironies *cliché*
one of the last remaining one of the last
ongoing *cut*
only time will tell *cliché*
open secret *cliché*
operative (adj.) *cut*
opt for *cliché;* choose
opt out decline
optimistic hopeful
optimization best, improvement
optimum best
order out of chaos *cliché*
orient adjust
orientate adjust
original source source
output production
over a period of years for years
over and above *cliché*
overview review, survey
overwhelming (majority, odds) *cliché*
own home home
own worst enemy *cliché*

P

paid the penalty *cliché*
painted a grim picture *cliché*
(pair of, two) twins twins
pale as a ghost *cliché*
Pandora's box *cliché*
parameters limits, boundaries, variables
paramount issue *cliché*

part and parcel *cliché*
participate take part
participate in the decision-making process have a say
party person
passed (away, on) died
passing phase phase
past (experience, history) experience, history
patience of Job *cliché*
pay (off, out) pay
paying the piper *cliché*
penetrate into penetrate
per a, according to
perceive see
perfectly clear clear
perform a task do
perhaps *can often cut*
permanent importance *cliché*
personal (experience, friend) experience, friend
personalize make more personal
personally (involved, reviewed) involved, reviewed
personnel staff, workers
peruse read, examine
phase *cut*
physical size size
physician doctor
picture of health *cliché*
pie in the sky *cliché*
pitched battle *cliché*
pizza pie pizza
place put
place in the sun *cliché*
plan (ahead, for the future, in advance) plan
play hardball *cliché*
play it by ear *cliché*
play the race card *cliché*
pleased as punch *cliché*
pocketbook purse
point with pride *cliché*
polemics arguments
polish up polish
ponder consider
populace people, population
position job
possess own, have
postpone until later postpone
powder keg (used as a metaphor) *cliché*

powers that be *cliché*
preceded in death died earlier
present a report report
present incumbent incumbent
presently soon
pretty as a picture *cliché*
primary first, main
prior to before
prioritize rank
problem *cut*
proceed go, move ahead
process *cut*
process of *cut*
prohibit forbid
promoted to the rank of promoted to
proposition *cut*
protrude out protrude
provide give
provided if
puppy *cliché in reference to things other than dogs and their relatives*
purchase buy
pure as the driven snow *cliché*
purloin steal
pursuant to following, in accordance with
pursue chase
pushing the envelope *cliché*
put a lid on it *cliché*
put emphasis on stress
put into effect start

Q

qualified expert expert
quality time *cliché*
question of *cut*
quick as a wink *cliché*
quiet as a mouse *cliché*
quite *cut*

R

radical transformation transformation
rain (couldn't, didn't) dampen the (spirits, enthusiasm) *cliché*
raise up raise
rapprochement reconciliation
rarely ever rarely

rat race *cliché*
rationalization excuse, reason, explanation
raze to the ground raze
reading material books, pamphlets, etc.
really *cut*
really unique unique
rear taillight taillight
reason is because because
reason why reason, why
(recall, recede, refer, remand, retreat, revert) back recall, recede, refer,
    remand, retreat, revert
receive get
(recur, repeat, resume, restate) again recur, repeat, resume, restate
red-hot *cliché*
red-letter day *cliché*
reduce down reduce
refer back to refer to
referred to as called
register approval approve
register (complaint, objection) complain, object
register stamp of approval to approve
regret are sorry
regular (monthly, weekly) meeting (monthly, weekly) meeting
reign of terror *cliché*
reigns supreme *cliché*
reins of government *cliché*
reinvent the wheel *cliché*
reliable sources sources
relocate move
remainder rest
remains to be seen *cliché*
remark say
remedy the situation *cliché*
remunerate pay
renowned *cut*
repeated again repeated
requires asks for, calls for, needs
reside live
residence house, home
resigned her position as resigned as
resource center library
respond answer
rest up rest
resultant effect effect
results achieved results
retain keep

reveal show
reverted back reverted
revise downward lower
right stuff *cliché*
ripe old age *cliché*
rise up rise
road to recovery *cliché*
rode roughshod over *cliché*
root cause cause
rose to (new, the) heights *cliché*
rose to the (cause, defense) of supported, defended
round of applause *cliché*
rushed to the hospital *cliché*

S

sadder but wiser *cliché*
salt of the earth *cliché*
scored a gain gained
sea of (upturned) faces *cliché*
seal off seal
seamy side of life *cliché*
seasoned (journalists, observers, reporters, etc.) *cliché*
seat of the pants *cliché*
second to none *cliché*
secondly second
seldom ever seldom
select few *cliché*
self-confessed confessed
selling like hot cakes *cliché*
senseless murder *cliché*
serious (crisis, danger) crisis, danger
seriously (consider, inclined) consider, inclined
settle up settle
sharp as a tack *cliché*
shattering effect *cliché*
sheet of rain *cliché*
shift into high gear *cliché*
shopping list (of desired programs, for example) *cliché*
short (minutes, years) minutes, years
shot in the arm *cliché*
shrouded in mystery *cliché*
sigh of relief *cliché*
silhouetted against the sky *cliché*
simple life *cliché*
single unit unit

sink down sink
situated (in, at) in, at
situation (as in classroom situation, crisis situation) *cut*
($64, $64,000) question *cliché*
skirt around skirt
sky-high *cliché*
slick as a whistle *cliché*
slow as molasses *cliché*
slowly but surely *cliché*
small in size small
smart as a whip *cliché*
smoking gun *cliché*
smooth as silk *cliché*
snatched victory from the jaws of defeat *cliché*
snug as a bug in a rug *cliché*
social amenities *cliché*
soiree party
something fishy *cliché*
sort of *cut*
speak volumes *cliché*
spearheading the campaign *cliché*
spell out explain
spirited debate *cliché*
spliced together spliced
split apart split
spotlight the need *cliché*
spouse husband, wife
sprung a surprise surprised
square peg in a round hole *cliché*
staff of life *cliché*
stand up stand
staple together staple
start up start
started off with started with
states says
states the point that says
staunch supporter supporter
steaming jungle *cliché*
stern warning *cliché*
stick to your guns *cliché*
sticks out like a sore thumb *cliché*
still (continues, persists, remains) continues, persists, remains
stinging rebuke *cliché*
stolen loot loot
storm(s) of protest *cliché*
storm-tossed *cliché*

straight as an arrow *cliché*
straight (losses, games, wins) in a row straight (losses, games, wins)
straight-and-narrow path *cliché*
strangled to death strangled
straw that broke the camel's back *cliché*
stress the point that stress that
stretches the truth *cliché*
strife-torn *cliché*
strong, silent type *cliché*
stubborn as a mule *cliché*
submit send, give
subsequent later
substantial big, great, large
substantially largely
succeed in doing accomplish, do
such is life *cliché*
sufficient enough
sum and substance *cliché*
sum total total
summer (months, season) summer
summoned to the scene summoned
sunny South *cliché*
superhuman effort *cliché*
supportive helpful
supreme sacrifice *cliché*
surrounding circumstances circumstances
sustain suffer
sweat of his brow *cliché*
sweeping changes *cliché*
sweet 16 *cliché*
swing into high gear *cliché*
sworn affidavits affidavits

T

take into consideration consider
take place happen
take the bull by the horns *cliché*
take them one at a time *cliché*
tangled together tangled
tarnished image *cliché*
team player *cliché*
telling effect *cliché*
temblor earthquake
temporary reprieve reprieve
temporary respite respite

tender mercies *cliché*
tendered her resignation resigned
terminate stop, end
textbook example *cliché*
that *can often cut*
that dog won't hunt *cliché*
the above cut; *repeat the antecedent*
the area of *cut*
the fact is *cut*
the fact that *cut*
the field of *cut*
the limelight *cliché*
the month of *cut*
the truth is *cut*
therein *cut*
thereof *cut*
thereon *cut*
there's the rub *cliché*
thick as pea soup *cliché*
thirdly third
this day and age *cliché*
thorn in the side *cliché*
thorough investigation *cliché*
threw caution to the wind *cliché*
through their paces *cliché*
throughput *cut*
throw a monkey wrench into *cliché*
throw in the towel *cliché*
throw support behind support
thrust main idea
thunderous applause *cliché*
tied together tied
tight as a drum *cliché*
time (immemorial, of one's life) *cliché*
tip of the iceberg *cliché*
to be sure *cut*
to summarize *cut*
to the tune of *cliché*
today's society *cliché*
ton of bricks *cliché*
tongue (firmly planted) in cheek *cliché*
too numerous to mention *cliché*
took to task *cliché*
torrent of abuse *cliché*
total (extinction, operating costs) extinction, operating costs
total strangers strangers

totally (demolished, destroyed) demolished, destroyed
tower of strength *cliché*
transport carry
trapped like rats *cliché*
trials and tribulations *cliché*
triggered *cliché;* prompted
true colors *cliché*
true fact fact
tumultuous applause *cliché*
tuna fish tuna
turn thumbs down *cliché*
12 (midnight, noon) midnight, noon
two alternatives alternatives, choices
two-way street *cliché*

U

ultimate final, last
ultimate (conclusion, end, outcome) conclusion, end, outcome
uncharted sea *cliché*
underground subway subway
underlying purpose purpose
undertake a study study
uneasy (calm, truce) *cliché*
unexpected surprise surprise
uniformly consistent consistent
united together in holy matrimony married, wed
universal panacea panacea
unpaid debt debt
unprecedented situation *cliché*
untimely end *cliché*
untiring efforts *cliché*
up (in arms, the air) *cliché*
upcoming coming, impending
updated current
upset the apple cart *cliché*
uptight *cliché*
user-friendly easy-to-use
usual custom custom
utilization use
utilize use
utterly indestructible indestructible

V

vanish into thin air *cliché*
various and sundry *cliché*

vast expanse *cliché*
vehicle car, truck
very *cut*
viable workable
viable (alternative, option, solution) alternative, option, solution
view with alarm *cliché*
violence erupted *cliché*
violent (assault, attack, killing, murder, rape, slaying) assault, attack,
    killing, murder, rape, slaying
vitally necessary necessary
voiced (approval, objections) *cliché;* approved, objected

W

walk(s) of life *cliché*
warm as toast *cliché*
war-torn *cliché*
was employed worked
was in possession of had
watchful eye *cliché*
watershed *cut*
watery grave *cliché*
wealth of information *cliché*
wear and tear *cliché*
wear many hats *cliché*
wee, small hours *cliché*
weighty (matter, reason, tome) *cliché*
well-known *cut*
wellness health, prevention
went up in flames burned
were scheduled to would
what makes (her, him, them) tick *cliché*
where there's smoke, there's fire *cliché*
whether or not whether
which are *can often cut*
which is *can often cut*
while at the same time while
whirlwind (courtship, romance, tour) *cliché*
white (as snow, stuff) *cliché*
who are *can often cut*
who is *can often cut*
who said said
whole nine yards *cliché*
wide-open space *cliché*
widespread anxiety *cliché*
(widow, widower) of the late widow, widower
will be a participant in will participate in

will hold a meeting will meet
win out win
winds of change *cliché*
wipe the slate clean *cliché*
wish(es) (he, she, they) had that one back *cliché*
with bated breath *cliché*
witness see
word to the wise *cliché*
words (can't, fail to) express *cliché*
world-class *cliché*
worse for wear *cliché*
worst ever worst
wrapped in mystery *cliché*
write down write
writing on the wall *cliché*

Y

you know *cut*
young juvenile juvenile

Z

zoo animals animals *(if context is clear)*

Web Resources

NEWSPAPERS

There are several major professional associations for newspaper journalists. They cater to individuals at various points in their professional careers and to newspapers of various sizes.

- American Society of Newspaper Editors
  www.asne.org

- Associated Press Managing Editors
  www.apme.com

- National Newspaper Association (community papers)
  www.nna.org

- Newspaper Association of America
  (daily newspapers, including metros)
  www.naa.org

- Society of Professional Journalists
  (not limited to newspaper journalists)
  spj.org

CHAPTER 13

Sexism, Racism and Other "isms"

"Welcome to the world of After."

— Paul Greenberg, Tribune Media Services, Oct. 29, 2001

"As far as a---s* go, yours is kinda sweet."

— Dr. Jordan Cavanaugh, the female lead in "Crossing Jordan,"
primetime drama series on NBC, Oct. 10, 2001

"Fast is fine, but accuracy is everything."

— Wyatt Earp, 1860's Western gunslinger

These three quotes outline the tough-to-navigate Language Triangle: new social change, new language standards, new journalism requirements. These three mind-benders will stretch you every time you work to communicate the truth. Why? Because what is true keeps changing.

1. **New social change—"the world of After."** (Greenberg) Language changes to get in step with power shifts. For instance, after civil rights legislation was passed, labeling an adult black man as a boy was wrong. After women attended colleges and universities more than men in this country, describing women as physical objects and men as powerful actors was inaccurate. After coverage of the AIDS epidemic focused heavily and unfairly on homosexual men, the media drew heavy criticism. Gay and lesbian groups formed in news organizations, demanding more equitable treatment in the news. Immediately after the Sept. 11, 2001, terrorist attacks on New York and Washington, top news organizations rushed to develop relevant language to avoid racist descriptions of terrorists, Muslims and U.S. citizens born in Middle Eastern countries. (See the discussion later in this chapter.) Global changes shape us daily, and you —as a journalist—must see quickly what has changed, then respond in language that portrays current reality.

---

*This is your challenge: In a world where nothing is *not said*, how do you choose appropriate language?

2. New standards of language—the world of entertainment and the Internet. ("Crossing Jordan") Prime-time network TV shows now contain many words that used to be forbidden. (The "Crossing Jordan" quote is one of the less offensive.) Kids and teens are bombarded with millions of cruel, coarse, violent and sexual words in online games, popular music, cable TV programs and movies. You have to learn to communicate with a public numbed to actual pain and violence because it is confronted with these daily in language and the media.

3. New journalism requirements—the world of constant coverage. (Earp) "Always on" describes today's computer networks and today's journalism. The world keeps speeding up. Journalists communicate in a global culture of accelerating change. You must perform in the two ways journalism is deemed valuable: fast and accurately.

If you understand what forces today's reality in the Language Triangle, you will be able to deliver words, ideas and information in sync with what's really going on. In sum, you will be able to produce believable journalistic work.

The new global culture of accelerating change sometimes looks and feels like chaos. Language has trouble catching up. It's your job as a journalist to think through, then communicate change in today's language.

Today's language wells up in a broad spectrum of media, including more than 521 satellite TV channels; millions of Web sites; global music, online games, 24-hour updates on news sites; and myriad magazines, newspapers and other publications. In the competitive explosion of sound, programming, words and music, the extremes stand out.

In this new cauldron, writers, webcasters and broadcasters translate the now to global publics. Journalists struggle to craft intelligent work that reflects current reality, not stereotypes and labels from an out-of-date time frame. When you pay attention, you'll find even the best of communicators relying on old assumptions that miss new realities. Journalists in the United States are forced to be more sophisticated about the power of at least nine once-invisible groups:

- Women
- African-Americans
- Hispanics
- Asian-Americans
- Native Americans
- People with disabilities
- People over 50
- Gays and lesbians
- Globans (global citizens)

Weiner, Edrich, Brown, Inc., a futurist company in New York City, has coined the term *Globan* to identify a new category of citizenry emerging as the world morphs into interdependency. A Globan lives in more than one national culture and may or may not be a U.S. citizen. The Globan is conversant and comfortable in multiple geographies. Companies from all developed countries are multinational, with opportunities for employees to live almost simultaneously in two cultures. For instance, more than 3 million U.S. citizens reside outside the country. U.S. companies have branches in more than 163 countries. The golden arches of McDonald's restaurants appear throughout the world, serving the traditional hamburger along with local foods (such as squid tempura in Japan).

Don't Be Ridiculous

Unexamined assumptions can make newspeople appear to be naive. Here are some 21st-century realities to help you examine your own assumptions.

American does not mean *white*. *American* doesn't even mean *a citizen of the United States*. Instead, *American* refers to *someone from North or South America*. Period.

Gangs come in all colors. Most unwed teen mothers in the United States are white. The single-parent family makes up only 9 percent of U.S. households. There are more Muslims in the United States than Episcopalians. One in eight people in the United States was born in another country. At least another 300,000 illegal immigrants add to the diversity. In the Los Angeles consolidated school district, 87 languages are spoken. In New York, 119 languages can be heard.

Ideas that were radical a few years ago (equal pay for equal work in the 1980s, for example) have been transformed into trends. Hillary Rodham Clinton, a professional from the baby-boom generation, represents her generation's professional presence of women. Yet much of journalistic writing about her reflects assumptions common among people of older generations: "uppity woman," "pushy broad" and "stand by your man." From 1993 to 2001, as the wife of President Bill Clinton, Hillary Rodham Clinton's approval ratings went up only as she shut up, when press coverage relegated her to nonpolicy, symbolic or motherly activities.

The Associated Press required reporters to ask women quoted in their stories if they were married so that they could be tagged with their marital status—*Miss* (unmarried) or *Mrs.* (married)—unless the woman requested that she be referred to as *Ms.* Men's marital status was mentioned only if it was relevant to the story. This out-of-date practice sprang from a time in U.S. history when women could not own property, vote nor publish. Marital status, even in the early 1900s, cemented a woman's place in society.

Only a few days before Hillary Rodham Clinton entered the U.S. Senate race in February 2000, the AP had finally decided to eliminate courtesy titles for women from its stories. Even so, today, Sen. Hillary Clinton, D-N.Y., is portrayed differently from Sen. Chuck Schumer, R-N.Y. Clinton's attire, emotions, weight and facial expressions receive comment. Yet no one seems to care what Schumer wears, how he shows his feelings, whether he has put on a few pounds or what his facial expressions are.

Language Turns to the Future

Since the 1990 census, when the growing multicultural change could be seen in the statistics, journalists and their audiences have been forced to cope with the fastest iteration of change in history. The 2000 census spun out a story of even faster change. Then, the immigration reports after the Sept. 11 terrorist attacks portrayed a leaky-sieve policy, as individuals from every land alight in the United States and get lost in the mobile millions of other immigrants. In addition, international migrations reshape the globe, surprising demographers, much less citizens. All these changes pose special challenges for journalists.

Futurists tell us that:

- There has been more change in the past 50 years than in the preceding 100,000.
- Language began only 100,000 years ago.
- Today's everyday language transformations provide one of the best measures of the driving force of social change.

Many of the spelling, grammar and punctuation rules covered in this book evolved from Latin, a language that is dead. The concepts discussed in this chapter evolved during the past three decades, many in the past few years. The issue, then, is how a language grounded in Latin copes with such change.

The answer is that Latin may be dead, but English isn't. Like all living languages, English constantly evolves and changes to fit new, uncomfortable realities. In their classic book, "The Elements of Style," E.B. White and William Strunk Jr. state: "The language is perpetually in flux: It is a living stream, shifting, changing, receiving new strength from a thousand tributaries, losing old forms in the backwaters of time."

Since "Working With Words" was first published in 1989, everyday language has shifted to be more inclusive and less dismissive. Yet hate speech has grown. Why? Because power now also resides with the "outsiders." As women fill college classrooms, and then professional jobs, they accrue power. As "minorities" become a larger proportion of U.S. society—and become the majority in many communities, not only in California—they also amass power.

New Players in the New Millennium

Women and members of racial, ethnic and immigrant groups continue to move from the sidelines to the headlines. Unprecedented numbers reshape the labor force, higher education and public life. These facts make obsolete traditional assumptions that males of European descent should be more important. Multiculturalism now defines the United States. Meanwhile, U.S. language lives by updating to accommodate new reality.

Today, new constructions replace the old sexually biased *he* to describe those who act as leaders, teachers, attorneys, pilots, factory workers, managers and executives. As recently as 1989, *he* was commonly used to mean all. Why the change? Increasingly, women fill jobs and assume roles once assumed to belong to men. For instance, 33 percent of today's U.S. Air Force and half of the students enrolled in medical schools are women. Similarly, men move to roles once thought reserved for women. For example, now 40 percent of all grocery shoppers are men, and men account for a growing percentage of students in nursing programs.

The driving force of social change accelerates. Tracing five "undercovered" groups of newspaper readers shows how they have shifted in power, causing language to shift.

1. *Women:* They now make 80 percent of consumer decisions and own 40 percent of all U.S. businesses.
2. *Young adults:* Many resent the label "slackers," and they face a muddy economic future.
3. *Racial/ethnic and immigrant groups:* These are the new entrepreneurs and the future of international business. Estimates are that "minorities" will be the majority throughout the United States by 2032.
4. *Those over 50:* They are lifetime learners and seekers. At the beginning of 1900, the average age of death was 47. At the beginning of 2000, the age was 76.
5. *Children and teens:* A century ago, elders lived in poverty. Today, proportionally more children than elders live in poverty, with endless consequences.

All these shifts remold our society. But change does not happen without comment. As women of all races and men of color have taken on more visible roles in a society of diminishing paternalism, there has been a lot of "noise." Much of this comment comes through journalism that resists change and hangs on to the status quo.

In resistance to the shift in power, more inclusive language is discounted as being "politically correct" by those losing power. In fact, many of the preferred terms listed later in this chapter have been pejoratively labeled "PC."

In a world in which we are bombarded by sounds and images, journalism's credibility will rely more and more on its ability to see current reality and report it. Fortunately, that credibility can be ensured by living out a basic tenet of good journalism: Get it fast, get it right (Earp). Ridding media messages of sexism, racism and other "isms" requires only that journalists report accurately. Then relevant coverage can emerge.

With the social shifts already in place and with those yet to come, the journalist's job of using clear, non-psychologically loaded language is more important and difficult than ever before. Subtle "isms"—the unconscious use of insulting, out-of-date terms, biases and assumptions about whole groups of people or individuals in those groups—are harder to eliminate than blatant sexism and racism. Why? Although we may hold nonsexist and nonracist beliefs, we may unconsciously fall into the trap of using dated sexist, racist, ageist and dismissive language.

Today, as the world reorganizes because of new transportation, communication and business systems, new groups can now be vocal and heard. Ethnic, racial, lifestyle and international communities connect globally through the Internet. They demand that their unique voices be heard. But to understand what is necessary to embrace (and what is necessary to eradicate) in today's language, we need to examine the past.

A Brief History of "isms"

In Western civilizations, society for centuries dismissed women and children of all races and men of color as peripheral, using those groups as unpaid workers, servants and, sometimes, slaves. Language today displays a bias against women and minorities and reflects a history of inequality.

When the Pilgrims settled in Massachusetts Bay, they brought English common law with them. When Blackstone's Commentaries on the Laws of England was imported to this country as the basis of the U.S. legal system, women and children (particularly female children) were legally on a par with the master's cattle, oxen and dogs. And when slavery was institutionalized into the country's laws, black women, men and children were given the same legal status accorded white women and children. All were property belonging to white men.

It can be argued that black men gained citizenship when they got the vote after the Civil War in the 1860s. White women and women of color were elevated to citizen level when they won the vote in 1920. Realistically, men of color and women of all races began to gain equal access to employment, credit and education only in the mid-1960s.

Documents serving as the foundation of this country's government held white males in higher value: "We hold these truths to be self-evident, that all men are created equal."

For those who would argue that *men* was generic then and included everyone, remember that two constitutional amendments were required to bring adults other than white males into the voting process. So, what journalists are faced with in today's usage is centuries of authoritative language diminishing the roles and lives of women and minorities.

But society changes. Accelerating social revolutions are partly about renaming what is. Language must catch up to a world in which the poor, people with disabilities, women, gays and lesbians, African-Americans, Asian-Americans, Native Americans, Hispanics, Latinos and Chicanos demand full citizenship, authority and viable economic power.

Future Realities: More Language Transformation Coming

Language transforms as the realities of U.S. society change. We can anticipate what the future holds for language by considering these major demographic shifts:

- By 2005, one-half of those leaving the work force will be white males, and 38 percent of the work force will be non-Hispanic white men, compared with 43 percent in 1990.
- By 2007, women in the work force age 55 and older will increase by 54 percent; men age 55 and older will increase by 36 percent.
- By 2008, women in the work force will increase by 26 percent.
- By 2010, the oldest non-Hispanic, white baby boomers will start retiring.
- By 2010, married couples will no longer make up a majority of households.
- By 2025, those older than 64 will outnumber teen-agers 2 to 1.
- By 2030, the youngest boomers will reach 65 and more than 20 percent of Americans will be older than 65.
- By 2050, life expectancy is expected to increase to 82.1 years.

Dealing With Reality

To reflect today's reality, and the realities of the future, we should avoid the following "isms" both in specific words and in areas of coverage.

Sexism

Sexism is usually thought of as fixed expectations about women's appearance, actions, skills, emotions and "proper" place in society. Sexism also includes sex stereotyping of men.

Instead of adequate and varied portrayals of individual women, five common stereotypes of females emerge in news coverage. They cloud today's reality. In most cases, these dismissive categories are to be avoided.

1. *Mother/nurturer:* woman as caregiver. Examples: grandmother, prostitute with a heart of gold, fairy godmother.
2. *Stepmother/bitch:* woman as non-nurturer. Examples: iron maiden, aggressive woman, aloof executive, female boss.
3. *Pet/cheerleader:* woman as appendage to a man or children. Examples: first lady, the little lady, soccer mom.
4. *Tempter/seducer:* woman as sexpot (a term used only for women). Examples: Madonna, gold digger, victim of sex crime who "asked for it."
5. *Victim:* woman as incompetent. Examples: damsel in distress, helpless female, rape victim.

Three stereotypes for men have emerged in language and should also be avoided.

1. *Macho/007:* man as battler. Examples: financial warrior, political strongman (no parallel word exists for women), master criminal, gang hero.
2. *Wimp/enlightened man:* man as sensitive. Examples: mama's boy, househusband, caregiver, sissy, single father.
3. *Demon/pervert:* man as "perp." Examples: child molester, rapist, murderer.

Because women are the majority in the United States, *she* more adequately conveys everyone than *he.* Some major publications now use *she* throughout as the generic pronoun, in direct opposition to the generic *he,* to convey information about all people. In many ads and company communications to the mainstream, the construct *he or she* reflects those companies' understanding of the majority audience. Many publications sprinkle *he* and *she* throughout, in an effort to balance acknowledgment. It's usually easiest to rewrite a sentence in the plural *they,* however, being concise, grammatical and nonsexist. (See Pages 27-46.)

In reality, making language relevant is fairly simple.

○ Use *man* only when referring to a man or a group of men. When a word describes a group that includes women and men, or could include men and women, say so. Almost any word ending with the suffix *man* can end with the suffix *woman.*

Racism

Racism is discrimination against ethnic or racial groups based on the notion that one ethnic group is superior to all others. Individual African-Americans, whites, Asian-Americans, Native Americans, people of Spanish-speaking ancestry and any other racial or ethnic group can be racist.

These are common stereotypes to be avoided.

1. *The secondary:* people of little consequence who serve the powerful. Examples: domestic help, migrant farmers, service workers, immigrants.
2. *The ignored/invisible:* people whose achievements are trivialized. Examples: slum or reservation residents, the underclass.
3. *Achievers:* exceptions to the "norm." Examples: model minority, credit to one's race.
4. *The despised/feared:* outsiders, criminals, suspects. Examples: welfare cheats, illegal aliens, drug addicts, "animals."

It appears that racial bias in U.S. crime reporting is increasing, not decreasing. Race is usually played up, not down. Often, those outside the white power framework are portrayed as villains without human characteristics attributed by default to whites.

The invisibility of racial and ethnic groups is perhaps most vividly apparent in accounts of an event that were corrected decades after the fact. For generations, history books noted that the only survivor of Custer's last stand at the Battle of the Little Bighorn in Montana was a horse, Comanche. Almost a century after the battle, in the 1960s, demonstrating students at the University of Kansas (where the stuffed Comanche resided in a glass case) pointed out that several thousand Sioux and Crow also survived that day.

What major facts are you getting wrong because of your latent prejudices? When members of racial and ethnic groups are made visible, the reference is sometimes gratuitous and fosters old stereotypes: *Police in Kansas City are searching today for a black man in his 30s who is suspected of taking part in a convenience store robbery late last night.*

How many black men in their 30s live in Kansas City? The report is not a description. If height, weight and distinguishing characteristics such as scars or speech patterns were used, enough information would be given on which to base an identification. The gratuitous addition of *black* simply adds a label.

The all-too-common assumption that "minority" issues are the same as "black-white" issues ignores the country's movement from melting pot to mosaic to kaleidoscope. Limiting the dialogue in that way leads to scapegoating, not factual reporting.

In today's United States, immigration is and will be an issue worthy of coverage. But it also is an issue that is multilayered, complex and frequently emotional. This new force for social change can and must be covered without falling back on old, outdated assumptions. To cover it objectively, journalists must face facts.

For instance, in the 1995 Oklahoma City bombing, early reports pointed to the possibility that international terrorists were responsible, and there were reported sightings of Middle Eastern people who were antagonistic to the United States, violent and sinister. All proved to be false. Needless stereotyping invaded and distorted media reports. The bomber was a white man, born in the United States.

Six years later, in September 2001, when Middle Easterners flew U.S. commercial jets into the World Trade Center, killing almost 3,000 people, news organizations had to scramble to find ways to describe the groups and individuals involved.

As we move toward a changing future, you probably will face similar situations. One side of the Language Triangle will shift, and as a professional journalist, you will have to respond quickly.

For instance, after Sept. 11, faced with new complexities about how to avoid racism while identifying terrorist threats, allies and Muslim U.S. citizens, even the most respected news organizations quickly had to develop non-racist standards.

Here's an example of how the shift on one side of the Language Triangle led to a race to develop relevant language in September 2001. At The Wall Street Journal, a memo containing the following information was sent to all reporters, swiftly responding to the need for sensitive, truthful and appropriate language standards that would avoid racism yet lead to clarity:

al Qaeda Lowercase the *al* in the name of bin Laden's terrorist network except starting a sentence or a line in a headline.

Arab and Islamic The terms aren't interchangeable. Many Arabs, particularly in the United States, are Christian, and a number of Muslim states (including Afghanistan, Iran and Pakistan) are not Arab.

Hamas The common name for the Islamic Resistance Movement, a militant Islamic group with the aim of establishing a Palestinian state incorporating Israel and the West Bank.

Hezbollah The Shiite Muslim militant group opposing Israelis in Lebanon, with Iranian support. The name means "Party of God."

Islamic extremists and Islamic militants These terms are appropriate in referring to zealots involved in terrorist activities, while the term *Islamic fundamentalists* should be avoided. Many Muslims who consider themselves fundamentalists are not supporters of the terrorist acts. For example, the Saudi Arabian government is fundamentalist in the sense that it supports a form of Islamic governance, but it is often portrayed as fighting "Islamic fundamentalists." And some nations and organizations that are suspected of complicity in terrorist acts do not embrace religious fundamentalism. The government of Iraq, for instance, has secular socialist roots, and some radical Palestinian organizations are motivated more by nationalism than by religious zeal.

jihad The religious struggle or war against nonbelievers in Islam.

Muhammad Preferred over *Mohammed* for the founder and chief prophet of the Muslim religion, also known as Islam.

Mujahedeen This is the preferred spelling for the plural noun for those engaged in a jihad, or Muslim holy war.

normalcy While *normality* has long been considered the preferred noun, this variation seems to have taken over among officials and commentators addressing the nation's attempts to return to the one-time status quo.

Osama bin Laden Lowercase *bin*, meaning "son of," in the name of the terrorist leader, except starting a line in a headline.

Sunni Muslims, Shiite Muslims The main branches of Islam. [Most Afghans are Sunnis.]

Taliban The Islamic movement that overran Afghanistan in 1996. The term, literally meaning "students," is construed as plural.

terrorists They attack civilian targets, such as the World Trade Center, while *guerrillas* attack military or government establishments.

Ageism

Ageism is discrimination based on age, especially discrimination against middle-aged and elderly people.

In a culture dominated by baby boomers, youth has been idealized and age has been posed as an issue for men and women. But the focus on age is usually not necessary and gets in the way of the greater reality, as in these examples:

> The spry 65-year-old salesman works five days a week in the job he's loved for the past 30 years. [The story later says he founded the company.]

> Grandmother Wins Election as Centralia Mayor [headline]

In the first example, *spry* gives the impression that the salesman is unusually active for his age. The assumption is unfair and ageist. In the second example, *grandmother* is both ageist (it focuses unduly on age) and sexist (it focuses on a woman's tie to her family rather than on an appropriate accomplishment—being elected mayor). You're unlikely to see this headline: *Grandfather Wins Election as Centralia Mayor.*

Today, only Japan and Europe have an older average age than the United States (median age is 36 and going up). The World War II generation and their children, the baby boomers, form large blocs of society. Both groups are active shapers of new power and won't be dismissed easily in language. Nor will the members of the large Gen Y age cohort.

The "young old" of the 70- to 85-year-old group continue to retire but also to be employed, form companies and lead communities. For instance, Clint Eastwood at 72 stars in movies, golfs competitively and plays with his 9-year-old. The "old old," ages 85 to 100, still vote, subscribe to newspapers and invest in the stock market. Some parents and children now live in the same nursing homes.

Other Stereotyping

Stereotyping denies the individuality of people or groups by expecting them to conform to unvarying patterns. For example:

> Jones said that after a woman who identified herself only as a "Jewish mother" complained that she and several co-workers were upset because of the lack of day care, the company began making plans to survey employees.

Even when a source uses a stereotype, such as *Jewish mother,* it is not the journalist's job to perpetuate that stereotype. In this example, it would be a simple matter to drop the offensive labeling. It's hard to imagine that the label is in any way necessary to the story.

Such labeling makes it easy for the narrow-minded to engage in discrimination. Perpetuating sexism, racism, ageism and other forms of stereotyping in the language helps contribute to such discrimination against individuals and groups.

Sexist, racist and ageist labels that creep into writing not only are unfair to groups and individuals but also are inaccurate. To repeat the obvious — but obviously neglected, or this chapter would not be necessary — *a journalist's job is to reflect reality.*

The Nonbias Rule

The history of inequality in Western culture has led to a language that stresses white men as the standard and considers others as substandard. One simple rule eliminates most language biases.

⬤ **Ask yourself, "Would my wording be the same if my subject were an affluent white man?"**

The expectation is that white men are leaders and that leaders who are not able-bodied white men are aberrations. Yet the reality is that leaders in communities, corporations and the nation are women; gays and lesbians; members of racial, ethnic and immigrant groups; people with disabilities; and people older than 70.

Often, reporters treat men and women unequally, patronizing women by describing them or their dress when the same would not be done to a man. For example: *The attractive, 35-year-old mother of three wore an all-business suit on her first day as managing editor.* Would anyone have written: *The handsome, 38-year-old father of three wore an all-business suit on his first day as managing editor?*

Other inequitable media treatment is evident when individuals or groups are labeled by race. For example: *Black poet Maya Angelou spoke to 500 people about her new book.* Would anyone have written: *White poet Tom McAfee is memorialized in one of his students' poems?*

Apply the nonbias rule to test whether you write fairly. When you use a "colorful," "catchy" or "cutesy" phrase, the interpretation may be derogatory. A headline describing Sen. Diane Feinstein, D-Calif., as "Fiery, Feisty Feinstein" is sexist. Just imagine applying the same adjectives to Gov. Gray Davis.

Straightforward, factual writing builds credibility. Adjectives and characterizations are always opportunities for derision. Drop as many as possible. Don't label a person as a member of a specific gender, age or racial group.

Symbolic Annihilation

Sources for stories today still are "mainly male, mainly pale." The media rarely query more than 60% of the population (women or people from ethnic or racial minorities) except when the story is about women's rights, racial profiling, Black History Week, etc. To give audiences a more realistic look at themselves, multi- and varied sources must be quoted.

As both George Gerbner and Gaye Tuchman, sociologists who independently study the media, point out, if a group is not represented in media messages and the language, that group is not part of the picture we carry around in our heads. When a group is invisible, absent, condemned, trivialized or ignored in writing, people in that group are symbolically "zapped" from existence.

And although white men have always been presidents of this country and chiefs of the FBI, it is unrealistic to assume that the sex, age, race and physical abilities a person holds will neatly fit that person into old stereotypes. Janet Reno was the longest-term U.S. attorney general in the 20th century. Elizabeth Dole ran a serious campaign for the U.S. presidency in 1999. As of early 2002, there were 13 women serving in the 100-member U.S. Senate, 61 women serving in the 435-member U.S. House of Representatives, and five women serving as governors of their states.

Many African-Americans are middle-class, which runs counter to journalistic reports placing African-Americans in poverty. More than half the women in the country are employed outside the home, which runs counter to the out-of-date image of women as the only audience using food information. Mentally disabled people are no longer shut away from participating in the world. Disabled people may be no more handicapped than the "temporarily abled." Native Americans are not of one tribe. Citizens of Spanish-speaking ancestry are not a monolithic group; they are Cuban-Americans, Mexican-Americans, Puerto Rican-Americans and others whose roots are in Spain, Latin America and Spanish-speaking Caribbean nations, all with differing cultural backgrounds. Asian-American students are not all stereotypically at the head of the class. Nor are Asian-Americans of one monolithic group; they may be of Japanese, Chinese, Korean, Vietnamese, Thai or other ancestry (including Tiger Woods, whose mother is Taiwanese and whose father is African-American).

Ignoring the individuality of people does not fit today's writing. The Seattle Times developed this diversity checklist for reporters and editors:

- Have I sought diverse sources for this story?

- Have I allowed preconceived ideas to limit my efforts to include diversity?

- Am I employing "tokenism," allowing one minority person to represent a community, or am I seeking true diversity?

- Am I furthering stereotypes as I seek diversity?

- Am I battling stereotypes?
- Am I being true to my other goals as a journalist as I seek diversity? If not, what are my alternatives?
- If there are ethical concerns, have I sought out other points of view?
- What are the likely consequences of publication? Who will be hurt and who will be helped?
- Will I be able to explain clearly and honestly, "not rationalize," my decision to anyone who challenges it?

Dumping Today's Stereotypes

There are some terms to avoid (many of them are considered slurs) or to include when writing or editing stories. *Even when preferable terms are suggested, they should not be used except when germane to the story.* Usually, you should identify everyone, or no one, by race, age, sex, and so on.

Ask the source.

Generally, the best way to determine whether a term is prejudicial is to ask the person(s) it covers. For instance, many members of tribes object to the term *Indian,* although some groups retain it. Many prefer being identified by tribal name; some prefer the term *Native American* or *American Indian.* Ask the person her or his preference. That's the only way to ensure accuracy.

Eliminate labels.

Eliminate labels that stereotype. Stereotyping all people in a group as acting or being like all others in that group only blinds us to individuals' possibilities and characteristics. Expecting every white male to be like all other white males is just as racist and sexist as expecting all African-American females to be like all other African-American females.

Respect all subjects.

Be on the lookout for unconscious bias. The most punishing stereotypes are subtle. For instance, research documents that 3-year-old boys are more encouraged to risk and fail than are 3-year-old girls (Michael Lewis, Steven M. Alessandri and Margaret W. Sullivan, "Differences in Shame and Pride as a Function of Children's Gender and Task Difficulty," Child Development 63, No. 3 [1992]: 630-38). Parents, teachers and others reinforce two different expectations without realizing the difference, and this subtle double standard takes a toll on both boys and girls.

Drop race, sex, age or disability tags.

Don't provide someone's racial, ethnic or religious background; sex or sexual orientation; or age or disability unless it's relevant to the particular story. The days of the "she's a college professor, but she's black" story are over.

● Pay attention.

Remember: Fair, objective language cannot be determined solely by popular usage or rules in books that can have the effect of freezing current understanding. Language changes daily as it responds to an increasingly global culture that changes at an accelerating speed.

The constant revision of language is not easy, as seen by arguments over acceptable and unacceptable language in a globally interdependent society. The controversy over what terms are "politically correct" will grow as the world slouches toward multilevel multiculturalism.

The following list of preferred terms is controversial. As soon as it is published, some of it may be out-of-date. Each time we publish the list, we add and delete terms. The first core set of examples was provided by permission of the Multicultural Management Program at the University of Missouri School of Journalism, which constructed a Dictionary of Offensive Terms with the help of multicultural journalists from across the nation. Other examples are drawn from observation of language in today's media.

Racism, sexism and other "isms" are unfair, period. Avoid using racist, sexist, ageist and other stereotyping terms, even in quotes. As language changes fast, keep current with changes by using Web resources named at the end of this chapter. Watch your language.

⌐──── A ────⌐

actor Not *actress*. Most members of the acting community prefer *actor* for either a man or a woman, but this usage has not become common otherwise, and the Oscars still have categories such as "Best Actress" and "Best Supporting Actress."

advertising representative Not *adman*.

African People or language of a continent, not a country; of or pertaining to Africa or its people or languages. Not a synonym for *black* or *African-American.*

African-American Usually interchangeable with *black* but more universally accepted. Don't use the terms *articulate, intelligent* and *qualified* as modifers for *African-American;* you would not use those terms to describe whites in the same context.

AHANA Acronym coined by Dr. Robert S. Knight, late professor at the University of Missouri School of Journalism, to reflect the country's rapid move away from the term *minorities;* stands for African-American, Hispanic, Asian-American and Native American.

AIDS victim Do not use; *person with AIDS* is preferred.

airhead Do not use; objectionable description, generally aimed at a woman.

alien Do not use; *illegal immigrant* or *undocumented immigrant* is preferred.

all people are created equal Use instead of *all men are created equal* unless you need to quote the Declaration of Independence.

alumnae and alumni Not *alumni* for a group of men and women who have attended a school. Specifically, *alumna* (plural *alumnae*) is correct for a woman (women); *alumnus* (plural *alumni*) for a man (men). Your editor, backed by the AP Stylebook, may tell you that *alumni* is the correct term for a group of men and women. However, just as *man* does not stand for men and women, *alumni* does not stand for women and men who attended a school.

Amazon Do not use; characterizes women as predators of men; also refers to size.

American Applies to persons from both North and South America; should not be used to refer to citizens of the United States of America.

American Indian Interchangeable with *Native American;* ask source to determine preference; use correct tribal name if possible. *Wampum, circle the wagons, warpath, warrior, powwow, scalping, tepee, brave, squaw, savage* and other similar terms offend.

anchor Even though the AP Stylebook calls for *anchorwoman* or *anchorman,* use *anchor* for all people anchoring the news.

Anglo Always capitalized. Used interchangeably with *white* in some parts of the United States; in others, *white* is preferred.

Arab A native of Arabia or any of a Semitic people native to Arabia but now dispersed throughout surrounding lands. Not interchangeable with *Arab-American* nor persons from Middle Eastern countries.

articulate Offensive when referring to a member of a minority group and his or her ability to handle the English language; usage suggests that "those people" are not considered well-educated or articulate.

artisan Not *craftsman.*

Asian Refers specifically to things or people of or from Asia; not interchangeable with *Asian-American.* Some Asians regard *Asiatic* as offensive when applied to people.

Asian-American Preferred generic term for U.S. citizens of Asian descent. Be specific when referring to particular groups: *Filipino-Americans, Japanese-Americans, Chinese-Americans* and so on. *Serene, quiet, shy, reserved* and *smiling* are disparaging stereotypes of Asian-Americans, as are *buck-toothed, delicate, obedient, passive, stoic, mystical, China doll* and *dragon lady.* Also avoid references to the *Asian invasion* describing Asian immigration.

assembly member Use for all people elected to an assembly (also *assemblywoman* or *assemblyman*).

author Not *authoress.*

aviator Not *aviatrix.*

(B)

babe Do not use; offensive term referring to a woman.

ball and chain Do not use; offensive phrase that refers sarcastically to a man's loss of freedom because of a woman.

banana Do not use; offensive term referring to an Asian-American who allegedly has abandoned his or her culture. Just as objectionable are *coconut* for a Mexican-American and *oreo* for an African-American.

bandito Do not use; often applied derisively.

barracuda Do not use; negative generalization of a person without morals and/or ethical standards or judgments; many times directed at a woman.

basket case Do not use; term began as British army slang for a quadruple amputee who had to be carried in a basket but has come to mean anyone who is incapacitated. When someone says, "I was so drunk, I was a basket case," what is implied is, "I was so drunk, I was as useless as a quadriplegic." Many people consider the term offensive.

bastard Do not use; also do not use *illegitimate*.

beaner Do not use; offensive term referring to someone of Latin descent.

beauty Avoid descriptive terms of beauty when not absolutely necessary. For instance, use *blond* and *blue-eyed* for a woman only if you would use the same phrasing for a man.

beefcake Do not use; offensive term referring to male physical attractiveness.

bellhop Not *bellman*.

bi Do not use; offensive term derived from *bisexual*.

Bible-beater, -thumper, -whacker Do not use; unacceptable terms for evangelical Christians. Acceptable terms are *fundamentalist Christian* or *born-again Christian;* ask source.

Bible Belt Do not use for sections of the United States, especially in the South and Middle West.

bimbo Do not use; offensive term referring to a woman.

birth name or given name Not *maiden name*.

bisexual Term describing a person sexually attracted to members of both sexes; use carefully if at all.

black *African-American* is the term preferred by many people and publications. Do not use *colored*.

blond Use one spelling, *blond*, in all instances. Do not repeat or refer to jokes where blond-haired people are assumed to be stupid.

blue-haired Do not use; offensive phrase applied to an older woman.

boy Insulting when applied to an adult male, especially a man of color.

brave Do not use as a noun referring to a Native American male.

broad Do not use; offensive term for a woman.

brotherly and sisterly love Not *brotherly love*.

brunet Use only one spelling, *brunet*, in all instances.

buck Do not use; derogatory word for an African-American or Native American male.

burly Do not use; adjective too often used to describe a large African-American man, implying ignorance; considered offensive.

business professional Use for all those in business (also *businessman* or *businesswoman*).

buxom Do not use; offensive reference to a woman's chest size.

C

camera operator Use for all people operating video cameras.

Canuck Do not use; derisive term for a Canadian.

career woman Do not use; offensive. Just report her business title.

Caucasian Always capitalized. Defines a race of people, not a specific ethnic group or nationality; Mexican-Americans are Caucasians.

chairperson, convener, presider, coordinator, chair Use for all those chairing meetings (also *chairwoman* or *chairman*).

Charlie Do not use; a derisive term popularized in the Vietnam War by U.S. soldiers to refer to a Vietnamese.

cheesecake Do not use; objectionable; refers to female physical attractiveness.

Chicano/Chicana Popular terms in the 1960s and 1970s to refer to Mexican-Americans; could be offensive to older Mexican-Americans; check with source.

chick Do not use; offensive term referring to a woman.

Chico First name inappropriately applied to a Mexican or Mexican-American; do not use generically. Also avoid *José, Pancho* and *Julio.*

chief Offensive when used generically to describe a Native American; use only when title is applicable.

Chinaman Do not use; unacceptable racial epithet for an Asian-American or Chinese.

Chinatown Refers to some Asian-American neighborhoods; avoid as a blanket term for all Asian-American communities.

chink Do not use; unacceptable racial epithet for an Asian-American or Chinese.

coconut Do not use; offensive term referring to a Mexican-American who allegedly has abandoned his or her culture. Just as objectionable are *banana* for an Asian-American and *oreo* for an African-American.

codger Do not use; offensive reference to an elderly person.

coed Do not use; comes from the days when men were the dominant gender in college. Today, women outnumber men in college enrollments and graduations. Use *student.*

cojones Do not use; vulgar Spanish word for testicles, often used to indicate machismo; offensive.

colored In some societies, including the United States, the word is considered derogatory and should not be used except when part of an official title, as in *National Association for the Advancement of Colored People.* In some African countries, *colored* denotes individuals of mixed racial ancestry. Whenever the word is used, place it in quotation marks and provide an explanation of its meaning.

common person, average person Not *common man, average man.*

community Do not use; implies a monolithic culture in which people act, think and vote in the same way, as in *Asian-American, Hispanic, African-American* or *gay community.* Be more specific: *Hispanic residents in a north-side neighborhood.* You are not the judge of whether a group is a community.

congressional representative, member of Congress Use for a member of Congress (also *congressman* or *congresswoman*).

conjoined twins Not *Siamese twins.*

coolies Do not use; refers specifically to a Chinese laborer in the 19th-century United States; objectionable then, objectionable now.

coon Do not use; highly objectionable reference to an African-American.

coot Do not use; offensive reference to an elderly person.

councilor Use for a member of a council (also *councilwoman* or *councilman*).

cracker, hillbilly, Okie, redneck Do not use; offensive, even when people refer to themselves this way.

craftsman Do not use; *artisan* is preferred.

crip Do not use; derogatory term for a person with a disability.

cripple, crippled Do not use; also do not use *handicapped. Disabled* is preferred; see *disabled.*

cybergeek Do not use; derogatory reference to an inventor, programmer and technical expert. Also avoid *nerd* and *techie.* Use the person's title.

D

dago Do not use; derogatory reference to an Italian.

deaf, hearing impaired and speech impaired Not *deaf and dumb, deaf and mute.* Deaf people are not dumb.

dear A term of endearment objectionable to some. Usage such as *He was a dear man* or *She is a dear* are your judgments, which are to be avoided.

deliverer, delivery person Not *deliveryman.*

dingbat Do not use; objectionable term referring to a woman.

disabled Because a disabling condition may or may not be handicapping, use *disabled* and *disability* rather than *handicapped* or *handicap.* Don't use *disabled* as a noun. Do not use *crippled, crip* or *invalid.* Use *person (people) with a disability (disabilities)* or check with the individual.

ditz Do not use; objectionable term implying stupidity.

divorced Not *divorce* or *divorcee;* say a person *is divorced,* if it's relevant. A person's marital status seldom is pertinent to a story. Especially be careful when you start to state a woman's marital status. Women continue to be tagged with marital identifiers more than men.

dizzy Do not use; offensive adjective for a woman.

door attendant Not *doorman.*

drafter Not *draftsman.*

dragon lady Do not use; highly objectionable characterization of an Asian-American woman, depicting her as scheming and treacherous.

Dutch treat Do not use; implies that Dutch people are cheap. Use *separate checks.*

dyke Do not use; offensive term for a lesbian.

E

English Not *Englishmen.*

Eskimo Many people referred to as *Eskimo* prefer *Inuit* (those in Canada) or *Native Alaskan;* ask source for preference.

every person for himself or herself Not *every man for himself.*

F

factory worker Not *factory man.*

fag, faggot Do not use; offensive term for a gay man or lesbian. Do not use even if members of the group refer to themselves by the term.

fairy Do not use; offensive term for a gay man.

female Do not use in place of *woman* (the noun). Do not use *woman* or *female* as an adjective. Do not identify by gender unless it is pertinent to the story.

feminine Can be objectionable to some women.

feminine wiles Do not use; insulting.

fiance Language is moving toward one spelling, *fiance,* for all instances. As with the issue of *divorce,* extra care is necessary so that overemphasis is not placed on a woman's marital status.

firefighter Use instead of *fireman* or *firewoman* for one who puts out fires.

fisher Not *fisherman.*

flip Do not use; derogatory term for a Filipino or Filipino-American.

foreman, forewoman Not *foreman* for both sexes.

foxy Do not use; offensive description of a woman's physical appearance.

fragile Do not use; offensive description of a woman's physical attributes.

French Not *Frenchmen.*

fried chicken Do not use as a stereotypical reference to the cuisine of African-Americans. Also avoid *watermelon.*

frigid Derisive when used to stereotype or characterize women; usually applied to women viewed by men as aloof or distant.

fruit Do not use; offensive term for a gay man or lesbian.

full-figured Do not use; offensive description of a woman's physical appearance; additionally, use physical descriptions only in sports stories.

G

gabacho Do not use; derogatory Spanish word applied to whites.

gaijin Do not use; exclusionary Japanese term referring to foreigners.

gal Do not use to refer to a woman.

gay Preferred term for homosexual men. A person's sexual orientation should be identified *only* when pertinent to the story.

geezer Do not use; objectionable reference to an elderly person.

geisha Japanese woman trained to provide entertainment, especially for men; offensive stereotype when used as a blanket term or caricature.

gender enders Avoid these terms: *actress, comedienne, executrix, heroine, poetess* and *starlet.* Instead, use gender-neutral terms such as *actor, comedian, executor, hero, poet* and *star.*

ghetto Avoid; stereotype for a poor minority community.

ghetto blaster Do not use; offensive and stereotypical. Use *portable stereo* or *boom box.*

girl Do not use to refer to a woman.

gold digger Do not use; characterizes a woman as a predator of men. Also avoid *Amazon* and *barracuda.*

golden years Avoid; characterizes people's later years as uniformly idyllic.

gook Do not use; unacceptable term for a Vietnamese or other Asian-American.

gorgeous Avoid giving your judgments of the physical attributes of women.

greaser Term used in the 1950s for those with a specific hairstyle and dress; derogatory when applied to Hispanics.

gringo Do not use; derogatory Spanish term applied to whites.

Guido An Italian first name; offensive when used to denote membership in the Mafia or as a description of street punks.

gyp Do not use; offensive term meaning "to cheat"; derived from *gypsy.*

(H)

handicapped Do not use; see *disabled.*

handmade, synthetic Not *man-made.* Also use *manufactured, constructed, fabricated* or *created.*

harebrained Do not use; offensive.

harelip Do not use; offensive term for *cleft lip.*

harem Do not use; derisive when used to describe a gathering of women.

heap big Do not use; stereotypical phrase denoting size; offensive to Native Americans.

heathens Do not use; derogatory, especially in this country when applied to Native Americans.

hero Not *heroine.*

Hiawatha Character popularized in a Longfellow work. Offensive when applied generically to describe or characterize Native Americans.

high yellow Do not use; objectionable when used to refer to lighter-colored black persons. Avoid any description of skin color or degrees of color. Also avoid *mulatto* and *half-breed.*

hillbilly Do not use; offensive term applied to people generally from Appalachia or the Deep South.

Hispanic Term referring generically to those with Latin American or Spanish heritage; not necessarily interchangeable with *Chicano, Latino, Mexican-American* or other specific Hispanic groups. Ask source which term is preferred and use ethnic background *only* when extremely pertinent to the story.

Holy Roller Do not use; offensive term used to refer to an evangelical Christian.

homemaker Not *housewife.*

homosexual Use *gay. Homosexual* connotes a clinical illness and evokes the pejorative *homo.* Preferred terms are *gay* for a homosexual man and *lesbian* for a homosexual woman. Terms such as *dyke, fruit, fairy* and *queer* are highly objectionable. Do not use them, even if members of the group refer to themselves by any of these terms. Also, use *sexual orientation* rather than *sexual preference.*

honey Do not use; objectionable. Also do not use *dear* and *sweetie.*

honorifics Usually not useful. Women and men are identified on first reference with full name; on second reference, use last name. *Ms.* is the courtesy title preferred for a woman if *Mr.* is used for a man; *Ms.* does not focus on marital status just as *Mr.* does not. Use evenhanded treatment for women and men; women often are inappropriately described by family roles—wife, mother, parent—but men are not.

hotblooded Latin Do not use; derisive stereotype of Latinos as hot-tempered and violent.

hours of work Not *man-hours.*

house worker Not *maid.*

humanity, humankind, people Not *mankind.*

hunk See *"The Myth."*

hymie Do not use; derogatory term for a person of the Jewish faith. Also avoid other disparaging terms for Jewish people.

I

illegal immigrant, undocumented immigrant Not *illegal aliens.* Often used to refer to a Mexican and Latin American believed to be in the United States without a visa.

impotent Clinical term referring to male sexual dysfunction; not appropriate when used to stereotype or characterize males.

Indian Offensive term to many who call themselves *Native Americans* or who prefer their tribe's individual name. *American Indian* is acceptable unless specifically referring to residents or natives of India.

Indian giver Do not use; refers to someone who reneges or takes something back once given; highly objectionable.

Indochina Formerly *French Indochina,* now divided into Cambodia, Laos and Vietnam.

Injun Do not use; derisive term for a Native American.

inscrutable Adjective carelessly applied to Asian-Americans; avoid all terms that stereotype entire groups.

insurance representative Not *insurance man.*

invalid Do not use; see *disabled.*

Irish Not *Irishmen.*

Ivan Do not use; slur for a Russian.

J

JAP Jewish American Princess; do not use; a stereotype of a young Jewish woman.

Jap Do not use to refer to a Japanese or Japanese-American.

Jew boy Do not use; offensive to Jewish males of all ages.

Jew down Act of negotiating a lower price for services or goods; do not use; highly offensive and stereotypical.

Jew Person of the Jewish faith. Some people find the use of *Jew* offensive and prefer *Jewish person.* Always use as a noun, never as a verb.

jive Do not use; derisively applied to African-American slang or speech.

jock Term applied to both men and women who participate in sports; offensive to some.

john Do not use; not appropriate for a man who uses female or male prostitutes.

José First name inappropriately applied to a Mexican or Mexican-American; do not use generically. Also avoid *Chico, Pancho* and *Julio.*

joto Do not use; derisive Spanish term for a gay man or lesbian.

Julio First name inappropriately applied to a Mexican or Mexican-American; Do not use generically. Also avoid *Chico, José* and *Pancho.*

L

lamebrain Do not use; offensive.

Latin lover Avoid; stereotype alluding to Latino sexual prowess.

Latino/Latina Refers specifically to those of Spanish-American ancestry. Use ethnic identifiers for everyone in your story or no one.

layperson Member of the congregation as distinguished from the clergy (or *layman* or *laywoman*).

lazy Avoid labels; show what a person does rather than use value judgments. Especially avoid when describing nonwhites, who are commonly and unfairly stereotyped more often than whites.

leader Use with caution; implies the person has the approval of an entire group of people. Be more specific: *African-American politician.*

Leroy First name sometimes carelessly used to refer to all African-American males; do not use generically.

lesbian Preferred term for a homosexual woman.

letter carrier, postal worker Not *mailman.* Use for a man or woman who works for the Postal Service.

lily-white Any characterization of skin color should be avoided. Also avoid *paleface* and *redskin*.

limp-wristed Do not use; derisive description of a gay man.

line repairer Not *lineman*.

little woman Do not use; offensive reference to a woman.

M

Mafia, Mafiosi Secret society of criminals and its members; do not use as a synonym for *organized crime* or *the underworld*.

maiden name Do not use. Use *birth name* or *given name*.

mammy Do not use; antiquated term referring to an older African-American woman; highly objectionable.

man Do not use to denote both sexes. Use *humanity, a person* or *an individual*. Avoid *man and wife*. Use either *wife and husband* or *husband and wife; woman and man* or *man and woman*.

"The Man" A reference to the white establishment; could be offensive.

manhole Some have suggested that this term is sexist because women also work in these places. A more neutral term is *utility cover*.

man-made Better to use *handmade, manufactured* or *synthetic*.

maricón Do not use; derisive Spanish term for a gay man or lesbian.

matronly Do not use; offensive reference to an elderly woman.

meter reader Not *meter man* or *meter maid*.

Mexican From or of Mexico; not a substitute for *Mexican-American*.

Mexican-American Preferred term for U.S. residents of Mexican origin.

minority/minorities On its way to becoming out-of-date; use *racial, ethnic and immigrant group(s)* instead, or, better yet, drop racial labeling.

"The Myth" or "the male myth" Avoid any word, description or phrase contributing to the stereotype of African-American males as strictly athletic, well-proportioned or having a high sexual drive and exaggerated sex organs. Avoid *stallion, stud, hunk, womanizer* and *lady killer*.

N

Native American Often the preferred term; check with source; use correct tribal name if possible.

negress Do not use; objectionable and antiquated term for an African-American woman.

Negro Do not use. Use *African-American* or *black*, depending on the source's preference. Check stylebook for preferred local usage.

news carrier Not *newsboy*.

nigger Do not use even when people refer to themselves with this term; highly offensive term for an African-American.

nip Do not use; derogatory term for a Japanese or Japanese-American.

nurse Not *male nurse*.

O

Okie Do not use; derogatory term for a white person or, more specifically, for a person from a rural area.

old buzzard Do not use; derogatory term for an elderly person.

old maid Do not use; archaic term referring to an unmarried woman. Don't refer to a woman's marital status unless you would for a man in the same story.

old wives' tale Do not use. Use *superstition* or *tale of wisdom*.

old-timer Do not use; objectionable term for an elderly person.

operate (v.) Use *operate a machine* rather than *man a machine*. Also use *work, staff* or *serve*.

operational space flight Not *manned space flight*.

oreo Do not use; offensive term referring to an African-American who allegedly has abandoned his or her culture; derisively used to mean "black on the outside and white on the inside."

Oriental Do not use; use *Asian-American, Asian* or a specific term. Sometimes acceptable to describe things, such as *Oriental rug*.

P

paleface Do not use; objectionable term sometimes used by Native Americans to describe whites.

Pancho First name inappropriately applied to a Mexican or Mexican-American; do not use generically. Also avoid *Chico, José* and *Julio*.

peon A Spanish-American peasant; avoid; sometimes derisively applied to entire groups of Hispanics or others.

people at work Not *men at work*.

personnel Not *manpower*. Also use *staff, work force* or *workers*.

person-on-the-street interview Not *man-on-the-street interview*.

pert Do not use; offensive; adjective describing a female characteristic.

petite Do not use; can be offensive in reference to a woman's body size.

pickaninny Do not use; offensive term for an African-American child.

pimp Stereotypical characterization of African-American men; highly objectionable.

poet Not *poetess*.

Polack Do not use; derogatory term for a Polish person.

police officer Not *policeman*.

Pop Do not use; offensive reference to an elderly person.

postal worker Not *postman*. Also use *letter carrier* or *mail carrier*.

powwow Do not use; see *American Indian*.

PR Do not use; offensive acronym for *Puerto Rican*.

project Do not use, as in *public housing project;* has come to be a racial code word, as in *people in the projects*. Use *public housing development* or *subsidized housing*.

proper names Do not make wordplays on people's given names; see, for example, *Ivan, Hiawatha, Chico* and *Leroy.*

prosthesis, artificial limb Not *peg leg.* Also avoid *hook.*

Q

qualified minorities Do not use; unnecessary description that implies members of racial, ethnic and immigrant groups are generally unqualified.

queer Do not use; offensive term used to describe a gay man or lesbian.

R

redneck Do not use; offensive term describing some white people.

redskin Do not use; objectionable description of a Native American. Avoid any reference to skin color or shade.

refugee Do not use for people who are settled in the United States and no longer have refugee status. Use only to describe people who flee to find refuge from oppression or persecution while they have refugee status.

retarded Do not use; refer to a specific medical condition. Also avoid *stupid* and *ignorant.*

rubbing noses Do not use; stereotypically, an "Eskimo kiss." However, Eskimos (many of whom prefer *Inuit* or *Native Alaskan*) do not rub noses, and many object to the characterization.

Russian Use only to refer to people who are from Russia or of Russian descent and to the language spoken in the region.

S

sales representative Not salesman.

samurai As a term or caricature, can be offensively stereotypical; avoid unless referring specifically to the historical Japanese warrior class.

sanitation worker, trash collector Not *garbageman.*

savages Do not use; offensive when applied to Native Americans or other native cultures. Also avoid *heathen.*

sculptor Not *sculptress.*

senile Do not use; offensive to older people. *Dementia* is the correct term for the mental or physical deterioration of old age.

senior citizen Do not use for anyone under age 65. In general, give ages only when relevant. Do not describe people as *senile, matronly* or *well-preserved.* Do not use *dirty old man, codger, coot, geezer, silver fox, old-timer, Pop, old buzzard* or *blue-haired.* Do not identify people as grandparents unless it is relevant to the story. Many people object to the term *senior citizen* as "an unsavory euphemism"; alternatives are *the aged, the old, the elderly* and *the retired.*

shiftless Do not use; highly objectionable as a description of the poor.

shine Do not use; objectionable reference to an African-American.

shrew Do not use; derogatory characterization of a woman who competes in the workplace or whose behavior is seen as nagging.

siesta A Latin tradition of a midday nap; use advisedly. Do not use to denote laziness.

silver fox Do not use; objectionable term referring to an elderly person.

skirt Do not use; offensive term referring to a woman or girl.

"Some of my best friends are ..." Hackneyed phrase usually used by someone accused of racial bias or wanting to appear unbiased, as in *Some of my best friends are Hispanic.*

soulful Objectionable adjective when applied strictly to African-Americans.

spade Garden tool or card suit. Do not use in reference to an African-American; highly insulting.

Spanish The language or a person from Spain; not interchangeable with *Mexican, Latino/Latina* or *Hispanic.*

spastic Do not use as an adjective describing those with muscular dysfunctions, tics or jerky physical movements. Also do not use *spaz.* Use the correct medical condition: *has cerebral palsy.*

sped ed, spec ed Do not use; offensive reference to a child in a special education class.

spic Do not use; unacceptable term for *Hispanic.*

spokesperson Not *spokesman.*

spry Do not use; cliché describing the elderly that assumes most older people are decrepit.

squaw Do not use; offensive term for a Native American woman.

stallion Do not use; offensive sexual term for a man.

statuesque Do not use; avoid referring to a woman's appearance.

stud Do not use; offensive sexual term for a man.

stunning Do not use; avoid referring to a woman's appearance.

suffers from Do not use. A person has a disease, such as *has leukemia,* or *a person with AIDS.*

swarthy Do not use; objectionable reference to skin color. Other objectionable terms are *paleface, redskin* and *lily-white.*

sweet young thing Do not use; highly objectionable phrase that reduces a woman to a sex object.

sweetie Do not use; objectionable term of endearment. Also avoid *dear* and *honey.*

(**T**)

---

taco Do not use; objectionable reference to a Mexican.

telephone worker Not *telephone man.*

tepee See *American Indian.*

those people Do not use; objectionable phrase used by one group to refer to another group. Also avoid *you people.*

timber nigger Do not use; offensive term used by sporting enthusiasts and those in the tourist industry to describe a Native American involved in the fishing and hunting rights debate.

token Do not use; refers to someone hired solely because of race, ethnicity or gender; implies the person was not qualified for the job.

Tonto Do not use; unacceptable characterization of a Native American.

trades worker Not *tradesman*.

U

ugh Do not use; highly offensive sound used to mimic the speech of Native Americans.

Uncle Tom Do not use; derogatory term used to refer to an African-American who has abandoned his or her culture by becoming subservient to whites; objectionable because no person or group can claim exclusive power to define what it is to be African-American. Also avoid *banana* for an Asian-American, *coconut* for a Mexican-American and *oreo* for an African-American.

V

vegetable Do not use to describe someone in a comatose state or a person incapable of caring for himself or herself. *Persistent vegetative state* is the medical terminology, if applicable.

W

wampum See *American Indian*.

wannabe Refers to someone who mimics a style or behavior of another group or wants to be a member of another group; use advisedly. For instance, a person dressed in red or blue isn't necessarily a wannabe Blood or Crip gang member; nor is the person necessarily a gang member. Also use the term *gang member* advisedly for the same reasons.

warpath See *American Indian*.

WASP Acronym for white Anglo-Saxon Protestant; offensive to some.

watermelon See *fried chicken*.

welch, welsh Do not use; offensive term meaning to break an agreement.

well-preserved Do not use; offensive term applied to women and the elderly.

wench Do not use; derogatory term for a woman.

wetback Do not use; derisive term for an undocumented worker, specifically a Mexican who has crossed the Rio Grande.

wheelchair Do not use *wheelchair-bound* or *confined to a wheelchair*. Preferred expression is *uses a wheelchair*.

white trash Do not use; derogatory term for poor whites.

white-bread Do not use; term denoting blandness; can have a racial connotation.

whore Do not use; derogatory. A man's sexual status has no commensurate descriptor. Also avoid *trollop, tart, loose woman* and *hussy.*

wild Indian Do not use to denote unruly behavior; offensive to Native Americans.

without rhythm Do not use; a stereotype of whites; implies that other races have rhythm, also a stereotype.

woman Preferred term for a female adult; *girl* is appropriate only for those age 17 and younger. Do not use *gal* or *lady.* Avoid derogatory terms for women, such as *babe, ball and chain, bimbo, broad, chick, little woman* and *skirt.* Avoid adjectives describing female physical attributes or mannerisms, such as *buxom, feminine, foxy, fragile, full-figured, gorgeous, pert, petite, statuesque* and *stunning.*

wop Do not use; derogatory reference to an Italian.

worker Not *workingman* or *workman.*

workers' compensation Not *workmen's compensation.* About 50 percent of the work force is female.

Xmas Do not use; offensive to many Christians.

yanqui Do not use; derogatory Spanish term for a North American white. Also avoid *gringo.*

yellow Do not use; offensive term referring to skin color; also a derogatory term meaning "coward."

yellow peril Do not use; offensive term used in the United States in the 19th and early 20th centuries to elicit fear of Chinese or Asian immigrants.

you people Do not use; objectionable phrase used by one group to refer to another group. Also avoid *those people.*

Web Resources

SENSITIVE LANGUAGE

The following Web sites conduct studies, publish research and provide continuing updates on the coverage of women and different racial groups.

- Asian American Journalists Association
  www.aaja.org

- International Women's Media Foundation
  www.iwmf.org

- Journalism and Women's Symposium
  www.jaws.org/links.shtml

○ National Association of Black Journalists
www.nabj.org

○ National Association of Hispanic Journalists
www.nahj.org

○ National Association of Muslim Journalists
www.blackjournalism.com/namj.htm

○ Native American Journalists Association
www.naja.com

○ UNITY: Journalists of Color Inc.
www.unityjournalists.org

These sites provide tips and information to help you avoid offensive language and become more familiar with multicultural terminology.

○ **Gay and Lesbian Alliance Against Defamation**
www.glaad.org/org/index.html

○ **The Poynter Institute's Diversity Digest**
www.poynter.org/diversity/

○ **Words @ Random**
www.randomhouse.com/words/language/avoid_essay.html

PART FOUR

Writing Methods for Different Media

CHAPTER 14

Writing News That's Fit for Print

Newspaper and magazine writing does not have to be boring. Nor does it have to be written in a rigid, formulaic style devoid of flair. Consider this example, written by Bartholomew Sullivan, a reporter for The Commercial Appeal in Memphis:

> It killed first, then it came into town.
>
> With almost no warning, a tornado dropped from the skies over northeast Arkansas just before 3 a.m. Thursday, smashing the mobile home of 5-year-old Brittany and 2½-year-old Kasey Lomax just as warning sirens began to wail.
>
> Then it crossed a plowed but unplanted field, smashed a brake-parts factory and a Dollar General Store, and spun down Olympia Street, snapping 100-year-old trees like pencils.
>
> "It was one excellent, big, humming roar," said Larry Carpenter, 38, who saw what was coming and climbed into a Laundromat dryer to wait out the storm.
>
> The Lomax children died before rescue workers and their parents, Wayne and Candy Lomax, could lift the floorboards from their shattered bodies, a shaken and muddy Manila Police Chief Jackie Hill said later.
>
> "When you pick up two small kids and hold them in your arms—I've got kids—it breaks your heart," he said.
>
> The twister also injured 21 people—several seriously—and damaged or destroyed 163 homes and 25 other buildings in this usually quiet Mississippi County town of 6,410 about 70 miles northwest of Memphis.
>
> Gov. Mike Huckabee toured the town in the early afternoon and later declared Mississippi County—as well as Craighead, Lonoke and Pulaski counties, which suffered minor damage from tornadoes—a disaster area.
>
> After he met with the grandparents of the Lomax children, he said, he "walked away with the most helpless feeling," but vowed to commit the resources at his disposal to help those in need.
>
> Manila Mayor Jimmy White declared a dusk-to-dawn curfew to prevent looting as 30 National Guardsmen from the 875th Engineer Battalion, based in Jonesboro, began arriving in the late afternoon.
>
> "We had virtually no warning," White said. "But when you've got one that comes out of nowhere, you never have enough time."

That story was written on deadline. It was not a feature on which the writer worked for days or weeks. It demonstrates that good writing is possible even in the most trying circumstances and when the writer is under severe deadline pressure.

Close examination of the body of the story shows that Sullivan wrote it with a formulaic approach that is well-understood by the best newspaper and magazine writers. It's a formula that draws heavily on the *inverted pyramid,* the classic style of American news writing, but one that is adapted to improve readability.

Sullivan also used literary techniques that make the story much more than a mere recitation of facts, as a bare-bones inverted-pyramid story would be. He used a poignant lead to embark on a storytelling technique. Throughout, he made ample use of direct quotes to show the event's impact on ordinary people.

The story was one of several that led the American Society of Newspaper Editors to award Sullivan its top prize for deadline reporting. It shows that the best newspaper writing, though dependent on formulas to some degree, can be compelling to read.

Just as a knowledge of grammar—the structure of language—lets us write and edit sentences better, so a knowledge of news-writing formulas lets us write and edit stories more efficiently.

Talk of formulas inevitably ignites fears that someone is trying to take away the writer's creativity or turn the writer into a hack. That's not our purpose in discussing the most common newspaper-writing formulas in this chapter. We would never suggest that stories should be written like a paint-by-number picture. We simply note that the experience of thousands of journalists over the years has resulted in typical ways of doing things. You don't have to imitate slavishly these typical ways, but you should understand them as a starting point.

For example, if you were assigned to the police beat, after covering several accidents you'd figure out that there are certain things that always need to be in that kind of story. You'd also learn that there is a typical order of importance—deaths ahead of injuries, injuries ahead of damages unless the injuries were slight and the damages large. And you'd learn that there are certain pitfalls that need to be avoided, such as not assigning someone guilt for an accident if that person hasn't yet been convicted of a charge.

That doesn't mean every accident story should be written as a fill-in-the-blank report. Details will vary, and those details could require writing the story in an atypical way. But understanding what typically needs to be there and in what order would help you make sure the most important elements are covered, would help you write or edit more quickly and efficiently, and would help you know the difference between creative variations that grow organically from the material and variations that are merely the result of ignorance or inexperience.

In other words, these formulas, like the standard chord changes in a blues song, can actually free your writing to be more creative in ways that work.

News Leads

No matter what medium they work in, news writers share the idea that there should be a good introduction, or lead, to start each story. They also agree that there are two basic approaches: You should either get to the bottom line or dramatically grab the reader's attention.

Leads that stress summarizing the story and telling the reader the bottom line are called *hard-news leads* because they typically are used for hard-news stories such as crimes, accidents, government meetings, and political and economic news. Another name for them is *straight-news leads*.

Leads that stress attracting the reader's attention by using a dramatic grabber are called *soft-news leads* because they are typically used for soft-news stories such as personality profiles, sports, entertainment and lifestyle features, reviews and columns.

Before we turn to the specific order of elements in a lead, let's first consider how to pick the overall approach, or angle, for a story. This advice applies to both print and broadcast media.

Pick the Best Angle

Sometimes, journalists have trouble writing a lead because they can't figure out what *angle* to take in the story. That is, they're looking for the best overall approach to stress—the best way to focus the story. Once you decide what angle to take, the rest usually comes easily. You can make this decision in several ways.

○ Use the "Hey, did you hear about ... ?" approach, in which you simply ask yourself what you would tell a friend about the event.

What you would say after "Hey, did you hear about ... ?" is the angle to take. Broadcasters strongly recommend this approach, but print journalists use it, too.

○ Focus on basic news values.

This approach is presented in broadcast and print textbooks alike and includes the following news values:

Audience—who your audience is and what news it wants or needs from you.

NEWSPAPER WRITING

Impact—the number of people involved, the number affected or the depth of emotion people will likely feel.

Timeliness—how up-to-the-minute the information is.

Proximity—how nearby the story took place.

Prominence—how rich, famous or powerful the people involved are.

Novelty or oddity—how unusual the news item is.

Conflict or drama—how exciting the news is; the more conflict involved, the more dramatic the news is.

With this method, you ask yourself which of these values is appropriate to the story and lead with it. If there's more than one appropriate value, rank them, then bring them up in the order of their importance.

○ **Stress the angle you think would most affect or interest your audience.**

The strongest angle is always to tell readers, listeners or viewers about something that has a direct effect on them. Look for how this information will have an impact on people and tell them that. For example, will their taxes be raised, will people be laid off, will the price of meat go down or will the streets be safer?

If the story doesn't contain information that directly affects the audience, the next best lead is what would most interest them. Don't bury the most interesting parts where people are less likely to see or hear them. Move them toward the top of the story, where they'll attract more attention.

If a story has neither impact nor interest, you might ask why run it at all. Who cares? Often, however, if the story appears at first to fail these tests, it will pass if you rewrite it to stress people doing things rather than the things themselves. Words about a thing typically contain less built-in interest than words about a person. News is people; it's not an encyclopedia article about gastropods.

Once you've picked an angle, decide whether to write the story as hard news or soft news. Different formulas define the usual order of details, depending on whether the story is hard news or soft news, print or broadcast.

Hard-News Leads

Hard-news leads are found more often in newspapers than in magazines. They get to the bottom line, as people in business say. That is, they tell you in the first sentence the essence of the news. They boil it all down for you. If you read no further—and many readers won't—you'll still have the gist of the story.

It's a myth that the lead needs to tell the reader *who, what, when, where, why* and *how*. A lead with all that information would likely be too long and hard to read. (A lead should be only a sentence or two long, a maximum of 20 to 30 words.)

Most hard-news stories leave out the *why* and *how* because those elements are often more speculative and less objective. Only when *why* or *how* can be discussed objectively are they likely to appear. (Soft-news leads, as you'll see, stress drama more than information and may leave out even some of the basic four—the *who, what, when* and *where.*)

"The Five W's and an H" are worth remembering, however, because the order in which people typically recite them—*who, what, when, where, why* and *how*—is almost always their order of importance in a story. That means it's also the order in which details typically should appear in a lead. For example, the two most important details in a story are usually *who* did *what,* in that order. In some stories, the *what* may come first if it's more important to the particular subject. Next most important are *when* and *where. Why* and *how* come last in "The Five W's and an H" and are almost never found in the lead.

Many journalists prefer to think of the basic formula for the hard-news lead as *who, what, time, day or date,* and *place*—in that order. This corresponds to the well-known *who, what, when, where, why* and *how,* leaving out the *why* and *how* and breaking *when* into *time* and *day or date. Place,* of course, is the same as *where. Time, day or date,* and *place* often come not in the lead itself but in later paragraphs. In some stories, one or more of these three elements may not appear at all if unimportant.

As Bartholomew Sullivan's story at the start of this chapter shows, there's been a tendency over the past 20 years to use soft-news leads on some hard-news stories when a story has special drama. So, again we say: Don't slavishly imitate the following formula. Understand it and appreciate it, but use your discretion—and don't be afraid to try something different when you have a valid reason for doing so.

Here's the formula and how to use it.

Who Was Involved?

Ask yourself whether this person is well-known to your audience. If the person should be well-known to your readers by name, use what's called an *immediate-ID who*—that is, simply begin with the person's name:

> Madonna sang to a full stadium.

If the person should be well-known to readers of your newspaper but still could benefit from identification, place a short title in front of the name or a longer title following it:

> Johnson City Mayor Anne Williams said … .

> Melquiades Martinez, secretary of Housing and Urban Development, said … .

Note that official titles in front of a name are capitalized, but those following a name are not.

If the person isn't well-known to your audience, use what's called a *delayed-ID who*—that is, write down a label for the *who:*

An Ypsilanti man ... .

An area plumber ... .

After you finish the lead sentence using the delayed ID, start the second paragraph with the name of the person represented by the label in the first sentence:

A Petersburg man died in a two-car accident Thursday on U.S. 23.
   Wilbur Jeffers was southbound when ... .

What Happened?

You can describe the *what* in four ways:

1. The *single-element what,* in which only one thing happened or is the focus of the story, so there's no problem figuring out the *what*. The rest of the story will be filled with extra details about what happened:

Slain Israeli Prime Minister Yitzhak Rabin will be remembered today.

2. The *most-important-element what,* in which more than one thing happened but one is more important than the others. This is frequently the case with meeting stories. The rest of the story is filled with details about the main *what,* then a listing of and details about the other *whats:*

Police have arrested a suspect in last month's kidnapping of a Springfield girl.

The story may then update the audience on how the girl is doing a month after the ordeal and provide other information, but the focus in the lead is on the arrest.

3. The *multiple-elements what,* in which more than one thing happened, they're unrelated, and they're all roughly of equal importance. You're going to have to list them all in the lead before you turn to details about any of them. The list can be in the first sentence if it doesn't make the sentence too long and unwieldy. Or you may have to list each *what* in separate sentences. Remember to maintain parallel structure:

The City Council approved Monday night the widening of Main Street but rejected a proposal that would have required city employees to live in town.

In listing the separate elements, try to list them in the order of most impact or interest to your audience:

Iraq imposed a curfew following ... .

4. The *summary what,* in which more than one thing happened, all of equal importance, and they all have enough in common that they can be summarized without having to list all of them separately. You can summarize all the *whats* in one sentence in the lead:

> Most economic indicators rose in the third quarter.

Sometimes, the *what* seems more important than the *who*—as is often the case in a crime story—and the *who* and *what* are reversed:

> First National Bank in downtown Springfield was robbed this morning by two hooded gunmen who got away with more than $200,000 in cash.

If the *what* involves what someone said—such as in the coverage of a speech, meeting or interview—many newspaper writers start with the *what,* then go to the *who:*

> Mesa County needs to spend $1.5 million this year to repair roads and bridges, the public works director told the County Commission at Monday night's meeting.

In beginning with the *what,* however, reporters should avoid a misleading lead that begins with a startling statement that sounds as though it's being presented as a fact, then attributes it in the next paragraph:

> Odofile Guinn is guilty of killing his wife, Judith Dandridge, and her friend Joseph Goldfarb.
>   That's what Prosecuting Attorney Elaine Chu told a jury in Los Angeles today.

Here's another tip for stories in which the *what* summarizes a speech, meeting or interview: *State the summary as a thesis, not a mere topic.* That is, it should make a definite statement, as a headline does, not just be a word or phrase, like the title of a term paper. One of the worst leads for such a story would be one that tells us only that someone spoke without giving us a clue as to what the person said.

> NO TOPIC MENTIONED: A researcher from the University of Kansas spoke Tuesday night to an audience of local health-care providers.

> ONLY A TOPIC: A researcher from the University of Kansas spoke Tuesday night to an audience of local health-care providers about new developments in cancer treatments.

> THESIS: A researcher from the University of Kansas told an audience of local health-care providers Tuesday night that there are many exciting new developments in cancer treatments.

If you have trouble telling a topic from a thesis, here's a hint: *Anytime you've written that somebody discussed something, spoke on something or spoke about something, what follows is probably a topic, not a thesis. If, instead, you force yourself to write that someone said something, it's almost impossible to follow that with a mere topic instead of a thesis.*

NEWSPAPER WRITING

Good reporters follow the dictum that simple forms of attribution are the best. Almost always, that means sticking to *said* or *says*. Failing to do so almost invariably gets reporters in trouble because they seem to lose their objectivity. Here are some words to avoid when attributing information:

- Words that imply the reporter is a mind reader: *believes, feels, thinks*. How do you know the source believes, feels or thinks something unless he or she said so?

- Words that suggest the reporter's opinion: *admitted* or *conceded* (imply the person confessed or made a concession), *claimed* (expresses disbelief), *refuted* (expresses agreement with the person answering another's charges), *alleged* (can sound to a reader like disbelief and to an attorney as if the reporter is making the allegation).

When Did It Happen?

Time might not appear in the lead, but wherever it appears, assuming it does, it should precede *day or date*. Remember to avoid redundancy in expressing the time element in a story. You could write *6 p.m.* or *6 this evening* but not *6 p.m. this evening*.

In some stories, the lead might mention a general time frame, with the specifics coming later in the story. For example, a lead might say a fair will be held *this weekend,* with the exact times further down in the story.

Use the *day of the week* if the *what* will take place (or has taken place) within a week forward (or backward) of the publication date. Use the *date* if the event will take place (or has taken place) further ahead or back than one week. If the event happened exactly a week ago or will happen exactly a week away, you may use the date or a phrase such as *next Wednesday* or *last Thursday.*

Here are some additional guidelines:

○ Never use both the day and the date.

○ For an event happening on the day of publication, you may write *this morning, this afternoon, this evening, today* or *tonight,* as appropriate. But the wire services say never to write *yesterday* or *tomorrow;* they tell you to use the day of the week instead.

○ If the *what* involved what someone said or reported, or what a governing body did, the *when* (either the time or day or date) is often moved up in the sentence immediately following the verb:

> Alan Greenspan, chairman of the Federal Reserve Board, said today ... .
>
> Vice President Richard Cheney said Wednesday ... .
>
> The Board of Curators voted Wednesday ... .

Where Did It Happen?

The *place* may be the name of a street, building, institution, neighborhood, town or other location, as appropriate:

> The campus chapter of Women in Communication will meet at 7 p.m. Monday in Room 120 of the Shichtman Student Union.

Notice that this example uses the order of elements recommended for the lead of a story and that the order is based on what's typically most to least important among these five elements. Because news is people acting and reacting, you should begin with the presumption that the most important element is the *who* followed by the *what*, although on some occasions you may prefer to use the *what* and then the *who. Time, day* or *date,* or *place* is rarely, if ever, the most important element of a story, and therefore none of them should be the first element in a lead.

Some types of hard-news stories often use variations on the formula described here. For example, an obituary should begin with an *immediate-ID lead* even if the deceased was not famous, and the *place,* the deceased's address, is often given only as a town to eliminate the risk of a burglary during the funeral. Likewise, crime stories often begin with the *what* and follow with the *who* because the crime may be more significant than the perpetrator.

Problems With Hard-News Leads

○ Don't make the lead too complicated. Don't load it down with too many names, figures or details. Keep the lead sentence short —never more than 30 words and closer to 15 to 20 if possible.

TOO MANY NAMES: Gus Gish, manager of Springfield's Downtown Development Fund, said today at a Chamber of Commerce luncheon in Fairfield Village that this year's drive will be co-chaired by Carla Zim, Springfield National Bank vice president, and David Roche, Elmdorf Electronics Corp. general manager.

TO THE POINT: The Springfield Downtown Development Fund has named two people to co-chair this year's drive.
   Gus Gish, the fund's manager, said ... .

TOO MANY NUMBERS: The Springfield Board of Education voted 5-4 Tuesday night to place on the November ballot a proposed property tax increase of two mills, or $2 for every $1,000 of assessed valuation, up from the 10 mills property owners currently pay, to help cover the school district's 1996 budget of $13.2 million, which itself is up $350,000 over last year's.

TO THE POINT: Springfield voters will have to consider in November whether to raise their property taxes to pay for schools.
   The Board of Education voted 5-4 Monday night to ... .

NEWSPAPER WRITING

TOO MANY DETAILS: Pete's Brewing—maker of the brown, malty Pete's Wicked Ale—raised about $40 million in its initial public offering Tuesday, as well as an additional $12.5 million for its owners, a total of around 56 times its estimated earnings for next year, as it became the second specialty beer company this year, behind Redhook Ale Brewery of Seattle, to offer its stock to investors.

TO THE POINT: Pete's Brewing has become the second specialty beer company to go public this year.

The maker of Pete's Wicked Ale … .

○ Don't begin with the *time, day or date,* or *place.*

They are less important than the *who* and *what.* Hint: If your lead starts with a prepositional phrase, it's probably starting with *time, day or date,* or *place* and should be rewritten.

WRONG   At 11 a.m. this Thursday, the County Commission will hold a public hearing on allowing fireworks within the county limits.

RIGHT   The County Commission plans to hold a public hearing this week on allowing fireworks within the county limits. The meeting will be at 11 a.m. Thursday.

○ Don't begin with an empty, say-nothing expression or a generality that fails to distinguish this news from other news:

EMPTY

There were … .

In a report released today … .

According to … .

(Someone) spoke … .

(Somebody) held a meeting.

GENERALITY

Voters elected a mayor and six council members Tuesday.

Sen. Paul Hogan spoke to the Booster Club here last night.

The Student Council acted on four of its most pressing problems Tuesday.

○ Don't begin with a question if the question is answered in the story:

What does Ralph Nader have in common with Julia Child?

The question lead is one of many cliché leads seen too often in print and heard too often in broadcast. In the preceding example, it's better just to tell us what the two have in common—that would be startling in itself.

○ Don't begin with a direct quote if it's a full sentence or longer. Such quotes should first appear in the second or third paragraph of most stories.

WRONG   "This is the happiest day of my life," said the man honored as Chelsea's Man of the Year.

RIGHT   A man who rescued a family of four from a burning home was honored Tuesday night as Chelsea's Man of the Year.
           "This is the happiest day of my life," said Fred Winston ... .

Partial quotes in the first sentence are sometimes permissible, especially when a colorful phrase that aptly summarizes the theme can be excerpted from a speech:

Senate candidate Fred Hawkins told a Springfield Auditorium audience last night that "feminazis, compassion fascists and environmental wackos" are on the retreat as more Americans "see them for what they are."

○ Don't use a form of the verb *to be* in the lead, if you can avoid it:

WEAK   The County Commission was unanimous in approving ... .

BETTER   The County Commission unanimously approved ... .

○ Don't overstate the news in the lead, making it more dramatic than it really is:

OVERSTATED   A Springfield woman may have averted a holocaust today when she used her fire extinguisher to put out an inferno in a family's station-wagon engine.
             [The words *holocaust* and *inferno* overstate the situation.]

REALISTIC   A family of four has a Springfield woman to thank for putting out the engine fire in their station wagon this morning. [Thus reduced to reality, we might ask whether this is even worth a news item.]

For your lead, either state the "bottom line"—what it all boils down to—or use a grabber that dramatically attracts the reader's attention. Anything else, such as a long history of the problem, won't work.

Soft-News Leads

Soft-news leads—and increasingly some hard-news leads, as well—introduce the story dramatically.

Soft leads are also sometimes called *delayed leads* or *feature leads.* They take a storyteller's approach by setting the scene, describing a person, starting with dialogue or relating an anecdote before telling the main point straight out. Notice also that in soft-news leads, it is acceptable to use an immediate-ID lead even though the *who* may not be well-known.

> The young man in the Coast Guard uniform slumped forward.
>
> His forehead hit the microphone in front of him, sending an amplified "thunk" ringing through the still air of the hearing room. His slim body was racked with sobs as he buried his face in his hands.
>
> Patrick Lucas, 23, was reliving the night his ship sank and 23 of his friends died.

The Wall Street Journal has some of the best soft leads around in the far-left column of its front page each day. (Check the middle and far-right columns, also.) The Journal is excellent at taking abstract subjects such as the economy and personalizing them—showing how they actually affect people.

The Wall Street Journal formula begins with a person who is affected by the topic under discussion. The lead shows how the topic affects that person. Then, a *nut graf* makes a general statement—perhaps about the extent of the problem—that broadens the story's impact to others. The Journal presents facts, figures and analysis about the topic in general, then returns in the end to the person with whom it started.

Take a look at a few of The Wall Street Journal's front-page pieces for examples. Notice this construction, and see how effectively it enlivens what could have been a dull abstraction.

Soft-News Clichés

Don't confuse story types with clichés. Many stories fit into a recognized genre, but that doesn't mean all stories of a given kind should have the same cliché lead.

Cliché leads usually begin as someone doing something creative—someone taking a clever, soft-news-lead approach to a story. The problem arises when other reporters steal the idea and repeat it often and automatically. After you've heard it a few times, it's no longer clever—just annoying.

Here are some examples of the most common, most annoying leads.

○ **Avoid the one-word lead, especially when followed by an exclamation point:**

> Tired. That's how John Smith felt after winning his first marathon at the age of 56.

> Sex! Now that I have your attention, let's talk about birth control.

○ **Avoid the question lead:**

What is freedom? To Gunther Kling of what used to be East Germany, it means seeing his family again.

What do Bean Blossom, Ind., and Bill Monroe, the father of bluegrass music, have in common?

What would an extraterrestrial visitor or archaeologist from the future make of a television set? He'd probably think it was some sort of household god we worshipped.

Notice that in each of these examples, the question lead is phony — the reporter is merely rhetorically asking a question he or she intends to answer. The one place a question lead isn't phony and clichéd is when the question isn't answered in the story — that is, when the news is that there's an unanswered question:

What happened to the night clerk at Fred's QuikMart on Friday? That's what police investigators are asking this morning.

When the early-morning-shift clerk arrived, night clerk Terry Schmidt, 22, was missing, along with all the money from the safe. Police are uncertain whether this is an inside job or a case of robbery and abduction.

In short, don't lead with a question that's answered in the story.

○ Avoid the dictionary lead:

Webster's Dictionary defines freedom as ... . But to Denny Davison, freedom means ... .

○ Avoid the "good and bad" lead:

First the good news, then the bad.

○ Avoid the lead that labels what kind of story this is or isn't:

This is not another story about street people.

This is a story about people who have survived.

○ Avoid the "something came early" lead:

Christmas came early for the Philip Peters family of Lawrence.

Thanksgiving came early for Diego Ramirez this week.

○ Avoid the "you might think" lead:

You might think to look at the Victorian-style house that it's someone's comfortable home, perhaps filled with antiques. But you'd be wrong. The house actually is home to one of the city's high-tech software firms.

○ Avoid the "one thing's different" lead:

Like most kids his age, Billy Small goes to school, likes baseball and enjoys ice-cream cones. But one thing about him is different: He's a quadriplegic.

O   Avoid the "what a difference" lead:

What a difference a day makes. Yesterday, the Red Sox were in first place. Now, with a loss to the Angels, they've fallen to second behind the Yankees in the American League East.

O   Avoid the "rain couldn't dampen" lead:

Rain couldn't dampen the spirits of a capacity crowd at Comerica Park Saturday as Detroit won its season opener against Oakland 5-3.

O   Avoid the "all in the family" lead:

To Brian and Betsy Feintab and their three children, flying is all in the family. Each of them has a pilot's license.

O   Avoid the recipe lead:

Take one dash of love, sprinkle in a dash of excitement, and mix with a lifetime of commitment. That's the recipe for a 50-year marriage, say Ted and Ethel Peck, who celebrated their 50th anniversary today.

O   Avoid the "official" lead:

It's official: The Michigan Wolverines are the No. 1-rated football team in the nation, according to the latest Associated Press sports-writers poll.

O   Avoid the "funny thing" lead:

A funny thing happened to Al Gore on his way to the presidency.

O   Avoid the "not just for ... anymore" lead:

Country music isn't just for country folk anymore. It's become the fastest-growing segment of the recording industry.

O   Avoid the "little did she know" lead:

When Betty Smith walked up to the ATM machine at Seventh and Main to take out money for lunch, little did she know that a man waiting nearby in his car would force her at gunpoint to withdraw all her money and give it to him.

O   Avoid the truism lead.

Everybody has to eat.

○ Avoid the Snoopy lead:

> It was a dark and stormy night.

○ And one final chestnut we'd like to roast:

> Yes, Virginia, there is a Santa Claus.

What Comes After the Lead?

NEWSPAPER WRITING

In print, hard news is often written in the inverted-pyramid form, which means the main idea is told in the first sentence or two, then additional details are added in descending order of importance. The advantage of this style to readers is that if pressed for time, they can read only the headline and lead and still get the main information.

The advantage of this style to reporters and editors is that it gives them a mutual understanding of what should be cut from a story first when it's too long to fit. Because the reporter puts the information he or she thinks is most important at the top, editors can make quick cuts on deadline by chopping from the end without fear of "butchering" the story.

○ **Any detail that would be of particular interest to the audience should be moved toward the top of a story if it's not there already.**

The main mistake reporters make with story structure is simply not putting the items in the best possible order. For example, if a plane crashed and among the passengers was a local family, that detail should be part of the lead, not buried further down.

To take another example, a wire-service story about a man who one day went to a restaurant and shot 21 people included a detail near the bottom that should have been moved up. The man's wife told police her husband had called a local suicide hot line that morning but had been told to call back later. Because of funding cuts, there were not enough people on duty to answer all the lines.

That tragic irony (two words that shouldn't be used in an objective news account, by the way) deserved to be near the top of the newspaper version of the story—although, as we'll see in Chapter 15, it could have made a terrific ending for a broadcast version of the story.

○ **Paraphrases must be clearly attributed:**

> Perez says more than a third of American homes have a computer. But someone needs to worry about those too poor to join the information revolution.

NEWSPAPER WRITING

The second sentence in this example sounds like a gratuitous opinion offered by the reporter. Always make sure paraphrases are attributed to someone so the reader doesn't think you are editorializing.

By contrast, if a reporter quotes someone in the previous sentence, it's often clear that the same person is being quoted in this one, even without the attribution:

> "We don't see any compelling reason to change our product line this year," Kurlak said. "Our current models are exceeding our expectations."

⚪ **Use clear transitions to connect your points.**

Don't be afraid to start a sentence with *but* to show contrast. *And* can also be useful at the start of a sentence to introduce something additional. *Meanwhile,* though, is objectionable to many editors who think it's overused. Also, watch out for transitions like *as a matter of fact* and *undoubtedly,* which violate journalistic objectivity.

Features, commentaries, analysis pieces and other soft-news stories are not written in inverted-pyramid form. Soft-news stories don't follow the order of most to least important. Instead, they simply try to attract attention in the lead; supply details, analysis or opinion in the middle; and end with a memorable conclusion. For that reason, editors should never shorten a soft-news story by cutting from the end, as they would with a hard-news story.

Web Resources

JOURNALISM REVIEWS

The best-known national reviews that cover and critique the practice of American journalism are the Columbia Journalism Review and American Journalism Review. The Quill, magazine of the Society of Professional Journalists, does similar work, as does The American Editor, a publication of the American Society of Newspaper Editors.

⚪ **The American Editor**
www.asne.org/kiosk/editor/tae.htm

⚪ **American Journalism Review**
ajr.org

⚪ **Columbia Journalism Review**
www.cjr.org

⚪ **The Quill**
spj.org/quill

CHAPTER 15

Writing News for Broadcast

Print journalism and broadcast journalism don't always organize sentences and stories alike. We speak differently with friends than with teachers, bosses or parents, and we write differently for a newspaper or magazine than for radio or television. Whether we're speaking with different people or writing for different media, we use the same language but different dialects.

Some of the differences among print and broadcast media are apparent. Newspapers and magazines stress the written word but may contain illustrations and still photographs. Radio stresses the spoken word and has no pictures at all other than the mental ones it stimulates through sound portraits. Television stresses moving pictures and the sound of the spoken word.

Less obvious to casual readers, listeners and watchers is that different media require different wordings of news stories. A sentence that reads well in a newspaper or magazine might be hard to understand when read aloud on the radio. Likewise, something that might be conversational on radio or television could look wordy in print.

Print journalism students who have received news most of their lives mainly through television and radio often have to learn to adjust to the different wording of print. Broadcast students, meanwhile, have to learn how to write for the ear and not for the page, which can go against the more formal, less conversational style they have learned while writing term papers in school.

Sometimes, students take classes in both print and broadcast and get confused by differing advice they hear in their classes, not realizing that the discrepancies may stem from differences in the natures of the media. Underneath it all, print and broadcast news writing have much in common, but they also have their differences.

Some journalism students choose to learn about writing for other media as a way to expand their job opportunities. Some journalists do it in search of tips from a related field that they may be able to apply to what they're already doing. In the future, more of us may have to learn skills outside our own fields as technology changes.

Already, many newspapers are experimenting with dial-in voice updates of stories in the paper, as well as online editions on the Internet. Many futurists, such as George Gilder and Nicholas Negroponte, are predicting that print and electronic media will increasingly "go digital" and merge into new multimedia such as we see now on the World Wide Web and CD-ROMs, which can carry full text, audio, and still and moving pictures. With such changes, it will be helpful to know why different media require different writing styles. By comparing broadcast news writing with that of newspapers, we may better understand our own chosen medium.

Print vs. Broadcast News

Print news is written for the eye and is typically longer, whereas broadcast news is written for the ear and is typically shorter. But when you pop the hoods, you find that the two vehicles for news have more in common than they have differences. That shouldn't come as too big a surprise, given that broadcast news writing was pioneered by print journalists who moved to radio and television as new opportunities arose.

Broadcast writing requires knowledge of fewer style rules and editing symbols than does print, so people who are considering careers in both should hold themselves to meeting the greater demands of the print media in these areas. But that doesn't mean writing for broadcast isn't as demanding. It can be just as—or even more—demanding of a journalist's knowledge and skills.

For example, broadcast journalists need to pay more attention to how words sound. They must be even more concise and more conversational in their writing. They also need to know in what order the details should be presented to be understood best by someone listening—someone who doesn't have the luxury of being able to look back to the previous sentence or paragraph if something important slipped by unheard. Of course, the time constraints of broadcast news, as well as the frequent need to match words with audio and video, place additional demands on broadcast writers.

It would be a good idea for students studying print journalism to take a class or two in broadcast and perhaps even volunteer to write news at the campus radio station. This not only gives you an opportunity to hear additional journalists' viewpoints and get more practice in writing, but it also can help you write more conversationally, focus your angle on people, tighten your writing and, when necessary, cut stories quickly while keeping them focused on the main points.

Here are some of the major differences between writing for print and writing for broadcast.

Use a Conversational Style

Broadcast news must be written for the ear. When it's read over the air, it should sound conversational, not stilted. Keep the sentences short — around an average of 15 words, rarely more than 25. Keep the sentence structure as simple as possible, and use active-voice verbs whenever you can. Read your copy aloud (or at least faintly mumbling to yourself) to make sure it doesn't sound awkward or artificial.

Broadcast news should sound informal, not stuffy. The following suggestions are especially useful in broadcast, although there is nothing wrong with using most of them in print, too — except in the most formal situations.

○ Try to keep sentences only one thought long. It's usually better not to tack on additional thoughts:

> NOT CONVERSATIONAL: A local student, Latisha Green, who is one of only 10 selected nationally, will get to shake hands with the president today.

> CONVERSATIONAL: A local student will get to shake hands with the president today. Latisha Green is one of only 10 students selected nationally.

○ Avoid vocabulary or wording that people don't usually use in conversation:

> PRINT WORDING: The three youths ... .
> [Does anyone actually say *youths?* Wouldn't somebody instead say *teen-agers* or something similar?]

> PRINT WORDING: Judith Cushing, 33, said ... .
> [Again, no one would say it that way. That's just the way newspaper reporters write. People would say something more like *Judith Cushing is 33.* But ages are seldom used in broadcast news, anyway, except in describing children.]

> NOT CONVERSATIONAL: One should use caution today when driving on Interstate 94 near downtown.

> CONVERSATIONAL: Drivers should use caution today when driving on I-94 near downtown.

> CONVERSATIONAL: You should use caution today when driving on I-94 near downtown.

○ Use contractions — that's how people talk.

> TOO FORMAL: The president says he cannot attend.

> BROADCAST STYLE: The president says he can't attend.

BROADCAST WRITING

○ It's OK to start a sentence with *And* or *But:*

> And that was just in the first game.

> But economists are saying next year could be worse.

○ It's OK to use dashes for dramatic pauses:

> CNN reports that since the verdict, ratings have dropped 80 percent —from a rating of 3.5 down to 0.7.

Personalize the News

Broadcasters' voices and faces are familiar to their audience, and part of their success or failure can be attributed to how the audience relates to them personally. By contrast, print journalists usually establish far less personal rapport unless they're columnists or highly skilled feature writers or sportswriters.

As a result, a broadcast audience may put pressure on the newscaster to be personally likable. This can result in more emphasis on personality in reporting, which can lead to a subtle blurring between news and commentary.

For instance, look under the previous rule at the examples suggesting that drivers should use caution on a particular highway. Those sentences aren't really objective because they are personal expressions offering advice. By contrast, here's a more objective statement, one that might follow such sentences in a broadcast story:

> Road work has reduced traffic to one lane in both directions.
> [No value judgment or advice is offered.]

But broadcast news generally allows more leeway for expressing personal judgments—especially ones that would get little disagreement, such as suggesting that drivers use caution. And such statements have increasingly found their way into print news, as well.

Strictly speaking, even value judgments and advice that few would disagree with are still nonobjective statements, and the best journalism— broadcast or print—strives to avoid them. (See also Chapter 11.)

Make It Easy to Understand

Broadcast news has to be written in an order that lets the audience catch the news in one hearing. We'll go into more detail later in this chapter about the order of information in a broadcast lead, but here are four general suggestions to help you write news for the listener's ear.

○ Get to the main point at the start of the sentence, not at the end.

Don't begin with a dependent clause, prepositional phrase or participial phrase that introduces details before we know the subject:

CONFUSING WHEN HEARD: Because of reports from the National Weather Service that a thunderstorm is on the way, you may want to take an umbrella along if you're going to the White Sox game.
[The dependent clause at the beginning makes this sentence difficult for a listener to follow.]

CLEARER WHEN HEARD: You may want to take an umbrella along if you're going to the White Sox game. The National Weather Service reports a thunderstorm on the way.

CONFUSING WHEN HEARD: In Ohio this weekend for a national meeting of law-enforcement officials, Sheriff Everette Watson is being honored by his peers.
[The extended prepositional phrase requires the listener to remember details before he or she knows what's being discussed.]

CLEARER WHEN HEARD: Sheriff Everette Watson is being honored by fellow law-enforcement officials this weekend at a national meeting in Ohio.

Avoiding such details before the subject of the sentence is introduced also fixes the problem of lack of attribution that sometimes creeps in when writers begin with a participial phrase:

NO ATTRIBUTION: Believing that Gov. Sam Wilson is vulnerable because of his abortion-rights stand, a second candidate has announced she'll run in the Republican primary.
[The reporter is not a mind reader, presumably, but the sentence never attributes how it is known what the candidate believes. Similar words that evade attribution are *thinking* and *feeling*.]

SUBJECT FIRST AND STATEMENT ATTRIBUTED: A second candidate has announced for the Republican primary. Jill Xavier says she thinks most voters disagree with Gov. Sam Wilson's abortion-rights stand.
[Notice that this wording also lets the reporter more easily expand on what before had been the dependent clause.]

● Start with a general statement to attract the audience's attention, putting listeners on alert for what's to come:

Area motorists are having trouble getting home tonight. Chicago police are reporting 33 fender benders already as that blizzard reduces visibility and makes roadways slick.

Most newspaper editors would cut the first sentence of a lead like that (even if a newspaper could report events as they were happening). In print, that sentence seems to be a delay and, perhaps even more, a comment rather than an objective observation. For most print journalists, the second sentence contains the real lead.

● Repeat key information for someone who has just tuned in or who may have caught part of a longer story but missed an essential element.

Especially in a longer or particularly important story, the broadcaster may repeat the name of the *who* involved, the *what* that happened (such as a key sports score) or the *place* where the event occurred.

○ **Rewrite phrases containing a word that has a *homonym* (a word that sounds like another word) that a listener could reasonably confuse with the intended word:**

>   *comity* of nations   [Or was it *comedy* of nations?]
>
>   steel *magnate*   [or was it steel *magnet?*]

Keep It Short

Both print and broadcast media stress tight, concise writing, although broadcast leads are often more general than print leads.

Newspaper and broadcast paragraphs and sentences are shorter than those in magazines and books, with those in broadcast being even a little shorter than those in newspapers, especially the sentences.

Newspaper and broadcast stories also tend to be shorter than those in magazines, with broadcast stories averaging the shortest. Most broadcast stories are told in 20 to 30 seconds. Rarely does a broadcast story go more than two minutes except on noncommercial public radio or commercial all-news stations.

Keep It Timely

News delivered electronically can be more up-to-the-minute than news that's been set in print and delivered by carriers. As a result, broadcasters use different conventions of news writing than do print journalists when it comes to time elements.

○ **Broadcast journalists write even hard-news stories in the present tense.**

Broadcast journalists tend to write about news happening this day, this hour, even this minute. Print news, especially in this age of morning-newspaper dominance, is often a day old.

○ **Broadcasters also are less likely to report news of events happening days or weeks away than newspapers are.**

All this means that getting verb tenses and time elements straight tends to be easier in broadcast than in print.

Make It Clear

Broadcast news uses fewer style rules and editing marks than print news. Many of the entries in the wire-service stylebooks are devoted to getting things right that could appear wrong when a reader looks at them. Broadcast style involves making things *look* clear to the newscaster, who must then make them *sound* clear to the listeners. Somehow, that translates into a thinner broadcast stylebook.

Students taking classes in both print and broadcast should note that in some cases, the style rules differ between the two fields. See the appendix and Page 327 for summaries of the most common rules for each.

Do Broadcasters Have to Know Grammar?

Yes. Don't let the fact that broadcast news is more conversational than print news fool you into thinking that all the rules of grammar can be ignored or thrown out the window.

Broadcasting textbooks advise students, for example, that if they want to improve their writing for radio and television, they should watch their usage and check their subject-verb agreement and pronoun-antecedent agreement. Broadcasters demand that the news be written in clear, simple sentences that avoid dependent clauses, and that adjectives and adverbs be cut as much as possible. How could anybody follow such advice if they didn't know enough grammar to know what was being asked of them?

Broadcast journalists, like print journalists, often bemoan the lack of grammar skills among young graduates looking for work. One of the best books we've seen on improving broadcast news copy is "Rewriting Network News" by Mervin Block, a former staff writer for the ABC and CBS evening news shows. His book looks at examples from 345 television and radio news scripts and demonstrates how they could be improved by closer attention to grammar, usage, tightening and order of details. The lessons are useful for print journalists, as well.

Good writing means knowing how to put the best words in the best order, and that's what grammar and usage are all about.

Broadcast Hard-News Leads

Broadcast hard-news leads typically present the same five main elements in the same order as do print leads, but the wording of these elements often differs. As with a newspaper lead, the first two items, *who* and *what*, are the most essential. *Time, date* and *place* may appear later or even occasionally not at all, depending on the nature of the story.

Start With the *Who*

- If there's any identification or title with the name, put the ID or title before the name:

> **PRINT STYLE:** Dennis Archer, former mayor of Detroit, will speak to the Legion of Black Collegians … .
>
> **BROADCAST STYLE:** Former Detroit Mayor Dennis Archer will speak to the Legion of Black Collegians … .

Although some print reporters would also write that sentence in the broadcast style, the second example would be clearly preferred in broadcast. Many print journalists would insist on the first wording, saying that the word *former* is confusingly placed in the second, seeming to imply *former Dennis Archer* as well as *former mayor.*

○ **Always put the attribution at the beginning of the sentence and before the verb:**

> **PRINT STYLE:** Home sales rose in September to the highest level since January 1998, according to a report Wednesday from the National Association of Realtors.
>
> **BROADCAST STYLE:** The National Association of Realtors reports home sales rose in September. They were up to the highest level since January 1998.

○ **If the *who* involves a number of people, don't start the lead with the number because the reader has not yet heard what subject the number modifies.**

For example, a newspaper lead might read like this:

> **PRINT STYLE:** Five people died and 15 more were injured when an Amtrak train left the tracks near St. Louis this morning.

That lead conforms to the injunction in newspaper journalism that you should lead with what's most important—in this case, that five people died and 15 were injured, not that a train had left the tracks. But broadcasters would typically write something like this:

> **BROADCAST STYLE:** An Amtrak train left the tracks near St. Louis this morning. Five people were killed, and another 15 were hurt.

What Happened?

○ **Use the present tense or present progressive as much as possible, as opposed to the past tense or present-perfect tense used in newspaper and magazine hard-news stories:**

> **PRINT STYLE:** The Republicans *have called* for Medicare cuts.
>
> **BROADCAST STYLE:** The Republicans *are calling* for Medicare cuts.

In this regard, broadcast news is like a print soft-news story. This also stresses an advantage broadcast news has over print news: Broadcast can be more timely and up-to-the-minute.

When attributing quotes, don't write someone *said* but someone *says:*

PRINT STYLE: Columbia Mayor Darwin Hindman said … .

BROADCAST STYLE: Columbia Mayor Darwin Hindman says … .

○ If the past tense must be used in the lead, include the time element after it:

Speaker of the House Dennis Hastert said last night … .

○ Don't forget to put a verb in the lead, as in any other sentence.

Some news directors won't allow any fragments in news copy at their stations. Some permit an occasional fragment if it sounds conversational, but most object to fragments being overused.

For example, some broadcasters have overreacted to the common advice that they should avoid the verb *to be* in leads whenever possible and end up with nongrammatical leads like this:

A consortium selling the St. Louis Cardinals.

Without the *is* in front of selling, that sentence has just a participle, not a verb. Try this instead:

A consortium says it wants to sell the St. Louis Cardinals.

Granted, some broadcasters occasionally leave out the verb *to be* for some punch:

Another victory in progress at Fenway Park.

But couldn't that fragment have just as much punch if it were recast into a sentence?

It looks as if the Red Sox can chalk up another victory.

Other Points to Remember

○ Don't say *today* if you can avoid it.

Stress timeliness, and give the story the most up-to-the-minute news peg you can. Say *this morning, this afternoon* or *this evening.*

○ If the news comes from a previous day, it's probably not news in broadcast. An upcoming event more than a week off would probably not be in today's broadcast.

Most references to other days are likely to be within the upcoming week and will simply be referred to as *Thursday, Saturday* and so on. An event further off would most likely be referred to as *next week, in three weeks, next month* and so on.

○   Street addresses of people or businesses in the news are not used in broadcast in the routine way they are in print.

In broadcast, a person's address would typically be given only as the name of a city. A business address would typically be given only when a news event was taking place there and people might want to know how to get there.

Broadcast Story Structure

Broadcast news is typically written to an assigned length of time, often 20 to 30 seconds. This means the journalist writes the average number of words that could be read in the time allotted.

After the lead come the most important and interesting details—as many as will fit conversationally in the time slot. Broadcast stories are like feature stories in print because they need not only a strong beginning but also a strong ending. In broadcast, the last sentence is called the *snapper*, and, as the name implies, it must have some snap to it.

The snapper may be the punch line for a humorous story, a simple re-statement of the main point, a statement putting the story in context or telling the audience what it means, a line quoting a different side of a dis-pute or a subject stating "no comment" in a controversial story. The one requirement is that the snapper give the listener a definite sense of closure—that it sound like an ending. Consider these types of snappers:

1. Punch-line snapper:

    Next time, she said, she'll take the bus.

2. Restatement snapper:

    Once again, Secretary of State Colin Powell says he won't run for president in 2008.

3. "What it means" snapper:

    That would mean property taxes on an average $120,000 home would go up $120 a year.

4. "Other side" snapper:

    Pettit says he'll appeal.

5. "No comment" snapper:

    We asked the commissioner to respond to the allegations, but he said, "No comment."

Some snappers have been done so often, they're as stale as the cliché leads we discussed in Chapter 14. Here are a few canned snappers we'd like to see tossed:

1. The "one thing's certain" ending:

   The election results are a week away, but one thing's certain: The winner will be left-handed.

2. The "only time will tell" ending:

   So will it be global warming or global cooling? Only time will tell.

3. The "riding the elephant" ending:

   At the zoo, this is Bill Gahan for Eyewitness News.
   [The camera pulls back to reveal the reporter is riding an elephant.]

The late Charles Kuralt, famous for his "On the Road" series, once said this last ending was one of the biggest clichés he noticed in local TV news as he traveled the country. That was years ago, but it's still the case that reporters too often think it is clever for the final shot of a feature story to show them good-naturedly participating in an event they are covering, especially if it shows them doing something ridiculous.

Broadcast Style Summary

Preparing Your Manuscript for Radio

- Most stations want you to triple-space your news copy.
- In the upper-left corner, type the story's slug on the first line, the time of the broadcast on the second, the date of the broadcast on the third and the reporter's name on the fourth. Also at the top, or at the bottom at some stations, you should put a colon followed by the time in seconds it takes to read the story, then circle the time.
- The story should start 2 to 3 inches from the top of the page and stop at least an inch or two from the bottom. If the story is longer than that, put the word *MORE* in parentheses at the bottom center of the page. At the top of the next page, as the last line of the heading, type *FIRST ADD, SECOND ADD* and so on. Type *ENDS* at the bottom of the last page of a story.
- The copy should be set 70 characters a line. For the purpose of timing, figure that the newscaster will read aloud about 15 lines a minute on average.
- Don't split words at the end of a line. Instead, move the word to the next line. Also, don't split sentences across pages. If a sentence won't fit on one page, move it to the next.

Preparing Your Manuscript for Television

- Triple-space the copy.
- Across the top, on one line, write the time of the broadcast, the date, the story slug and the reporter's name.

- Set the copy at 40 characters a line on the right side of the page. It should take the newscaster a minute to read about 25 lines.

- Beside the news copy to the left, type in all caps a description of the video and audio, the timed length and any instructions, such as whether the sound should be turned off or a title superimposed.

- If the story goes more than one page, type *MORE* in parentheses at the bottom center of the page. At the top of the next page, under the slug, type *FIRST ADD, SECOND ADD* and so on. Type *ENDS* at the bottom of the last page of a story.

- Don't split words at the end of a line. If a word won't fit, move the whole word to the next line. Likewise, don't end a page in the middle of a sentence. Move the whole sentence to the next page.

Editing and Other Symbols

○ For the most part, broadcasters don't use the traditional copy-editing symbols used in the print media.

Instead, they simply mark a line through an error and write the correction above it. If a passage has several errors close together, it's better to cross out and rewrite that whole section of mistakes rather than make the reader's eyes go up and down between errors.

○ Some of the few copy-editing symbols that have carried over from print to broadcast are those for deleting and inserting, closing spaces, and separating and connecting paragraphs.

○ Broadcasters don't use the ¢ symbol for *cents,* $ for *dollars* or % for *percent.* They write out the word after the number and use a hyphen between them:

> 3-cents
>
> 25-dollars
>
> 13-percent

Pronunciation

○ Write the pronunciation of any difficult names phonetically in parentheses after the name. This is to help the newscaster avoid sounding like a fool:

> Dmitri Shostakovich (duh-ME-tree shaw-stuh-KO-vich)

○ To make words easier to pronounce, many news writers add hyphens to words that don't have them in the dictionary:

> hydro-electric
>
> wood-stove

○ To indicate that a word should be stressed in a sentence, either underline it or write it in all caps:

What do you think about that?

Despite the rain, the parade WILL go on.

Abbreviations

○ Generally speaking, writers avoid abbreviations in broadcast copy.

That includes no abbreviations for states, days of the week, months, military titles or countries other than the United States.

○ Some abbreviations are acceptable:

C-I-A, F-B-I, F-C-C, G-O-P, I-B-M, N-C-double-A, N-double-A-C-P, U-N, U-S
[Note the use of hyphens.]

a.m., p.m.

Dr., Mr., Mrs., Ms.

○ When abbreviations form acronyms pronounced as one word, no hyphens or periods are used:

NATO

○ Interstate highways are almost always called by their abbreviated form in broadcast, even on first reference:

I-94

Numbers

As is generally the case with newspaper style, write out single-digit numbers, as well as *eleven,* which sometimes poses problems when written as *11.* The numbers *10* and *12 through 999* should be written as numerals. For larger numbers, use a numeral up to three digits long followed by a hyphen and the word *thousand, million, billion* or *trillion:*

6-thousand

160-billion

○ Write sports scores and stock index numbers as numerals even if they are in single digits:

score of 6 to 4

Dow Jones index up 2 points

- Write out fractions in words:

  one-half

  two-and-three-eighths

- Write out decimal numbers in words:

  twenty-point-six

  one-point-five-trillion

- Break street addresses and years into pronounceable units of numerals:

  13-0-1 East William Street

  the year 20-02

- Add *nd, rd, st* or *th* to the end of numerals whenever the number would be pronounced that way:

  July 20th

  14th Amendment

Punctuation

The only punctuation marks broadcasters typically use are the comma, hyphen, dash, period and question mark.

- Broadcasters use a dash in place of parentheses, a colon or a semicolon.
- Because broadcast copy is written to be performed, it often makes sense to put in dashes or ellipses for longer, dramatic pauses.

  At stores like this one, you can buy anything from special hiking shoes ... to backpacks ... to canoes. But most sales are of items like sleeping bags and down jackets—items that are practical even for those who only faintly hear the call of the wild.

- Most broadcasters don't use quotation marks in their copy because it's awkward to convey where a quote begins and ends.

Saying "quote" at the beginning and "unquote" at the end of a quotation sounds too awkward and formal, although some broadcasters will say "quote" without the "unquote" or use a phrase such as "to quote the mayor." It's better to paraphrase a quote to avoid the problem or, when the exact words are required, to write something like "what he termed," "as he put it" or "in his words" to alert the newscaster that it's a quote.

- Use a hyphen between a numeral and the word *cent* or *cents,* *dollar* or *dollars, percent, thousand, million, billion* or *trillion:*

    20-dollars

    3-percent

    105-thousand

    6-million

Names

- Unlike in print style, it's not always necessary to give famous names in their entirety on first reference:

    President Bush

    Gov. Engler

- Unlike in newspapers, middle initials should be used only to distinguish someone with a name similar to another's, and a nickname should be used only with the last name, not following the first name:

    George W. Bush [to distinguish from his father]

Spelling

Why worry about spelling when your audience will never know whether the words they hear read were spelled the way the dictionary says? Because misspelled words may cause the newscaster to stumble, pause or mispronounce the word. Even if the spellings are vaguely recognizable, they will lower the respect your colleagues in the newsroom have for you.

Web Resources

BROADCASTING

The Professional association for broadcast journalists is the National Association of Broadcasters. Another leading industry group is the Radio and Television News Directors Association.

- National Association of Broadcasters
  www.nab.org

- Radio and Television News Directors Association
  www.rtnda.org

CHAPTER 16

Writing for the Online Media

The traditional news media—newspapers, magazines, radio and television—once dominated information dissemination in the world. They still do, but a new medium, the Internet, is making significant inroads. Millions of Americans and others across the globe now get news and information from the Internet's user-friendly World Wide Web.

That's particularly true when a major story breaks. When terrorists flew airplanes into New York's World Trade Center and Washington's Pentagon on Sept. 11, 2001, the world's attention focused on two nontraditional means of getting information, cellular telephones and the Web. Flight attendants and passengers aboard the doomed airliners provided critical information to the outside world through their mobile phones. And in the confusion that followed, the Web became a significant source of information for family members searching for missing loved ones or other information not readily available on the mainstream media. Thousands of New Yorkers became reporters and supplied information that was not available elsewhere to the rest of the world.

Increasingly, experts recognize that the Web has a combination of advantages the traditional media do not:

- Distribution is instantaneous, as it is with radio and television but not with newspapers and magazines.

- Information is often thorough and detailed, as in newspapers and magazines but not radio and television.

- Users not only can partake of what editors offer but also can sift through original information themselves.

- The presentation of information is nonlinear. That is, users don't have to read a story from top to bottom or start to finish. They can jump around to bits and pieces of the story or related material as desired.

Thus, the Web combines the near-instantaneous dissemination characteristics of the broadcast media with the thoroughness of the print media. It even adds a new dimension by making original source information available. There are, however, a couple of significant problems with this new medium:

- No one is quite sure how best to write for it.
- In a medium in which anyone can become a publisher, there are significant concerns about how to evaluate the reliability of the information being offered.

Let's examine this new medium, and its online cousin, the public information utilities such as America Online and Prodigy, in more detail. Only then can we begin to understand the prevailing thinking about how to write for it.

Online Media Are Unique

When radio and television came along, the first newscasters simply read news over the air just as it was written for newspapers. That often was the medium from which they came, and they understood the art of crafting a news story for print.

It soon became obvious, however, that the writing formula had to change for radio, and even more for television. The way we speak is not the way we write, and broadcast journalism had to make those adjustments. For the most part, they weren't dramatic differences but subtle ones. The tone had to be more conversational, and tough-to-pronounce phrases had to become more casual. When television arrived, the words and pictures had to be melded to tell a story. But through it all, the basics of good journalism remained: Be correct. Be concise. Be consistent. Be complete.

Just as the arrival of radio and television required journalists to rethink the way news was presented, so, too, has the arrival of the online media. Consider these realities, placed in the context of the four basics:

1. *Correctness* results in credibility for the information provider, and in the online media credibility is one of the keys to success. There's an old axiom in journalism that's as true today as ever: "First, get it right." It's easy on the Web to find confirming or contradictory sources of information, and if one source is consistently wrong, or even often wrong, its credibility wanes. Credibility is one of the things that keeps people coming back for more. Ironically, although people responding to opinion polls give the media in general low marks for credibility, they almost always give high marks to their own newspapers or television stations. Little research has yet been done on what makes a Web site credible.
2. *Conciseness,* as in broadcast news, is a virtue. That's because hooking a consumer on an item presented must be accomplished in one computer screen of information. Links beyond that page provide volumes

of depth, or what those who write for the Web call *layering*. But if the reader isn't hooked on Page 1, he or she will never get to the rest of the story, no matter how good it may be.

3. *Consistency* takes on a new meaning in the online media. To be sure, consistency within a story and from story to story is just as important here as in the traditional media. But equally important is consistency of presentation—or consistency from story to story in what the consumer should expect. Equate that to consistency in navigating the site.

4. *Completeness* also takes on a new meaning. In being complete, the new media can blow away the traditional media. Deep links to related information can provide context and background that not even The New York Times has the space to provide. The Internet, with its virtually unlimited capacity, has a real strength here.

Let's examine each of these issues in more detail.

Correctness and Credibility

The traditional media like to think they offer an accurate, or correct, accounting of the day's news and therefore have credibility with the public. As noted earlier, polls show otherwise. The credibility of journalists in such polls usually compares to that of used-car salespeople and is only slightly above that of politicians.

That's disturbing because one thing the traditional media should have is credibility. Recently, the traditional media have learned that the public often considers their information no more reliable than that provided by a dedicated-topic junkie on the Internet. Sometimes, that's true; sometimes, it isn't. Yet building credibility as a reliable information source would seem to be more important than ever.

Ironically, despite the public's apparent confidence in the Internet's content, the Internet is full of false information or information provided by people with a cause to promote. Sorting fact from opinion can be difficult. If the source is a respected organization such as The New York Times or The Washington Post, most journalists, at least, would consider the information to be trustworthy. But if it is an organization promoting a cause, there is ample reason to be wary. Whether the average consumer recognizes the difference is a topic of much debate.

In 1998, for example, Pierre Salinger, a respected news veteran and former press secretary to President John F. Kennedy, was ridiculed when he publicly proclaimed that a document blaming the U.S. government for shooting down a TWA jetliner was written by the French intelligence service. The document, found on the Web, was a fake.

Online journalists can go wrong in two ways. First, like print or broadcast reporters, they can use information from unreliable sources. Second, they must be wary of providing World Wide Web links to unreliable sources. Stan Ketterer, a journalist and journalism educator, suggests that journalists evaluate information on the Internet by following the same journalistic practices they use for assessing the credibility and accuracy of any other information. He developed these guidelines.

○ Before using information from a Web page in a story, verify it with a source.

There are exceptions to this rule. They include taking information from a highly credible government site, such as the Census Bureau, or when you can't contact the source on a breaking story because of time constraints. An editor must clear all exceptions.

○ In most cases, information taken from the Web and used in a story must be attributed.

If you have verified the information on a home page with a source, you can use the organization in the attribution—for example, "according to the EPA" or "EPA figures show." If you cannot verify the information after trying repeatedly, attribute unverified information to the Web page —for example, "according to the Voice of America's Web site." Consult your editor before using unverified information.

○ If you have doubts about the accuracy of the information and you cannot reach the source, get it from another source, such as a book or a contact person. When in doubt, omit the information.

○ Check the extension on the site's Internet address to get clues as to the nature of the organization and the likely slant of the information.

The most common extensions used in the United States are *.gov* (government), *.edu* (education), *.com* (commercial), *.mil* (military), *.org* (not-for-profit organization) and *.net* (Internet administration). Most of the government and military sites have credible and accurate information. In many cases, you can take the information directly from the site and attribute it to the organization. But consult your editor until you get to know these sites.

The same is true for many of the sites of colleges and universities. If college and university sites have source documents, such as the Constitution, attribute the information to the source document. But beware: Personal home pages of students often have *.edu* extensions, and the information on them is not always credible. Do not use information from a personal home page without contacting the person and without the permission of your editor.

○ In almost all cases, do not take information directly from the home pages of commercial and not-for-profit organizations and use it without verification. Verify and attribute all information on those pages.

○ Check the date when the page was last updated. If no date appears, if the site has not been updated for a while or if it was created some time ago, do not use the information unless you verify it with a source.

The date generally appears at the top or bottom of the first page of the site. Although a recent date does not ensure that the information is current, it does indicate that the organization is paying close attention to the site.

Using the Internet as a source of information is no riskier than using books, magazines or other printed material, provided you use common sense. Remember, too, that material on the Internet is subject to copyright laws. Taking care to use only credible sources and to abide by copyright laws will enhance your own credibility.

Conciseness

On the surface, conciseness would seem to conflict with our fourth dictum, completeness. Yet the Web is ideally suited to deliver both qualities. On the Web, more than any other medium, it's possible to be both concise and complete.

Typically, an online site has an index up front. Sometimes, that index is roughly equivalent to the newspaper headline or magazine article title. More often, there is a secondary headline or sentence that gives the consumer more information as a tease to read the complete story. If the reader is hooked, he or she then clicks on the headline to get more information, usually a complete newspaper-length story and perhaps even audio and video links. Presenting the news this way is called *layering,* a technique relatively new to journalists.

Upon closer examination, all the skills involved in layering are used by those who work in the traditional media. Just as the newspaper headline writer or magazine title writer tries to capture the reader's interest, so does the online journalist. Writing a headline and summary sentence is an art.

Some online sites take the process a step further by summarizing the story on the second page in a one-page format, which amounts to little more than writing a brief newspaper or broadcast story. As any print or broadcast reporter knows, a well-crafted lead, brevity and clarity are the keys to successful writing.

From there, the online journalist has unlimited space. Unlike the broadcast journalist, who is greatly restrained by time, and the print journalist, who is greatly restrained by space, the online journalist has freedom to tell the story at whatever length seems best. Then, it's possible to provide *links,* which point the consumer to other stories on the same subject, to original source or background materials or to electronic bulletin boards where users explore the subject at hand.

It's also possible to link to audio or video clips of the event, which makes the online media the first full-spectrum news media. As the speed of the Internet improves, the use of video and sound is expected to increase, resulting in new media that encompass the best of the traditional media—the depth of newspapers and magazines, and the appeal of audio and video now found only on television.

Obviously, then, the skills needed to work in these new media are those of the newspaper headline writer, the print or broadcast reporter, the graphic artist and the videographer—all rolled into one. Those preparing for careers in online journalism must know something about all those skills. The new media are the first to be multimedia in nature.

Consistency

In the traditional media, consistency refers to conveying the message in ways that are not contradictory. Inconsistency creeps into a news report when we spell a person's name one way in the first part of the story and another way at the end. Inconsistency also results when numbers don't add up within a story or when we say one thing in the main story and another in a sidebar.

Writers and editors for the online media also must be diligent in maintaining that type of consistency. But equally important is maintaining consistency in the way consumers are asked to navigate a Web site. Good sites have guidelines to maintain that consistency, just as newspapers have stylebooks and design restrictions to achieve the same purpose.

Like newspapers, Web sites and other online services must have consistency of design. Care must be taken in the use of color, the shape and size of navigational devices, and the nature of links. Consumers have a right to know that the time and effort taken to follow a link will be worthwhile.

Completeness

The wonder of the Web is that the consumer gets to choose how much, or how little, he or she consumes. That, in today's busy world, is important. And though readers do just that with newspapers, magazines, radio and television, the online media make the process easier.

The Internet can open wide new horizons to news and information consumers. No matter what the subject, finding more about it on the Internet is relatively easy—and almost a sure bet. The online journalist has the luxury of writing as much as is necessary, then referring the true news junkie to the Internet for even more.

Earlier, we discussed the advantages of layering and linking. To that we can add the Internet's *research* capability. The new media have been described as being multimedia in nature—with text, graphics, audio, still photography and video, all linked to the world's largest research library, the Internet. Those who learn to take advantage of these considerable capabilities are in a great position for the future.

The Fifth C

Earlier, we discussed the *four C's* that must be used to produce good journalism. When discussing the new media, however, it is necessary to add a fifth C—*currency*.

Newspapers typically publish once a day, although multiple editions of big-city papers are commonplace. Even among these big newspapers, however, it's rare to see more than three daily editions.

Television news also airs infrequently, except in the case of the 24-hour national news channels such as CNN. Local news typically comes in the form of early-morning cut-ins on the networks' news show, a noon newscast, another in the early evening and another late at night. Radio may have more frequent newscasts, but they are relatively brief, usually no more than five minutes.

As a result, the traditional media always have been pressed to provide fresh news, adding an update or new information for the next newscast or next edition. Online media, however, have no deadlines and rush the news to their consumers as soon as it is available. Only 24-hour news networks and the big wire services such as The Associated Press and Reuters do something comparable, and relatively few journalists have this experience.

New-media journalists must learn to produce their product quickly and continuously throughout an eight-hour shift. It is a pace to which not all can adapt.

Frequent updating of news and other information is the lifeblood of online journalism. Without it, consumers soon lose interest in a news Web site. Many newspaper sites have not been popular with the public simply because they are updated only once or twice a day. Sites updated 24 hours a day, such as CNN and USA Today, are consistently ranked among the most popular with online users.

Writing and Presenting Online News

Writers and editors for online media typically work with *storyboards*, computerized blueprints that tell them whether the information they are compiling will fit in the allotted space.

Most online news stories are layered:

1. Headline or title.
2. One-sentence tease, or lead.
3. First page or quick summary of what happened, not unlike a short radio or television story.
4. Accompanying visuals, usually photos or graphics.
5. Accompanying audio and video, if any.

6. Depth report, perhaps further layered.
7. Links.

At a newspaper, magazine or broadcast station, the work of assembling those items usually is parceled out to reporters, graphic artists, photographers, videographers and editors. In a new-media newsroom, one person is likely to handle most or all of those functions. That's because the new-media journalist is expected to be a jack-of-all-trades who is equally adept at handling all aspects of multimedia journalism.

There is no one way to produce a story for the online media. Although it's true that traditional newspaper and magazine writing formulas may work in this environment, there may be better ways. A quick story may lend itself to the classic newspaper inverted-pyramid writing style. A more complex one may require links to audio, video and still photos, with multiple layers of text. Major projects may require even more complex forms of storytelling.

Online journalism is multimedia journalism. The journalist is required to select the best medium—text, graphics, photos, audio or video—for the story to be told. Almost without exception, the best way to tell any story is with a combination of these media.

The toughest part of preparing such a story is knowing how to prepare the text. Researchers John Morkes and Jakob Nielsen studied just that by taking a Web site's content and rewriting it. They presented both versions to Web users and found that users prefer writing that is concise, easy to scan and objective rather than promotional.

We've already discussed conciseness in this chapter and Chapter 12, and objectivity in Chapter 11. But what makes a story scannable? Morkes and Nielsen found that readers don't *read* the Web, they *scan* it. They scan the head, the first bit of text and perhaps some subheads, then read only what catches their interest. Most readers are unlikely to read long text articles. That means Web editors must present information in clearly understandable short bursts. Hooking people for a longer read is tough.

The finding that Web users prefer objective material is interesting because it suggests that readers appreciate objectivity and are prepared to identify promotional material and distinguish it from news. When Morkes and Nielsen's test site was rewritten for conciseness, scannability and objectivity, users reported a 159 percent increase in satisfaction.

To facilitate the scannability of their test site, the researchers made several changes to call attention to important pieces of text. They added tables of contents, section summaries, bullets, numbered lists, boldface type and colored text to highlight key words. They also added more subheads and shortened paragraphs. Users appreciated the results.

The Morkes and Nielsen study suggests that merely dumping text onto the Web, which has been the norm for most newspapers, magazines and broadcast stations, doesn't work too well. Instead, editors must adapt to the new media much as the early television broadcasters learned to make video work *for* them rather than *against* them.

ONLINE WRITING

People scan the Web for information. When they find that information, they *may* be willing to drill deeper. Web editors should make it easy for them to do just that. To do so, we suggest that you:

- Write concisely.
- Write paragraphs that are as short as possible.
- Write in chunks, or easily consumable bits of information.
- Add tables of contents.
- Add section summaries and subheads.
- Add bullets and numbered lists.
- Make ample use of colored or boldface text.
- Highlight key words.
- Layer information to increase scannability.
- Provide useful links.
- Give readers a chance to respond.

The art of linking is an important one to understand. One convention of traditional newspaper writing, for example, is to provide a summary of background information in each article. That's probably unnecessary when writing for the Web, where links are a better way to provide such background. Also important is making sure the reader is able to link back to the original site, thus avoiding navigation problems.

We also know from several studies that readers dislike scrolling through text. That's why conciseness and layering become important. If an article extends beyond a single screen, layering is preferable to requiring the reader to scroll.

What all that suggests is that the best Web writing is concise, should be divided into layered pieces and should be liberally sprinkled with subheads, key-word links and the like. There's also some evidence that casual writing, as opposed to more formal writing, works best on the Web.

And finally, there's one fundamental difference between writing for the online media and writing for the traditional media: Online media have two-way capability. Give your consumers the chance to respond directly to you or your publication. They are accustomed to such interaction on the Internet.

Clearly, writing for the Web differs from writing for other media. We're still in the process of testing, experimenting and learning how to do it better.

Online Media vs. Traditional Media

The online media deliver information in a way that is fundamentally different from the way the traditional media do. In a sense, newspapers, magazines and broadcast stations all *broadcast* the news. That is, they compile news and other information in one format, then offer that to a mass audience. Members of the audience then scan the available material, and each consumer reads or watches what's interesting to him or her. Think of it as selective consumption of information produced for a plethora of tastes and interests.

The online media, however, take advantage of their considerable database capabilities to provide access to information from millions of sources. In each case, they offer gateways to the Internet, where the quality of information ranges from authoritative to suspect to highly incredible. The thorough search capabilities of the online media make it easy for the consumer to do what he or she already does with the mass media—search for and read or watch only those items or subjects of interest. Rather than broadcasting, think of it as *narrowcasting*, or providing news and information to those most interested in the topic.

That raises this question: Are the new media a part of the mass media, or do they equate more readily to the thousands of magazines targeted to specific interests—boating, cars and sewing, to name a few—or to targeted radio and television—rock, classical, ESPN and QVC? The answer, it would appear, is both. When taken as a whole, the Internet is certainly a mass medium in terms of the number of people using it. But it more closely resembles targeted magazines or broadcast stations in the way it is used. Remember, though, that in the larger sense these, too, are considered part of the mass media. So, in the end, the distinction may be irrelevant.

What's clear is that people prefer to choose the news they consume—in either the online media or the traditional media. The difference is that the online media make that easier and provide access to thousands more sources of information on the topic at hand. It's no accident that the popularity of the Web continues to boom while the traditional media are mired in a slump. Television ratings are down, and newspaper circulation is relatively flat, despite an increasing population base from which to draw.

If people prefer choice, it's logical to conclude that information providers need to rethink the way news and information are offered. Does that mean traditional news providers are doomed? Certainly not. A significant part of the public still prefers to have someone sort the news and provide highlights. But the traditional media also must embrace that part of the audience that prefers the new way of doing things, and there is every indication they are doing so. Newspapers as traditional as The New York Times have a significant presence on the Web. The Times' Internet site is one of the most-used sites on the World Wide Web. So, too, are those of CNN and USA Today.

They are not alone. Thousands of new-media sites are produced and maintained by the traditional media. All the television networks and most of the nation's newspapers and magazines have their own sites on the Internet. They see themselves as information providers, and they are ready to provide information in whatever form the public prefers.

ONLINE WRITING

Web Resources

ONLINE MEDIA

The new media are revolutionizing the way journalists research and write news stories, and they are affecting the way readers access them. Here are three general sites dedicated to online journalism, as well.

- Internet Press Guild
  www.netpress.org

- Online Journalism Review
  www.ojr.org

- Online News Association
  www.onlinenewsassociation.org

In 2001, the Online News Association presented its Online Journalism Awards to the following two sites.

- BBC News Online (affiliated)
  news.bbc.co.uk

- Slate (independent)
  www.slate.com

Wire-Service Style Summary

Most publications adhere to rules of style to avoid annoying inconsistencies. Without a stylebook to provide guidance in such matters, writers would not know whether the word *president* should be capitalized when preceding or following a name, whether the correct spelling is *employee* or *employe* (dictionaries list both), or whether a street name should be *Twelfth* or *12th*.

Newspapers use the wire-service stylebooks to provide such guidance. For consistency, most newspapers follow rules in the Associated Press Stylebook. Many also publish their own lists of exceptions to AP style. There often are good reasons for local exceptions. For example, AP style calls for spelling out *First Street* through *Ninth Street* but using numerals for *10th Street* and above. But if a city has only 10 numbered streets, for consistency it might make sense to use *Tenth Street*.

This section is an abbreviated summary of the primary rules of wire-service style. (For more punctuation rules, see Chapter 9.) This summary should be helpful even for those without a stylebook, but we provide it assuming that most users of this book have one. Why?

Because this section includes only the rules used most often, arranged by topic to make them easier to learn. Only about 10 percent of the rules in a stylebook account for 90 percent of the wire-service style you will use regularly. You will use the rest of the rules about 10 percent of the time. It makes sense, therefore, to learn first those rules you will use most often.

Abbreviations and Acronyms

Punctuation

○ Generally speaking, abbreviations of two letters or fewer have periods:

600 B.C., A.D. 1066

8 a.m., 7 p.m.

U.N., U.S., R.I., N.Y.

8151 Yosemite St.

Exceptions include *AM radio, FM radio, 35 mm camera, the AP Stylebook, D-Mass., R-Kan., IQ* and *TV.*

○ Generally speaking, abbreviations of three letters or more do not have periods:

CIA, FBI, NATO

mpg, mph

One exception is *c.o.d.*

Symbols

○ Always write out % as *percent* in a story, but you may use the symbol in a headline.

○ Always write out *&* as *and* unless it is part of a company's formal name.

○ Always write out ¢ as *cent* or *cents.*

○ Always use the symbol *$* rather than the word *dollars* with any actual figure, and put the symbol before the figure. Write out *dollar* only if you are speaking of, say, the value of the dollar on the world market.

Dates

○ Don't abbreviate days of the week except in a table.

○ Don't abbreviate a month unless it has a date of the month with it: *August 1999; Aug. 17; Aug. 17, 2002.*

○ Don't abbreviate the five months spelled with five or fewer letters except in a table: *March, April, May, June, July.*

○ Never abbreviate *Christmas* as *Xmas,* even in a headline.

○ *Fourth of July* is written out.

People and Titles

A few publications still use courtesy titles *(Mr., Mrs., Ms., Miss)* on second reference in stories, although most seem to have eliminated them. Many publications use them only in quotations from sources. Others use them only in obituaries and editorials, or on second reference in stories mentioning a husband and wife. In the last case, some newspapers prefer to repeat the person's whole name or, especially in features, use the person's first name. The Associated Press suggests using a courtesy title when someone requests it, but most journalists don't bother to ask.

○ Use the abbreviations *Dr., Gov., Lt. Gov., Rep., Sen.* and *the Rev.,* as well as abbreviations of military titles, on first reference, then drop the title on subsequent references.

Some titles you might expect to see abbreviated before a name are not abbreviated in AP style: *Attorney General, District Attorney, President, Professor, Superintendent.*

○ Use the abbreviations *Jr.* and *Sr.* after a name on first reference if appropriate but do not set them off with commas.

Organizations

○ Write out the first reference to most organizations in full rather than using an acronym: *National Organization for Women.*

Exceptions include *CIA, FBI* and *GOP.* The acronym may be used on the first reference.

○ You may use well-known abbreviations such as *FCC* and *NOW* in a headline even though they would not be acceptable on first reference in the story.

○ Do not put the abbreviation of an organization in parentheses after the full name on first reference. If its abbreviation is that confusing, don't use an abbreviation at all but rather call it something like "the gay rights group" or "the bureau" on second reference.

○ Use the abbreviations *Co., Cos., Corp., Inc.* and *Ltd.* at the end of a company's name even if the company spells out the word. Do not abbreviate these words if followed by other words such as "of America." The abbreviations *Co., Cos.* and *Corp.* are abbreviated, however, if followed by *Inc.* or *Ltd.* (and, by the way, these latter two abbreviations are not set off by commas even if the company uses them).

○ Abbreviate political affiliations after a name in the following way:

Sen. Christopher Bond, R-Mo., said … .

○ Never abbreviate the word *association,* even as part of a name.

Places

○ Don't abbreviate a state name unless it follows the name of a city in that state:

Nevada

Brown City, Mich.

○ Never abbreviate the six states spelled with five or fewer letters or the two noncontiguous states: *Alaska, Hawaii, Idaho, Iowa, Maine, Ohio, Texas, Utah.*

○ Use the traditional state abbreviations, not the Postal Service's two-letter ones: *Miss.*, not *MS.*

Exception: Use the two-letter postal abbreviations when a full address is given that includes a ZIP code: *217 Ridgecrest St., Westminster, MA 01473.*

Here are the abbreviations used in normal copy:

Ala.	Fla.	Md.	Neb.	N.D.	Tenn.
Ariz.	Ga.	Mass.	Nev.	Okla.	Vt.
Ark.	Ill.	Mich.	N.H.	Ore.	Va.
Calif.	Ind.	Minn.	N.J.	Pa.	Wash.
Colo.	Kan.	Miss.	N.M.	R.I.	W.Va.
Conn.	Ky.	Mo.	N.Y.	S.C.	Wis.
Del.	La.	Mont.	N.C.	S.D.	Wyo.

○ Use state abbreviations with domestic towns and cities unless they appear in the wire-service dateline list of cities that stand alone.

Many publications add to the wire-service list their own lists of towns well-known in the state or region. Use nations' full names with foreign towns and cities unless they appear in the wire-service dateline list of cities that stand alone. Once a state or nation has been identified in a story, it is unnecessary to repeat it unless clarity demands it.

The lists of cities in the United States and the rest of the world that the wire services say may stand alone without a state abbreviation or nation are too lengthy to include here. Consult the appropriate stylebook. A handy rule of thumb: If it's an American city and has a major sports franchise, it probably stands alone. Likewise, if it's a foreign city most people have heard of, it probably stands alone.

○ Don't abbreviate the names of thoroughfares if there is no street address with them:

Main Street

Century Boulevard West

○ If the thoroughfare's name has the word *avenue, boulevard, street* or any of the directions on a map, such as *north* or *southeast,* abbreviate those words with a street address:

1044 W. Maple St.

1424 Lee Blvd. S.

999 Jackson Ave.

○ In a highway's name, always abbreviate *U.S.* but never abbreviate a state. In the case of an interstate highway, the name is written in full on first reference, abbreviated on subsequent ones:

> U.S. 63, U.S. Route 63, or U.S. Highway 63
>
> Massachusetts Route 2
>
> Interstate 70 [first reference]
>
> I-70 [second reference]

○ Never abbreviate *Fort* or *Mount.*

○ Use the abbreviation *St.* for *Saint* in place names.

Exceptions include Saint John in New Brunswick, Ste. Genevieve in Missouri and Sault Ste. Marie in Michigan and Ontario.

○ Abbreviate *United States* and *United Nations* as *U.S.* and *U.N.* when used as adjectives, but spell them out as nouns.

Miscellaneous

○ Use the abbreviation *IQ* (no periods) in all references to *intelligence quotient.*

○ Abbreviate and capitalize the word *number* when followed by a numeral: *No. 1.*

○ Use the abbreviation *TV* (no periods) only in headlines, as an adjective and in constructions such as *cable TV.* Otherwise, spell out *television.*

○ Use the abbreviation *UFO* in all references to an *unidentified flying object.*

○ Use the abbreviation *vs.* for *versus* except in the name of court cases, which use *v.*

Capitalization

Proper Nouns

○ Proper nouns are capitalized; common nouns are not.

Unfortunately, this rule is not always easy to apply when the noun is the name of an animal, food or plant or when it is a trademark that has become so well-known that people mistakenly use it generically. (See Chapter 3.)

○ When two or more compound proper nouns are combined to share a word in common made plural, the shared plural is lowercased:

Missouri and Mississippi rivers

Chrisman and Truman high schools

Geographic Regions

⚪ Regions are capitalized; directions are not:

We drove *east* two miles to catch the interstate to the *West*.

⚪ Adjectives and nouns pertaining to a region are capitalized:

Southern accent, Western movie, a Southerner, a Western

⚪ A region combined with a country's name is not capitalized unless the region is part of the name of a divided country:

eastern United States, North Korea

⚪ A region combined with a state name is capitalized only if it is famous:

Southern California, southern Colorado

Government and College Terms

Government and college terms are not always as consistent as you might think.

⚪ College departments follow the animal, food and plant rule: Capitalize only words that are already proper nouns in themselves:

Spanish department, sociology department

⚪ By contrast, always capitalize a specific government department, even without the city, state or federal designator, and even if it's turned around with *of* deleted:

Police Department, Fire Department, State Department, Department of Commerce

⚪ College and government committees are capitalized if the formal noun is given rather than a shorter, descriptive designation:

Special Senate Select Committee to Investigate Improper Labor-Management Practices

rackets committee

⚪ Academic degrees are spelled out and lowercased:

bachelor of arts degree

master's degree

Avoid the abbreviations *Ph.D., M.A., B.A.,* and the like except in lists.

○ Always capitalize (unless plural or generic) *City Council* and *County Commission* (but alone, *council* and *commission* are lowercased). *Cabinet* is capitalized when referring to advisers. *Legislature* is capitalized if the state's body is formally named that. *Capitol,* the building, is capitalized, but *capital,* the city, is not.

○ Never capitalize *board of directors* or *board of trustees* (but *Board of Curators* and *Board of Education* are capitalized). *Federal, government* and *administration* are not capitalized. *President* and *vice president* are capitalized only before a name.

○ Military titles *(Sgt., Maj., Chief Warrant Officer)* are capitalized before a name, as are *Air Force, Army, Marines* and *Navy* if referring to U.S. forces.

○ Political parties are capitalized, including the word *party:*

Democratic Party, Socialist Party

Be sure, however, to capitalize words such as *communist, democratic, fascist* and *socialist* only if they refer to a formal party rather than a philosophy.

Religious Terms

Religious terms are variously capitalized and lowercased.

○ *Pope* is lowercased except before a name:

the pope

Pope Gregory

○ *Mass* is always capitalized.

○ Pronouns for *God* and *Jesus* are lowercased.

○ *Bible* is capitalized when meaning the Holy Scriptures and lowercased when referring to another book:

a hunter's bible

○ Sacraments are capitalized if they commemorate events in the life of Jesus or signify his presence:

baptism, Communion

Titles

○ Formal titles of people are capitalized before a name, but occupational titles are not:

> President George W. Bush, Mayor Kwame Kilpatrick, Coach Bill Cowher, Dean Fred Wilson

> astronaut Mary Gardner, journalist Fred Francis, plumber Phil Sanders, pharmacist Roger Wheaton

Some titles, such as *managing editor* and *chief executive officer,* are not easy to tell apart. When in doubt, put the title behind the name, set off with commas, and use lowercase.

○ Formal titles that are capitalized before a name are lowercased after a name:

> George W. Bush, president of the United States

> Kwame Kilpatrick, mayor of Detroit

> Bill Cowher, coach of the Pittsburgh Steelers

> Fred Wilson, dean of students

○ Formal titles that are abbreviated before a name are written out and lowercased if they follow a name:

> Gov. Bob Holden; Bob Holden, governor of Missouri

> Rep. Lindsey Graham of South Carolina; Lindsey Graham, representative from South Carolina

Miscellaneous

○ Actual race names are capitalized, but color descriptions are not:

> Caucasian, Mongoloid, Negro

> white, red, black

○ The first word in a direct quotation is capitalized only if the quote meets all these criteria:

- It is a complete sentence. Don't capitalize a partial quote.
- It stands alone as a separate sentence or paragraph, or it is set off from its source by a comma or colon.
- It is a direct quotation (in quotation marks).

○ A question within a sentence is capitalized:

> My only question is, When do we start?

Numbers

Cardinal Numbers

Use cardinal numbers, or numerals, in the following cases.

- Addresses. Always use numerals for street addresses: *1322 N. Main St.*

- Ages. Always use numerals, even for days or months: *3 days old; John Burnside, 56.*

- Aircraft and spacecraft: *F-4, DC-10, Apollo 11.* Exception: *Air Force One.*

- Clothes size: *size 6.*

- Dates. Always use the numeral alone—no *nd, rd, st* or *th* after it: *March 20.*

- Decades: *the 1990s, the '90s.*

- Dimensions: *5-foot-6-inch guard* (but no hyphen when the word modified is one associated with size: *3 feet tall, 10 feet long*).

- Highways: *U.S. 63.*

- Millions, billions and trillions: *1.2 billion, 6 million.*

- Money. Always use numerals, but starting with a million, write like this: *$1.4 million.*

- Numbers: *No. 1, No. 2.*

- Percentages. Always use numerals except at the beginning of a sentence: *4 percent.*

- Recipes. All numbers for amounts take numerals: *2 teaspoons.*

- Speeds: *55 mph, 4 knots.*

- Sports. Use numerals for just about everything: *8-6 score, 2 yards, 3 under par, 2 strokes.*

- Temperatures. Use numerals for all except zero. Below zero, spell out minus: *minus 6, not -26* (except in tabular data).

- Times: *4 a.m., 6:32 p.m., noon, midnight, five minutes, 16 hours.*

- Weights: *7 pounds, 11 ounces.*

- Years. Use numerals without commas. A year is the only numeral that can start a sentence: *1988 was a good year.*

Numerals With Suffixes

Use numerals with the suffixes *nd, rd, st* and *th* in these instances.

- Political divisions (precincts, wards, districts):
  3rd Congressional District.

- Military sequences: *1st Lt., 2nd Division, 7th Fleet.*

- Courts: *2nd District Court; 10th U.S. Circuit Court of Appeals.*

- Streets after *Ninth.* For *First* through *Ninth,* use words:
  Fifth Avenue, 13th Street.

- Amendments to the Constitution after *Ninth.* For *First* through
  Ninth, use words: *First Amendment, 16th Amendment.*

Numbers as Words

Write out numbers in the following cases.

- Numbers less than 10, with the exceptions noted above:
  five people, four rules.

- Any number at the start of a sentence except for a year:
  Sixteen years ago … .

- Casual numbers: *about a hundred or so.*

- Fractions less than one: *one-half.*

Other Rules for Numbers

- Mixed numerals are used for fractions greater than one:

  $1\frac{1}{2}$

- Roman numerals are used for a man who is the third or later in
  his family to bear a name and for a king, queen, pope or world
  war:

  John D. Rockefeller III, Queen Elizabeth II, Pope John Paul II,
  World War I

Web Resources

WIRE SERVICE

The Associated Press provides wire news through the sites of its member
newspapers. To access the AP wire online, follow this link and select a
newspaper.

- The Associated Press
  wire.ap.org

Bibliography

Agnes, Michael, ed. *Webster's New World College Dictionary.* 4th ed. New York: Hungry Minds, 2001.

American Heritage Editors. *The American Heritage Dictionary of the English Language.* 4th ed. Boston: Houghton Mifflin, 2000.

Angell, David, and Brent Heslop. *The Elements of E-mail Style: Communicate Effectively via Electronic Mail.* Reading, Mass.: Addison-Wesley, 1994.

Arnold, George T. *Media Writer's Handbook: A Guide to Common Writing and Editing Problems.* Madison, Wis.: Brown & Benchmark, 1996.

Bendell, John, and Jason Ward. *National Lampoon Presents True Facts: The Big Book.* Chicago: Contemporary Books, 1995.

Berner, R. Thomas. *Language Skills for Journalists.* 2nd ed. Boston: Houghton Mifflin, 1984.

Bernstein, Theodore M. *The Careful Writer.* New York: Atheneum, 1977.

———. *Dos, Don'ts and Maybes of English Usage.* New York: Random House Value Publishing, 1999.

———. *Miss Thistlebottom's Hobgoblins.* New York: Farrar, Straus and Giroux, 1991.

———. *Watch Your Language.* New York: Simon & Schuster, 1989.

Botts, Jack. *The Language of News: A Journalist's Pocket Reference.* Ames, Iowa: Iowa State University Press, 1994.

Bremner, John B. *Words on Words.* New York: Fine Communications, 1998.

Brooks, Brian S. *Journalism in the Information Age: A Guide to Computers for Reporters and Editors.* Boston: Allyn and Bacon, 1997.

Brooks, Brian S., George Kennedy, Daryl R. Moen and Don Ranly. *News Reporting and Writing.* 7th ed. New York: Bedford/St. Martin's, 2002.

Brooks, Brian S., and Jack Z. Sissors. *The Art of Editing.* 7th ed. Boston: Allyn and Bacon, 2001.

Buckley, William F. Jr. *Buckley: The Right Word.* Samuel S. Vaughan, ed. San Diego: Harvest Books, 1998.

Callihan, E.L. *Grammar for Journalists.* 3rd ed. Radnor, Pa.: Chilton, 1979.

Cappon, Rene J. *The Associated Press Guide to Newswriting.* 3rd ed. Englewood Cliffs, N.J.: Prentice-Hall, 2000.

Catalano, Kevin, and James Pinson. *Editing Manual.* Columbia, Mo.: n.p., 1987.

353

Celce-Murcie, Mariane, and Diane Larsen-Freeman. *The Grammar Book: An ESL/EFL Teacher's Course*. 2nd ed. Boston: Heinle & Heinle, 1998.

Chalker, Sylvia, and Edmund Weiner. *The Oxford Dictionary of English Grammar*. Oxford: Oxford University Press, 1998.

Cohn, Victor, and Lewis Cope. *News and Numbers: A Guide to Reporting Statistical Claims and Controversies in Health and Other Fields*. Ames: Iowa State University Press, 2001.

Cooper, Gloria, and Columbia Journalism Review, eds. *Red Tape Holds Up New Bridge and More Flubs From the Nation's Press*. New York: Perigee Books, 1987.

———. *Squad Helps Dog Bite Victim: And Other Flubs From the Nation's Press*. Garden City, N.Y.: Dolphin Books, 1980.

Copperud, Roy H. *A Dictionary of Usage and Style*. New York: Hawthorn Books, 1964.

Dizard, Wilson Jr. *Old Media, New Media: Mass Communications in the Information Age*. White Plains, N.Y.: Longman Publishing Group, 1999.

Flesch, Rudolf. *ABC of Style*. New York: HarperCollins, 1980.

———. *Look It Up*. New York: Harper & Row, 1977.

Follett, Wilson. *Modern American Usage: A Guide*. Edited and completed by Erik Wensberg. New York: Hill & Wang, 1998.

Fowler, H.W. *The New Fowler's Modern English Usage*. 3rd ed. New York: Oxford University Press, 2000.

Garner, Bryan A. *The Oxford Dictionary of American Usage and Style*. New York: Berkley Books, 2000.

Gilder, George F. *Life After Television*. Revised ed. New York: W.W. Norton & Co., 1994.

Goldstein, Norm, ed. *The Associated Press Stylebook and Briefing on Media Law*. New York: The Associated Press, 2001.

Hale, Constance, and Jessie Scanlan. *Wired Style: Principles of English Usage in the Digital Age*. New York: Broadway Books, 1999.

Harnack, Andrew, and Eugene Kleppinger. *Online! A Reference Guide to Using Internet Sources*. New York: St. Martin's Press, 1999.

Harrigan, Jane T. *The Editorial Eye*. New York: Bedford/St. Martin's, 1993.

Holley, Frederick S. *Los Angeles Times Stylebook*. New York: New American Library, 1981.

Kennedy, George, Daryl R. Moen and Don Ranly. *Beyond the Inverted Pyramid*. New York: St. Martin's Press, 1993.

Kessler, Lauren, and Duncan McDonald. *When Words Collide*. 5th ed. Belmont, Calif.: Wadsworth, 1999.

Kilpatrick, James J. *The Ear Is Human*. Kansas City, Mo.: Andrews, McMeel & Parker, 1985.

———. *The Writer's Art*. Kansas City, Mo.: Andrews, McMeel & Parker, 1984.

Leno, Jay. *Headlines IV: The Next Generation*. New York: Warner Books, 1992.

———. *Jay Leno's Real But Ridiculous Headlines From America's Newspapers*. New York: Wings Books, 1992.

Lewis, Norman. *The New American Dictionary of Good English*. New York: Signet Books, 1987.

———. *30 Days to a More Powerful Vocabulary*. New York: Galahad Books, 1998.

Liljeblad, Fredrik. *Berlitz English Grammar Handbook*. Princeton, N.J.: Berlitz Publishing Co., 1999.

Lippman, Thomas W. *The Washington Post Deskbook on Style*. 2nd ed. New York: McGraw-Hill, 1989.

Lunsford, Andrea, and Robert Connors. *The New St. Martin's Handbook*. 4th ed. New York: Bedford/St. Martin's, 1999.

Manhard, Stephen J. *The Goof-Proofer*. New York: Simon & Schuster, 1998.

The Merriam-Webster Concise Handbook for Writers. Springfield, Mass.: Merriam-Webster, 1991.

The Merriam-Webster Dictionary of English Usage. Springfield, Mass.: Merriam-Webster, 1989.

Miller, Boyd. *Copy Editing: Making Good Writing Better*. Haslett, Mich.: Wordpic Services, 1992.

Miller, Casey, and Kate Swift. *Handbook of Nonsexist Writing*. 2nd ed. New York: iUniverse, 2001.

——. *Words and Women*. New York: iUniverse, 2000.

Mitchell, Richard. *Less Than Words Can Say*. Boston: Akadine Press, 2000.

Morris, William, and Mary Morris. *Harper Dictionary of Contemporary Usage*. 2nd ed. New York: HarperCollins, 1991.

Negroponte, Nicholas. *Being Digital*. New York: Vintage Books, 1996.

Newman, Edwin. *Edwin Newman on Language: Strictly Speaking and A Civil Tongue*. New York: Warner Books, 1980.

——. *I Must Say*. New York: Warner Books, 1988.

O'Conner, Patricia T. *Woe Is I: The Grammarphobe's Guide to Better English in Plain English*. New York: Riverhead Books, 1996.

Ogden, James R., and Research and Education Association Staff. *REA's Handbook of English Grammar, Style, and Writing*. Piscataway, N.J.: Research and Education Association, 1992.

Paulos, John Allen. *A Mathematician Reads the Newspaper*. New York: Basic Books, 1995.

Pinckert, Robert C. *Pinckert's Practical Grammar*. Cincinnati, Ohio: F&W Publications, 1991.

Prejean, Blanche G., and Wayne Danielson. *Programmed News Style*. 2nd ed. Englewood Cliffs, N.J.: Prentice-Hall, 1988.

Quinn, Jim. *American Tongue and Cheek*. New York: Pantheon Books, 1980.

Randall, Bernice. *Webster's New World Guide to Current American Usage*. New York: Webster's New World, 1988.

Ranly, Don, and Jennifer Moeller. *Publication Editing*. 3rd ed. Dubuque, Iowa: Kendall/Hunt Publishing Company, 2001.

Reddick, Randy, and Elliot King. *The Online Journalist: Using the Internet and Other Electronic Resources*. Fort Worth, Texas: Harcourt College Publishers, 2000.

Ross-Larson, Bruce. *Edit Yourself: A Manual for Everyone Who Works With Words*. 2nd ed. New York: W.W. Norton & Co., 1985.

Safire, William. *Fumblerules*. New York: Doubleday, 1990.

——. *I Stand Corrected*. New York: Times Books, 1984.

——. *Language Maven Strikes Again*. New York: Doubleday, 1990.

——. *On Language*. New York: Times Books, 1980.

——. *Power Language*. Boston: Houghton Mifflin, 1996.

——. *Take My Word for It*. New York: Times Books, 1986.

——. *What's the Good Word?* New York: Times Books, 1982.

——. *You Could Look It Up*. New York: Times Books, 1988.

Schwartz, Jane. *Kaplan Grammar Power*. New York: Kaplan Books, 2001.

Semmelmeyer, Madeline, and Donald O. Bolander. *The New Webster's Grammar Guide*. New York: Berkley Books, 1991.

Shertzer, Margaret. *The Elements of Grammar*. New York: Barnes & Noble Books, 2001.

Siegal, Allan M., and William G. Connolly. *The New York Times Manual of Style and Usage*. Revised and expanded ed. New York: Times Books, 1999.

Strunk, William Jr., E.B. White and Roger Angell. *The Elements of Style*. New York: Macmillan, 2000.

United Press International. *UPI Stylebook*. 3rd ed. Chicago: National Textbook Co., 1992.

The Vest-Pocket Writer's Guide. Boston: Houghton Mifflin, 1987.

Webster's Third New International Dictionary. Springfield, Mass.: G.&C. Merriam Co., 2000.

Wilson, Kenneth G. *The Columbia Guide to Standard American English*. New York: Fine Communications, 1998.

Zinsser, William. *On Writing Well: An Informal Guide to Writing Nonfiction*. 6th revised and updated ed. New York: Harper Trade, 2001.

Index